IT Architectures
and Middleware

IT Architectures and Middleware

Strategies for
Building Large,
Integrated Systems

Chris Britton

 **ADDISON-WESLEY**

Boston • San Francisco • New York • Toronto • Montreal
London • Munich • Paris • Madrid • Capetown
Sydney • Tokyo • Singapore • Mexico City

Many of the designations used by manufacturers and sellers to distinguish their products are claimed as trademarks. Where those designations appear in this book, and Addison-Wesley was aware of a trademark claim, the designations have been printed in initial capital letters or in all capitals.

The author and publisher have taken care in the preparation of this book, but make no expressed or implied warranty of any kind and assume no responsibility for errors or omissions. No liability is assumed for incidental or consequential damages in connection with or arising out of the use of the information or programs contained herein.

The publisher offers discounts on this book when ordered in quantity for special sales. For more information, please contact:

Pearson Education Corporate Sales Division
One Lake Street
Upper Saddle River, NJ 07458
(800) 382-3419

corpsales@pearsontechgroup.com

Visit AW on the Web: *www.awl.com/cseng/*

Library of Congress Cataloging-in Publication Data

Britton, Chris.
　　IT architectures and middleware: strategies for building large, integrated systems / Britton, Chris.
　　　　p.　　cm.
　　ISBN 0-201-70907-4
　　1. Computer architecture.　2. Middleware.　3. Information technology.　I. Title.
QA76.9.A73 B77　2000
004'3682—dc.21　　　　　　　　　　　　　　　　　　　　　　00-045376

Text printed on recycled and acid-free paper.

ISBN 0201709074

2　3　4　5　6　7　MA　　04 03 02 01

2nd Printing　　April 2001

To my wife, Judy,
and children, Katie and Alice

Contents

List of Figures   xv

List of Boxes   xix

Preface   xxi

Acknowledgments   xxvii

CHAPTER 1   The Nature of the Problem   1

1.1 Example: Moving to e-business   1

1.2 What is IT architecture?   5

1.3 Why is it different from what we did before?   7

1.4 The IT architecture approach   9

1.5 Alternatives   11

    1.5.1 Why not surround?   11

    1.5.2 Packages   13

1.6 How do we get there?   13

    1.6.1 Rewrite   13

    1.6.2 Evolution   15

    1.6.3 Bringing the techies
         and modelers together   17

1.7 Conclusions   18

**CHAPTER 2   A Short History of Middleware Technology—
From the Stone Age to Message Queuing   19**

2.1 Early days   19

2.2 Preliminaries   23

2.3 Remote procedure calls (RPC)   25

2.4 Remote database access   27

2.5 Distributed transaction processing   30

2.6 Message queuing   34

2.7 Message queuing vs. distributed transaction
     processing   36

2.8 What happened to all this technology?   39

**CHAPTER 3   A Short History of Middleware Technology—
Object Middleware   41**

3.1 Object-oriented concepts   42

3.2 Object middleware concepts   49

3.3 Object middleware technologies—
     DCOM and CORBA   52

3.4 Using object interfaces   56

3.5 Conclusions   58

**CHAPTER 4   A Short History of Middleware Technology—
Components and the Web   61**

4.1 Internet applications   62

4.2 Transactional component middleware   66

     4.2.1 COM+   69

     4.2.2 EJB   70

4.3 The issues of state   71

4.4 Conclusions   73

**CHAPTER 5   Middleware Classification and
Middleware Architectures   75**

5.1 Middleware elements   75

     5.1.1 Networking and interoperability   76

     5.1.2 The programmatic interface   77

     5.1.3 Server control   77

     5.1.4 System administration infrastructure   78

5.2 A technical classification of middleware?   78

     5.2.1 What is communicating?   78

     5.2.2 How they communicate   80

     5.2.3 What is the interface?   83

     5.2.4 Classifying middleware from technological
            principles   84

5.3 Vendor architectures   84

     5.3.1 Positioning   87

     5.3.2 Strawman for user target architecture   88

     5.3.3 Marketing   88

5.4 Implicit architectures   89

5.5 Conclusions   90

CHAPTER 6   **What Is Middleware For?**   **91**

6.1 Support for business processes   92

    6.1.1 Transactional, real-time   94

    6.1.2 Transactional, deferrable   95

6.2 Information retrieval   96

6.3 Collaboration   97

6.4 The presentation layer   98

6.5 The transaction server layer   100

6.6 The data layer   101

6.7 A generic functional architecture   103

6.8 Mediators   105

6.9 Conclusions   106

CHAPTER 7   **Resiliency**   **107**

7.1 Using backup servers   108

    7.1.1 Detecting failure   108

    7.1.2 Clean-up work in progress   110

    7.1.3 Activating the application   110

    7.1.4 Reprocessing "lost" messages   113

7.2 Dual active   114

7.3 Applying resiliency techniques
in practice   118

7.4 System software failures   119

7.5 Planned downtime   120

7.6 Application software failure   121

7.7 Developing a resiliency strategy   123

7.8 Conclusions   125

CHAPTER 8   **Performance and Scalability**   **127**

8.1 The un-slippery slope   128

8.2 Transaction processing   131

    8.2.1 Object interfaces   133

    8.2.2 Transactional component
containers   135

8.2.3 Two-phase commit   135

8.2.4 Message queuing   136

8.2.5 Using remote database access for real-time transactions   137

8.2.6 Conclusions on real time   139

8.3 Batch   139

8.4 Is distribution an alternative?   140

8.5 Load balancing   141

8.6 Business intelligence systems   143

8.6.1 Ad-hoc database queries   143

8.6.2 Data replication   144

8.7 Backups and recovery   144

8.8 Design for scalability and performance   146

8.9 Conclusions   147

CHAPTER 9   Security and Systems Management   151

9.1 Systems management technology   151

9.2 Security technology   156

9.3 Building application security   161

9.3.1 Circumventing security   163

9.3.2 Handling internal security violations   165

9.3.3 Existing applications   165

9.4 Application support for systems management and security   166

9.5 Conclusions   168

CHAPTER 10   Implementation Design and Components   171

10.1 Some general comments on design   171

10.2 Implementation design   178

10.2.1 The presentation layer   178

10.2.2 Mapping business objects to implementation objects   179

10.2.3 Grouping objects into components   181

10.2.4 Making reuse work   182

10.2.5 Completing the implementation design   187

10.3 Conclusions   188

CHAPTER 11   Implementing Business Processes   191

11.1 What is a process?   193

11.2 Business processes   196

11.3 The alternative view—functional analysis   197

11.4 Information and processes   199

11.5 Processes and computer applications   202

11.5.1 Business rules   202

11.5.2 Real time vs. deferrable   203

11.5.3 Data distribution   203

11.5.4 Long transactions   204

11.5.5 Generic business processes   206

11.5.6 Batch   206

11.6 Business process flexibility   206

11.7 Conclusions   207

CHAPTER 12   Information Access and Information Accuracy   211

12.1 Information access   211

12.1.1 Basic process information   214

12.1.2 Process management   215

12.1.3 Process improvement   216

12.1.4 Customer view   216

12.1.5 Marketing and strategic
business analysis   216

12.1.6 Summary of requirements for
information access   217

12.2 Information accuracy   218

12.3 Shared data or controlled duplication   220

12.3.1 Shared data   220

12.3.2 Controlled duplication   222

12.3.3 Hybrid strategy   224

12.4 Creating consistency in existing
databases   224

12.4.1 The technical problem   226

12.4.2 The data migration problem   227

12.4.3 The business process problem   227

12.5 The information controller   228

12.6 Conclusions   229

CHAPTER 13   **Change—Integration   231**

   13.1 Creating a presentation layer   234

      13.1.1 Screen-scraping task   235

      13.1.2 Interface size mismatch   235

      13.1.3 Turning existing applications into transaction servers   236

      13.1.4 Wrapping   238

      13.1.5 Building a middle tier   239

   13.2 Business processing change with new interfaces   240

   13.3 Changing the middleware between transaction servers   243

   13.4 Runtime integration products   244

   13.5 Extensible markup language (XML)   246

   13.6 Conclusions   247

CHAPTER 14   **Change—Flexibility   249**

   14.1 Understanding large applications   251

      14.1.1 Airline example   252

      14.1.2 Bank example   256

   14.2 Batch   261

   14.3 Conclusions   265

CHAPTER 15   **Building an IT Architecture   267**

   15.1 Integrated applications architecture   268

   15.2 Business process design   270

   15.3 Managing information   273

   15.4 The organizational and project management context   274

      15.4.1 Understanding existing systems   276

      15.4.2 Business process change design   277

      15.4.3 Application functional design   277

      15.4.4 Implementation design   277

      15.4.5 Implementation—coding   278

      15.4.6 Implementation—testing   279

15.4.7 Deployment 280

15.4.8 Project management 280

15.5 Breaking down the barriers 282

15.6 The future 283

Index 285

List of Figures

Figure 1-1   Example—before adding Web commerce server   2
Figure 1-2   Example—add Web commerce server   3
Figure 1-3   Example—add new interfaces   4
Figure 1-4   Application silos   8
Figure 1-5   Integrated Applications Architecture   10
Figure 1-6   Example—hardware box implementation
              of the architecture   10
Figure 1-7   Smother Architecture   12
Figure 1-8   The cost of rewriting   14
Figure 2-1   Distributed networking   20
Figure 2-2   The OSI seven-layer model   22
Figure 2-3   Remote procedure call (RPC)   25
Figure 2-4   Marshalling   26
Figure 2-5   Microsoft remote database access technologies   28
Figure 2-6   Remote database access message flow   29
Figure 2-7   An example of distributed transaction processing   31
Figure 2-8   The X/Open DTP model   33
Figure 2-9   Message queuing   35
Figure 2-10   Message queuing client/server   36
Figure 2-11   Debit/credit using distributed transaction processing   37
Figure 2-12   Debit/credit using message queuing   38
Figure 2-13   Debit/credit with reversal   39
Figure 3-1   Objects and classes   43
Figure 3-2   Class hierarchy   44
Figure 3-3   Polymorphism   45
Figure 3-4   What is an object?   47

Figure 3-5   Object middleware compilation and interpretation   51

Figure 3-6   The CORBA model   54

Figure 4-1   Web hardware configuration   64

Figure 4-2   COM+   68

Figure 4-3   Enterprise Java Beans   69

Figure 5-1   Middleware elements   76

Figure 5-2   Protocol categories   81

Figure 5-3   Microsoft Windows' DNA   86

Figure 5-4   J2EE   87

Figure 6-1   Typical use of transactional middleware   95

Figure 6-2   Information vs. timeliness   97

Figure 6-3   The presentation layer   100

Figure 6-4   Transaction and database servers   102

Figure 6-5   Business intelligence servers   103

Figure 6-6   The generic architecture   104

Figure 6-7   Mediators   105

Figure 7-1   Simple backup configuration   109

Figure 7-2   Lost messages   113

Figure 7-3   Clustered servers   115

Figure 7-4   The two-phase commit   117

Figure 7-5   Web configuration for resiliency   119

Figure 8-1   The un-slippery slope   128

Figure 8-2   The effect of improving the hardware architecture   129

Figure 8-3   An ideal transaction implementation   131

Figure 8-4   Rough OLTP network calculations   132

Figure 8-5   Rough OLTP disk calculations   132

Figure 8-6   Two-phase commit   136

Figure 8-7   Database server benchmark configuration   138

Figure 8-8   Database copy requirements   145

Figure 9-1   Distributed systems management   152

Figure 9-2   The presentation layer and servers   162

Figure 9-3   Network configuration   164

Figure 9-4   Vertical systems management   166

Figure 10-1   Tasks and phases   173

Figure 10-2   Functions and processes   175

Figure 10-3   Serendipitous reuse   183

Figure 10-4   Component dependencies   184

Figure 10-5   The range of reuse possibilities   186

Figure 10-6   Component layers   188

Figure 11-1   Parallel activities and sub-processes   194

Figure 11-2   Processes and data   200

Figure 11-3   Business processes for resource objects   200

Figure 11-4   Shared and copied tracking objects   201

Figure 11-5   Long transactions   209

Figure 11-6   ImpDiags: Implementation diagram   209

Figure 12-1   Data access users   212

Figure 12-2   Business intelligence server   213

Figure 12-3   Shared data vs. controlled duplication   220

Figure 12-4   Shared data configurations   221

Figure 13-1   Example—before   232

Figure 13-2   Example—high-level integration requirements   232

Figure 13-3   Example—the customer view   233

Figure 13-4   Adding a presentation layer to an existing application   234

Figure 13-5   The device size problem   236

Figure 13-6   The old and the new presentation layers   238

Figure 13-7   Example—two order entry processes   239

Figure 13-8   Example—flexible order entry   241

Figure 13-9   Process refinement   242

Figure 14-1   The relationship between design and implementation   251

Figure 14-2   A partial airline picture   253

Figure 14-3   Partial airline systems configuration   254

Figure 14-4   Banking systems   257

Figure 14-5   Products assembled from variants   259

Figure 14-6   The product layer   260

Figure 14-7   The shortening batch window   262

Figure 14-8   Batch processing vs. online transactions   264

Figure 14-9   Batch as a presentation layer   264

Figure 15-1   Order processing example   267

Figure 15-2   Integrated applications architecture   268

Figure 15-3   Shared data access   274

Figure 15-4   Cross-project IT functions   275

Figure 15-5   Project tasks   276

List of Boxes

What is IT Architecture?　5

SQL Parsing　29

X/Open DTP　33

OODB　46

CORBA　53

COM/DCOM　55

Layering　79

Two-Phase Commit　116

Queuing　133

How Fast Is Disk?　134

Locking　149

Function vs. Process　175

Process Implementation Diagrams　208

Historical Data and Format Changes　214

Quantum Management　283

Preface

All large organizations have complex, heterogeneous IT systems. All of them need to integrate their applications to support faster, more accurate business processes and to provide meaningful, consistent management information. All organizations are struggling to achieve this.

One reason for this struggle is that they are caught in the crossfire of an IT vendor war. In one corner is Microsoft. The strength of Microsoft is that they have a consistent technical strategy based on COM+ and Windows 2000. In the other corner, ranged against Microsoft, is a group that includes IBM, SUN, Oracle, and BEA. This group is focusing their resources around Enterprise Java Beans and CORBA. This is a battle over who will rule over middleware technology; a battle over how to implement distributed systems. Given the importance of the subject matter, it is a battle for the hearts and souls of IT for the next decade. Why? Because all large organizations have complex, heterogeneous IT systems that need to be brought together.

But vendor wars are only part of the problem. Scratch the surface of a large IT department and you will see many camps—in particular, workstation/departmental server "decentralizers" in one camp, and mainframe "centralizers" in another. Look from another angle and you will see two kinds of people, "techies" and "modelers." A techy will start a project by deciding what platform and software to use and will eventually get around to the boring bit, which is writing application code. A modeler will design the application with a modeling tool, generate a few programs and a database, and eventually will confront the (to him or her) trivial question of what platform it will run on. Modeling to a techy seems abstract and disconnected from reality. Technical issues to a modeler are tedious, and surely, soon we will be able to generate the application from the model at the press of a button, won't we? One of the keys to developing large distributed systems is to bring these people together.

Computer professionals are in general comfortable with developing applications on a single platform to a well-defined set of requirements. The reason is that the technology is well understood; the modelers know that what they design can be implemented and the techies know they can make it work. Large distributed systems are not like that. A system designed without consideration for the distributed implementation will flat out not work. Even worse, you will only discover that it doesn't work when you start scaling it up to production capacity. To add to our woes, we are now considering integrating multiple systems, each of which was a challenge to develop in the first place, and each of which is changing at a different speed, driven ever faster by the business. The notion of a "well-defined set of requirements" is not realistic; requirements will always be changing.

It is my contention that modelers need to know something about technology, and techies need to know something about modeling. Also, vendors, commentators, consultants, academics, and marketers need to know that their "solutions" lack either a modeling or a technical dimension.

This book is about IT architecture. IT architecture provides a framework for discussing implementation design, and it is in these discussions where techies and modelers should meet. Anyone with IT architect as part of their roles and responsibilities should know everything in this book. (Note I said "know" not "agree with.") They might like to read this book to see whether my approach to IT architecture is the same as theirs.

While IT architects are an important audience for this book, I have tried to write a book for IT management professionals as well. To be honest, I have assumed that the IT management professionals in my readership come from an IT background and not a business background; therefore, this book is not an introduction to IT. So why do IT management professionals need a book about IT architecture? Because it is here that so many of their concerns come together—application flexibility, information quality, resiliency, scalability and so on. One of my goals is to give IT management professionals the knowledge needed to challenge IT architects.

This book attempts to give an overview of the whole subject of building and running large distributed systems. It is a deliberate attempt to step above the detail and the infighting to examine what is important, what isn't important, and what we need to do differently now from ten years ago. My contention is that the difference between then and now is much more than simply that there are some new tools to play with. Building integrated systems is substantially different from building standalone applications, and it impacts everything we do in IT.

A major theme of this book is "enterprise computing." In the list of terms abused by the industry, "enterprise computing" has to be somewhere near the top. This book takes the view that enterprise computing is about being able to build systems that support the whole enterprise, which in large organizations means many thousands of users. It is obvious that systems supporting thousands of users must have resiliency, scalability, security, and manageability as major concerns. The enterprise computing mentality is about not being prepared to compromise on these objectives. An old mainframe application written in Cobol that gives you resiliency, scalability, security, and manageability is far superior to any implementation that does not.

This is not to say that you cannot build enterprise capable applications with modern tools like COM+ and Enterprise Java Beans. But to succeed we must understand the principles of building large, resilient systems. The principles that served us well for mainframe applications do not all apply for distributed systems and vice versa. So much has changed recently, especially in connection with the Internet, that I feel it is time the principles were reassessed and restated.

Unfortunately I have already discovered that many people see a discussion of principles as too abstract, and many people in IT, to my surprise, hate any sniff of an abstract concept. In a sense this is a value judgment; my important principle is your unimportant abstract concept. I have tried to avoid too dry a presentation style by giving many examples. In the earlier chapters the examples are very short—snippets of examples if you will. In later chapters, when I discuss modeling, the examples become more substantial.

Many organizations today are trying to avoid all these issues by buying third-party application packages. This is partially successful. When you buy a package, you buy an IT architecture, albeit only in the context of the package functionality. If you buy many packages, it is likely that you must lash them together somehow and for this you need an IT architect. If the packages are from different vendors, integration is a challenge. In this book, I give you the principles that should help in this task, but I have chosen not to address the challenge directly. The problem is there are so many packages, and I don't know them well enough to give a good account on package integration. The subject needs a book by itself.

This book is not for everyone. If you have no ambitions beyond programming, you will find this book short on product detail. It does not tell you anything about installation, there are no proper coding examples, there is no survey of products, and little in the way of product comparisons. This book will probably offend many IT vendors by mentioning their products either not at all or only in passing. I have no apology for any of these omissions. There are many books on coding, and product details change so fast the best place for comparisons is on the Internet. This book does not teach modeling. There are many books for that as well. But I hope application designers will read this book because the discussion on the principles for building enterprise systems is vital for them also. Finally, this book is not an academic book. There is little mathematics except for back-of-the-envelope style calculations to illustrate a few points. The aim is for a practical, wide-ranging discussion for IT professionals to help them understand what is going on so they can pick out the real issues from the imaginary issues and start building complex distributed systems with confidence.

An outline of the book is covered in the next section—How to read this book.

How to read this book

You can read this book straight through or as a work of reference. The purpose of this section is to explain the structure of the book, particularly for those who want to use the book for reference. If you are intending to use it for reference, and don't intend to read it through first, I encourage you to read at least chapters 1, 6, 10, 11, and 15.

This book is about four topics:

- Middleware technology alternatives
- Distributed systems technology principles
- Distributed systems implementation design
- Guidelines on the practice of IT architecture

The common thread that holds these topics together is a focus on IT architecture and implementation design. The structure of the book in greater detail is as follows.

Introduction

Chapter 1: The Nature of the Problem. This chapter is an introduction to the rest of the book. It takes an example and points out the main concerns of IT architecture.

Middleware technology alternatives

Chapter 2: A Short History of Middleware Technology—From the Stone Age to Message Queuing. This and the following two chapters are a historical survey of middleware technology. The topics are

- Remote procedures calls.
- Remote database access (ODBC, etc.).
- Distributed transaction processing.
- Message queuing.
- Comparison of message queuing with distributed transaction processing.

Chapter 3: A Short History of Middleware Technology—Object Middleware. The topics are

- A short introduction to object-oriented concepts.
- DCOM.
- CORBA.
- Using object interfaces over middleware.

Chapter 4: A Short History of Middleware Technology—Components and the Web. The topics are

- The difference, from an application implementation design angle, between Web browsers and workstations.
- COM+.
- Enterprise Java Beans.
- The issue of session state.

IT architecture guidelines / middleware

Chapter 5: Middleware Classification and Middleware Architectures. The topics are

- A technological classification of middleware. This section tries to answer the questions—is there additional middleware that has been overlooked, and how does middleware fit with other software?
- Vendor architectures like Microsoft DNA and Sun's J2EE.

Chapter 6: What Is Middleware For? The topics are

- A description of the functional requirements of middleware technology.
- An introduction to a high-level generic architecture (this is further broken down into components in chapter 10).

Distributed systems technology principles

Chapter 7: Resiliency. This chapter explains the principles of resiliency in distributed systems.

Chapter 8: Performance and Scalability. This chapter explains the principles of performance and scalability in distributed systems.

Chapter 9: Security and Systems Management. This chapter explains the principles of security and systems management in distributed systems.

IT architecture guidelines / distributed systems implementation design

Chapter 10: Implementation Design and Components. The topics are

- An explanation of the design context for IT architecture.
- A look at implementation design in more detail, in particular how to break the application into components.

Distributed systems implementation design

Chapter 11: Implementing Business Processes. The topics are

- A description of business processes.
- The relationship between business processes and data.
- The relationship between business processes and IT systems.

Chapter 12: Information Access and Information Accuracy. The topics are

- Information access requirements.
- Shared data or controlled duplication in new applications.
- How to change existing applications to achieve data consistency.

Chapter 13: Change—Integration. This and the next chapter are about changing existing systems. The topics are

- Creating a new presentation layer for existing applications.
- Integration of transaction servers.

Chapter 14: Change—Flexibility. The topics are

- Understanding and changing large, monolithic applications.
- Reducing reliance on batch.

Chapter 15: Building an IT architecture. This chapter summarizes the contents of the book and discusses how projects change when an IT architecture approach is followed.

IT architecture guidelines / conclusion

Throughout the book you will see text put into boxes with a heading in bold. You will also see references like this (see IT Architecture box). This reference indicates that the box on this subject has more information about the topic just being discussed. The text in the box contains a subject that is either more technical than the body of the text or that is on an esoteric subject I could not resist writing about.

Acknowledgments

I owe a debt of gratitude to many people who one way or another, sometimes inadvertently, made this book possible.

When I started on this book I was given great encouragement from the Unisys editorial board, in particular Tom Soller, Bob Vavra, Tom Freeman, Sridhar Iyengar, and Jim Senior.

The manuscript was reviewed by many people in its various stages of completion. I had many valuable comments from Peter Bye, David Howard, Gary Erickson, Marco Parilla, Sridhar Iyengar, Tony Morgan, Frank Schudde, Tom Mallon, Tom Tribble, Charles LeFevre, Tom Soller, and Bob Vavra. I must particularly pick out Tom and Bob since they clearly read everything and read it carefully.

I must thank the editorial staff. I was guided through the production process by Peter Gordon at Addison-Wesley and by Dot Malson, who manages the Unisys authors' program. Kathy Glidden had to keep me on the straight and narrow converting English English (my native tongue) to American English. Given the laxity of my grammar and spelling at the best of times, this was no simple task. Dot has done a tremendous job promoting the book internally and keeping the marketing side running smoothly.

I owe thanks to Kevin McHugh, Wayne Carpenter, Colin Gash, and Marc Lambotte—who are my managers at Unisys and who gave me the flexibility in my day-to-day work to write this book. (Well, I took the flexibility, at any rate.) I also owe a debt of thanks to the other members of the team in Europe who gave me encouragement and support.

The ideas behind this book came from many sources. I had long discussions with Peter Bye and Bob Richards—mainly in the Queen's Head—on what IT architecture is and why it is important. Others who have been particularly useful in providing insight into various technical and development methods issues have been David Howard and Tony Morgan. For me, ideas develop best with examples, and I am in debt to many organizations throughout Europe who have provided the raw material—the problems that have needed to be solved. I discussed these with numerous people both in and out of Unisys.

Finally, let me thank my family—Judy, Katie, and Alice—who have no interest at all in the contents of this book but had to put up with me taking the time out to write it. Katie and Alice will tell anyone who asks that this book is incredibly boring and can't possibly be of interest to anybody.

1

The Nature
of the Problem

This book is about making the link between business problems and IT solutions. It is about turning a functional design into an implementation design, deciding how to divide the functionality across programs, choosing the best middleware technology, and defining the requirements for supporting infrastructure code.

The IT industry has a habit of assuming this problem is solved, or at least easily solvable. Techies—programmers and systems specialists—don't think there is a problem because whenever someone tells them to make something work, they make it work. Modelers—application designers and business analysts—don't think there is a problem because they have tools that turn models directly into code.

And in many ways there wasn't a problem until the need for integration was recognized. The spur for an increased interest in integration was e-business.

To explain the need for integration, I will use an example.

1.1   Example: Moving to e-business

Suppose we have a company that markets and sells a range of products but does not manufacture them. It now wants to move to selling over the Internet.

The existing IT applications in this example are illustrated in Figure 1-1.

The original idea is to get an expert in Web development, build an interface to the Order Entry system, and then go gung ho to compete with Amazon.com, only pausing for an IPO. A moment's thought, however, and you realize you need to do more. To start with you need a number of additional interfaces. These are illustrated in Figure 1-2.

But building the interfaces is only part of the problem. The Web interface has now exposed to the outside world all the inconsistencies and complexities of the

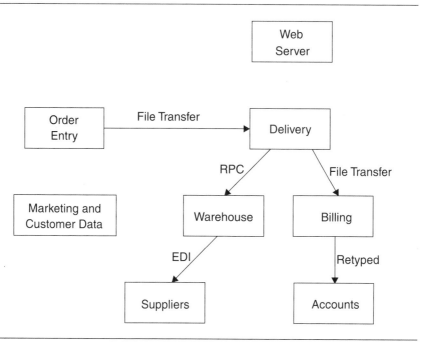

Figure 1-1   Example—before adding Web commerce server

system that up to now only the internal users had to contend with. Even if the Web interface is a good one, there are some fundamental issues that go much deeper, for instance:

- When the order information is being sent from the Order Entry to the Delivery system, there comes a time when it has been completed on one system but is still unknown on the other. The order has gone into limbo. The online user is left wondering what happened to it.
- Previously payment was after delivery. On the Internet they may need to take credit card details and process the payment before delivery. This means changes to the Order Entry, Delivery, and Billing applications.
- Product information is dispersed over the Order Entry, Warehouse, Delivery, Billing, Static Web Server, and Marketing applications. There is great potential for the information not to be consistent and therefore a danger that an online customer may order a product that isn't available or be unable to order a product that is available.
- Likewise, customer information is dispersed over the Order Entry, Delivery, Billing, and Marketing applications. There is a possibility that the customer's goods or invoice will be sent to the wrong address.

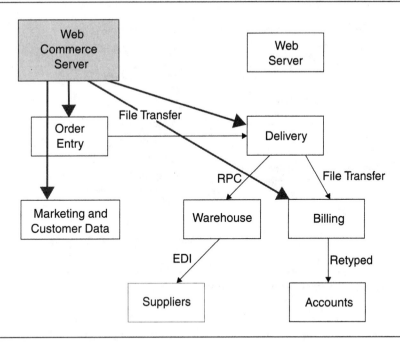

Figure 1-2   Example—add Web commerce server

If we look further ahead, we might want to implement WAP interface (for ordering over a mobile phone), a call center, one-to-one marketing, business-to-business (B2B) Internet communications, perhaps even a commerce portal. All of these interfaces are illustrated in Figure 1-3.

So how do we implement all these requirements?

First we need a structure to prevent chaos from breaking out. If we look more closely, there are three generic issues that need exploring.

First, the business process flow from order entry through distribution to billing needs to be controlled. The primary reason is that the customer wants to know what happened to his or her order. The solution could be an order tracking system linked to all the other systems. This solution could provide the basis for many other improvements. For instance, it might be possible to substantially improve the business process for order cancellation or delivery returns. The business might also be able to get a better handle on where the delays are in the system and improve the speed of service, perhaps to the extent of being able make a delivery time promise at the time of order placement.

Second, the data quality needs improvement. The fundamental issue is that there are many copies of one piece of information, for instance, product or customer data, dispersed over many databases. We need a strategy for either sharing the same data or controlling data duplication.

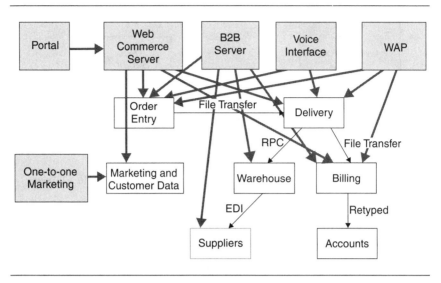

Figure 1-3   Example—add new interfaces

Third, an existing service needs to be opened up to additional end user devices. Figure 1-3 shows the Order Entry application being called from a Web Commerce server, from a WAP server, from the Call Center workstations, and from a B2B server. We not only want the Order Entry application to handle all these forms of access, but we also want it to be possible to start entering an order on a Web Commerce server and finish entering the same order over the telephone.

These three problems—improving cross-functional business process control, providing online information accuracy, and supporting multiple presentation devices—are typical of many IT organizations. IT architecture is a primary tool for solving all of these problems.

Of course these problems are not the only IT management concerns. Three other issues that stand out are

- Making applications more responsive to change
- Keeping costs down
- Finding skilled staff

IT architecture has a direct impact on the first of these problems and an indirect impact on the other two.

So what is IT architecture? Why is it different from what we did before? And how does it help us tackle the issues outlined above?

1.2   What is IT architecture?

IT architecture is generic implementation design (see IT Architecture box for more on the problem of definition).

Broadly speaking, building an IT system can be broken down into five tasks:

- Business process change definition
- Application functional design
- Implementation design
- Implementation
- Deployment

What is IT Architecture?

To answer this question, we must distinguish between the specific versus the generic, the narrow focus versus the wide focus, and the detailed versus the high level.

Narrow focus to wide focus: This is the move from considering a single project to considering multiple projects, eventually considering the total enterprise.

Detailed to high level: This is the move from the individual brush strokes to the big picture view. Note that, while high level and enterprise wide commonly go together, that does not have to be the case. You can have a very detailed, enterprise-wide network design, for instance.

Specific to generic: This is the move from the one to the many. Generic does not equal high level; generic is looking at points in common across the many, while high level is looking at one thing from a long way off.

To my mind, the word "architecture" in IT is best used for generic design. Thus architecture constrains, informs, or specifies an aspect common across many designs, and a design can have many implementations. A design is often said to implement an architecture, and an application implements a design. For instance, there is the Intel chip architecture, which has been implemented in many chip designs.

Even within the area of generic design there are an enormous range of possible architectures. Architectures can be classified by their scope and their precision.

The scope is defined by the answer to the question—what is this architecture for? Some possible answers might be: business processes design, application functional design, database design, and implementation design. I use the words "application architecture" if the scope is application functional design and "IT architecture" if the scope is implementation design, but it is possible in theory to define a subcategory of architecture for every design task.

(continued)

What is IT Architecture?   (*cont.*)

The precision of an architecture could be

* a guideline.
* a pattern.
* a formal model (for example, ISO seven-layer model).

(A pattern is more precise than a guideline and less inclusive than a formal model.) Because of the connotations of the word "architecture," there is a feeling that it should edge toward the formal model end of the precision spectrum. This is unfortunate because most of the useful points to be made about generic design are guidelines or patterns.

So, what does an IT architect do? The title implies that he or she should look after the IT architecture, but I believe the main task is to guide implementation design. What this book is about is doing implementation design with an architectural approach. In other words, enforcing generic principles and patterns across multiple projects. (As an aside, the use of the word "architect" here is also closer to the use of the word architect for buildings. In the same vein, IT architecture is closest to the notion of an architectural style like "gothic style" or "Palladian style.")

To be honest, I think calling designlike things "architectures" in IT has caused more confusion than it has shed any light. But I don't have a good alternative and in the end, what matters is consistency. So long as everyone uses the word in more or less the same way, the word is useful.

Implementation design sits in the middle. Implementation design is about high-level IT design decisions, all the key IT implementation decisions you make without actually writing any code. These decisions include: how to divide the functions into components and programs, data distribution, choice of technology, development tools, and programming rules. I personally would take it to the level of detail where the required components are identified and to take a first cut at defining the interfaces. I would not go further; I would not for instance define the operations in pseudo code.

To do implementation design well, you must understand what is going on around it. Clearly you must understand implementation and deployment issues—understand the nature of the things you are designing. But you must also be able to understand and critique the application design to truly understand the requirements.

Implementation design however cannot be done in a vacuum and that is where IT architecture comes in. There are many concerns, for instance:

* Ensuring the design is compatible with the high-level design of the IT systems across the enterprise to address issues such as shared user interfaces and shared data.

- Ensuring IT infrastructure code is reused (for example, security code, interface to e-mail systems).
- Ensuring design patterns are reused (for example, for switching to a backup server in the case of failure).
- Optimizing skills and resources.

There is a great temptation to develop a one-off "IT architecture" and to assume that this answers all the questions posed in implementation design. This is neither practical nor desirable. It is not practical because the document must be many times larger than this book to cover all the eventualities. It is not desirable because project teams will simply ignore it.

My alternative is to instigate the role of an IT architect who has responsibility for guiding the implementation design and has approval authority for the design going into implementation.

To do all this, the IT architect must understand

- The technology alternatives.
- The capabilities of the development staff in the technologies.
- The technology principles—how the technology can be used to create systems that are scalable, resilient, secure, and manageable.
- The "functional" requirements—what the application must do.
- The "nonfunctional" requirements—like the scalability, resiliency, and security requirements of the application.
- The business process change that will be implemented by the design.
- The factors that make applications flexible and easy to change.
- The existing systems that need to be changed.

The point about understanding business processes might seem surprising, but the reason why IT systems need to be integrated is because business processes are integrated. In particular, one business process may initiate others and business processes share data, as we saw in the previous section. Business processes and their relationship to implementation design is a subject I will explore in detail in Chapter 11.

Also, as I hope I shall make clear in later chapters, understanding the business processes is key to understanding the nonfunctional requirements like resiliency, scalability, and security.

1.3   Why is it different from what we did before?

The most obvious difference between IT now and IT ten years ago is the amount of new technology that has been introduced, especially technology that supports the Internet. But let us suppose for a moment that all the latest hardware technology, software technology, and modeling and development tools had been available for the last twenty years: would IT systems be in a substantially better position than they are today? I believe that they would not. Put another way, if we had had Enterprise Java Beans ten years ago, then although we might have had more IT systems, the systems themselves would be just as unresponsive to business change, hold just as much inaccurate information, be just as impervious to new interfaces, and probably be no cheaper. In no way is this to trash the new technology. It is just that new technology by itself does not solve the major underlying problem, which is managing complexity.

The major source of complexity is that most organizations simply have too many standalone applications, each with its own presentation layer, business processing logic, and database. I will call these "silos." (Others call these "stovepipes," but in U.K. English we call stovepipes "chimneys," and "chimney architecture" sounds rather strange.) Silo applications are represented in Figure 1-4.

The earlier example illustrates the problem. This company had six silos: Order Entry, Delivery, Warehouse, Billing, Accounts, and Marketing information. The problems described in this example are typical; inconsistencies in the data, difficulties in creating a single user view across multiple silos, and the lack of business process integration. Sixty silos would be more typical of a large commercial organization.

Silo applications were paid for and built on behalf of departments in the organization and were tuned to their requirements. Typically, those requirements were to computerize paper-based systems designed to make that single department's life easier. Now, several reorganizations later, the departmental boundaries are different. What worked then does not work now.

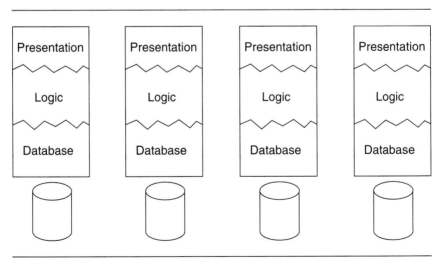

Figure 1-4   Application silos

Observe that new tools and clever techniques such as reuse make it easier to develop new silos even faster. Thus, whereas in the past we developed a few hundred applications using old tools, if we had had the new tools then, we could have developed a few thousand more applications. Yes, the business would have more functionality in its IT applications, but the problems of fast response to business change and information accuracy would be just as intractable.

Silo thinking is deeply embedded. Reasons include:

- Departments don't want to lose power.
- Project management wants self-contained projects to control.
- Development methodologies are silo based.
- There is a fear of large integrated systems.
- There is a fear of changing large existing applications.

Clearly, I think the fears are to some extent unjustified, otherwise I would not be writing this book. But there is genuine fear and uncertainty nonetheless, and I will return to this subject in the last chapter.

1.4   The IT architecture approach

An alternative to silo applications I shall call the **Integrated Applications Architecture**. This is illustrated in Figure 1-5.

This architecture is justified in Chapter 6. Note however that these boxes indicate functional areas and not a single program. In practice, there would be many presentation layer devices and servers, many transaction servers, and many business intelligence engines. A possible "box" view of the system is illustrated in Figure 1-6.

The key points of an Integrated Applications Architecture are:

- There are multiple user interfaces to the same underlying function.
- The transaction server and business intelligence logic can be used by any interface.
- Within the "boxes" there are many components.
- The databases can be shared by the transaction servers (but, as explained in Chapter 12, typically by using a component interface rather than directly through remote database access).
- There are well-defined, well-documented interfaces throughout.

An important issue that is not clear from the diagram is how business processes and business objects map to components. This is a key topic, if not "the" key topic of implementation design, and I will discuss it from various angles in the latter part of the book.

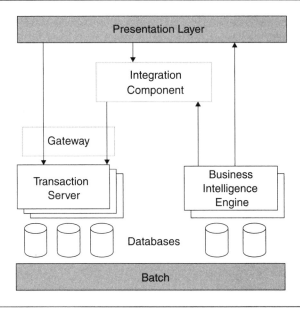

Figure 1-5   Integrated Applications Architecture

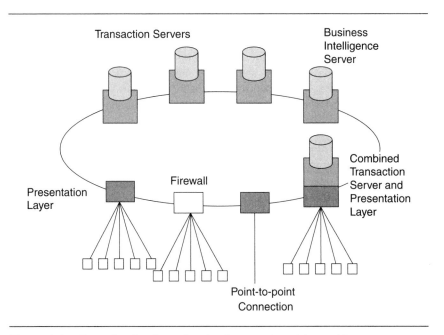

Figure 1-6   Example—hardware box implementation of the architecture

The Integrated Applications Architecture has broken away from silos by stressing the independence of the presentation, transaction server, and database layers. We can start to see how we might tackle the IT management problems described in the example, in particular:

- Responding quickly to business change—by aligning the components and the transaction servers with the organizational business processes, we will get to the root of the issue of responsiveness to business change.
- Providing accurate and accessible information—with a clear understanding of how data is used by many processes we can eliminate uncontrolled data duplication either by sharing data or by implementing controlled data duplication.
- Opening up the applications to new forms of interface, like the Web— with a clean separation of presentation and processing we make it easier to add a new interface.

I will cover business processes in Chapter 11, information accuracy in Chapter 12, and building for new interfaces in Chapters 6 and 13.

There are design consequences of the Integrated Applications Architecture. New development is no longer about building another silo but about adding and modifying components.

There are technical consequences of the Integrated Applications Architecture. If two logic components require different middleware standards, the presentation component must support both. This is clearly inconvenient, to say the least, so a technical consequence is a drive toward greater standardization. But standardization does not have to be total. You can put gateways or wrappers (discussed in more detail in Chapter 13) in front of the logic component to take messages from one middleware technology and resend them through another.

So long as it is not taken to excess, standardization is good. The effort required for system integration is great and is a significant proportion of the total project cost. Standardization is one tool for reducing cost. It enables reuse of system integration program code and skills.

1.5   Alternatives

The Integrated Applications Architecture is sufficiently radical for people to propose "easier" alternatives.

1.5.1   Why not surround?

Organizations are loath to change their existing applications and are therefore looking for ways of gaining the benefits of integration without the pain of touching the existing code. There is an alternative; I call it the "Smother Architecture." It is illustrated in Figure 1-7.

The idea is to surround the existing applications with a front end and a back end.

Before I go any further, let me point out that in some cases this kind of architecture is inevitable. If the application is bought from an external software vendor and can only be changed by them, then this kind of integration may be your only choice. If the application actually resides in a different organization, in other words, your organization is part of an alliance, this kind of architecture may also be inevitable. Also, silos are a natural consequence of mergers and acquisitions.

But the smother technique should be kept to a minimum. A front-end hub can be easily built to cope with 5 transaction types from one application and 20 from another. But if you try to reshape the interface for 200 transaction types in one application and 400 in another, the list of rules will balloon to enormous proportions. Furthermore, recovery issues make the front-end hub much, much more complex. For instance, suppose your new presentation interface takes one input and processes 10 back-end transactions. What happens if the sixth in the set fails? You have to programmatically reverse the transactions of the previous five that succeeded.

Finally, the hub is a potential bottleneck and a single point of failure, though these problems are fixable with a big enough checkbook.

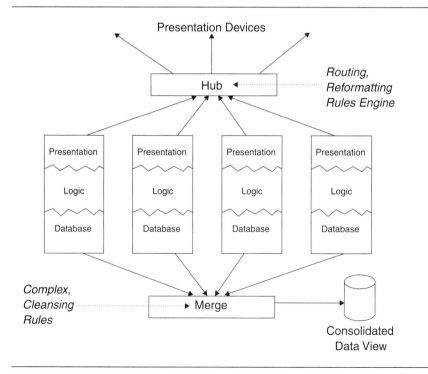

Figure 1-7   Smother Architecture

Turning to the back end, I am not against data warehouses, but a data warehouse is much more effective if the data is clean. The notion of taking data from multiple sources and reconstructing the correct form is unrealistic. Do you take the name from one database, the address from another, the phone number from a third and reconstruct a correct record? How do you know John Smith in one database is J. Smith in another? If there are two phone numbers for the same person, which one is the correct one? Of course, the last input data is the most likely to be correct, but how do you know which one is the last by looking at the data? You can't!

1.5.2 Packages

Many organizations have a policy that they will use third-party application packages for IT applications as much as is reasonably possible.

All the problems described with silo applications exist for packages as well. Sometimes the package itself is enormous and there is good integration within the product. But it is rare that an organization can run using only one package, so some level of integration is likely to be needed. For instance, in the earlier example, perhaps the billing application is from a third party; the challenge now is to integrate it with the Web commerce server.

Many of the techniques described in this book can be used on packages as well as standalone applications. The big difference is that you are constrained in your technology choices. Since the architecture principles I will be describing do not rely on a single technology or even a short list of technologies, most of them apply for packages. For instance, in Chapter 12 on information I describe the notion of achieving data accuracy by having a primary database and controlled duplication of the data to one or more secondary databases. This technique can often be implemented on packages. Let us suppose the data in question is the customer information. You might have to write some code to create the flow of messages from the primary database to the package applications, and you might have to write code to process these messages as updates on the package database, but it can be done with some work. What is probably harder to do is to make the package database the primary, but, of course, how much harder depends on the package.

1.6 How do we get there?

There are two options: rewrite or evolve.

1.6.1 Rewrite

It is wise to be cautious about the notion of rewriting simply to keep up with technology. If you had done so in the past, you would have first rewritten the application into DCE, then again into CORBA, and would now be rewriting it again into

EJB or Microsoft DNA. One reason why IT architecture got a bad name is because many organizations have already had an IT architecture study done that is sitting on a shelf gathering dust. A major problem with such exercises has been that they have recommended technology-driven change.

What about occasional rewrites? There are again good reasons to be cautious:

- The existing application works.
- All those concerns about scalability, resiliency, and security may have already been solved.
- Rewriting is lengthy and expensive during which time the business cannot move forward.
- Rewriting is risky.

In the long term, rewriting can never be a strategy for success; at some stage or other your organization will have to embrace evolutionary change. To understand why, look at the graph in Figure 1-8.

Over time, the amount of functionality in a system will increase and the rewrite will become larger and longer. The only escape is if the rewrite can use new tools that are an order of magnitude better than their predecessors. Suppose ten analysts and programmers have spent ten years extending an application; they have spent one hundred staff years on the application. For the same ten people to rewrite the system in one year will require tools that deliver ten times the productivity of their old tools.

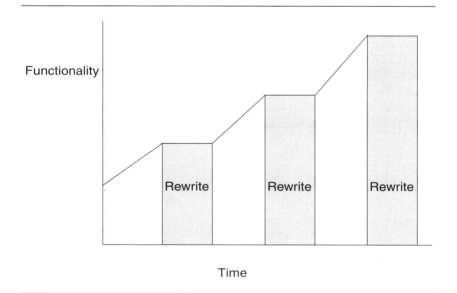

Figure 1-8 The cost of rewriting

I expect everyone with a passionate commitment to one of the latest development tools is at this point jumping up and down shouting—yes, it can, yes, it can! Of course, it could be true. If the old system is a built-in assembler with a hand-crafted databases system, modern tools will be at least ten times more productive. On the other hand, if the system uses Cobol and a relational database or even a network database system, call me a skeptic. Two times maybe, ten times—I don't think so. Mind you, if you did rewrite the application today, then the next rewrite in ten years time will require a tool ten times more productive than even that. Eventually rewrites are impossible.

There are many, many disasters in organizations that have chosen to rewrite, but the only ones that make the headlines are the ones in the public sector. Let me assure you that smugness in the private sector is entirely unwarranted. I know of situations where tens of millions of dollars have been spent on rewrites only for the whole project to be canceled. These disastrous projects made barely a ripple in the press. For large, core systems the practical alternative to evolving the existing application is to buy a package, not to rewrite. Even then, the experience many organizations have had implementing ERP packages like SAP, is that implementing a package demands a complete overhaul of all your business processes, albeit in many cases for the better.

Rewriting is not always bad. There are two cases for considering a rewrite. First, rewrite when the technology is so old that there are serious issues with support, such as a lack of skills. Second, rewrite when the business functionality has changed so much that it may be easier to rewrite than to modify.

1.6.2   Evolution

The alternative to rewriting can be summed up in one word: evolution.

Evolution is inevitable. Look back at the Integrated Applications Architecture and imagine introducing a major new piece of functionality, for instance, changing to a new delivery process. This might require a change to the Web interface, a new module in the delivery application, and some changes to the database. These changes cannot be implemented by writing a new silo application. The only practical way to move the Integrated Applications Architecture forward is evolution. I discuss this subject in more detail in Chapters 13 and 14.

But evolution is not only inevitable—it is desirable. IT organizations know this when they are software buyers, but somehow seem to forget this when they are software developers. We all know never to buy a product in its first release. We all know that when other people develop software, it needs several releases to turn a good idea into something usable in practices. We even talk about software "being mature." It is hard to find a major software product that has not developed significantly since the first release, certainly no operating system—all major operating systems have roots that go back ten, twenty years or more—and certainly none of the major database products.

I would even state this point more strongly and claim that evolution is the only proven methodology for developing large complex IT systems. There are two reasons. First, requirements change and therefore cannot be anticipated up front. Second, when you have a large number of requirements it is almost impossible to balance functionality against cost, against performance, against resiliency, against security, and against manageability. In a nutshell, if you are setting off on a large system development project and you think you know what the end result will look like, you are almost certainly wrong.

At the moment most IT practices are contrary to the spirit of evolution. For instance, there is the divide between the "exciting" development phase and the "boring" maintenance phase. But let us embrace evolution and try to make it work better.

So how do matters change when we try to design for evolution?

There are technical aspects to designing for evolution. For instance, I think we can be reasonably confident that there will be new technology in the future. Let us therefore try and build for maximum technological flexibility. Some techniques are:

- Using **mediator** routines (my term) to hide the middleware, operating system, or database system interfaces from the application logic.
- Ensuring that there are well-defined interfaces so a component can change without requiring changes to all the other components.
- Ensuring that the design is expressed in nontechnological terms. For instance, instead of saying this interface is an RPC interface we say it is a real-time interface which leaves open the option that it can be implemented in DCOM, Corba, EJB, or even message queuing used the right way. (I will explain what RPC, DCOM, etc., are in the next few chapters.)

Also, while we cannot write some Cobol in such a way that it can be easily translated to Java, we can document the design properly and keep it in sync with the code. Okay, forget the last sentence—I'm dreaming.

There are application aspects to designing for evolution. The basic idea is to exploit the fact that components can evolve at their own speed (so long as they don't break the interface). Application logic and data components should be split along business process boundaries to allow business processes to change with minimal disruption to other business processes. We could put fast changing parts into their own component and slower changing parts into other components. In practice, presentation logic will almost certainly change at its own (fast) speed and should be isolated out. At the other end of the spectrum, database logic, especially data such as customer data or product data that is used everywhere, will change slowly and should be behind the protective wall of a component interface to ensure its integrity stays intact.

There are project management aspects to designing for evolution. For instance, when partitioning the requirements into deliverables, let evolution work for you. Do not work too hard getting the last detail of the business requirement in the first deliverable. Instead, develop an application that can evolve, that is, that has

- a simple structure that can support change.
- a good user interface that can be extended easily in any direction.
- an architecture that is scalable and resilient.
- good support for security and system management.
- a minimum of functional requirements—avoiding frills and cleverness.

Then find out the real detailed functional requirements by seeking user feedback. User acceptance comes more from a system that works well and is easy to use, than from having a vast collection of features. The original Web browser is a classic example of this principle in practice. So produce a basic product and then act on the feedback. The great advantage of this approach is that it is easier to break the work into a number of small projects.

1.6.3   Bringing the techies and modelers together

Having established that there needs to be an Integrated Applications Architecture and hence a group to manage it, who is going to be in this group? Most organizations would either put it under the control of the application development section, and pack it full with modelers, or put in under the technical section, and pack it full of techies. Neither alternative works well.

Converting a model directly into code typically generates an application that works well with one user on a portable PC but works poorly with 1,000 users on a server. Some of the traps are

- expecting to use remote database access technology like ODBC for large scale transaction processing.
- having a large number of indexes on a volatile database table, leading to large numbers of additional IOs.
- having long transactions, locking out the data from other users.
- using a component interface in such a way that causes excessive network traffic, for instance by "getting" and "setting" attributes individually.
- using an unnecessarily large number of two-phase commits.
- having large search programs running alongside online work.
- requiring session state to be moved from the primary system to the backup system in the event of a failure.
- not having a consistent and well-thought-through security policy and implementation.
- not providing hooks to monitor performance or record error conditions.

These points are explored in Chapters 7, 8, and 9 on resiliency, performance, and systems management.

There are a large number of different middleware technologies and none of them does everything. The best middleware for doing an ad-hoc report is not necessarily the best for transaction processing. The best middleware that links a bank teller with the backend transaction processor is not necessarily the best for sending expense reports to a payment system. You need to have a blend of different technologies to build successful integrated applications. Modeling as currently practiced is usually insensitive to these issues; they all get bundled into the general category of object calls object. We need people capable of looking at a model, understanding it, and figuring out the best implementation. This requires modelers who understand the principles of enterprise-scale technology and techies who can read and understand models (and who also understand enterprise-scale systems).

Techies without modelers are also dangerous. While modelers have a propensity for delaying the design until the existing system is fully modeled, techies have a propensity for going for the quick kill. For instance I have seen excellent techies propose strongly that a customer should build a middleware interface to their data handling routines, thereby enabling new tools to access old data. This might be a good idea, but it might not, and the techy was not engaging in the discussion to find out. For instance, a downside is that you would lose the opportunity of reusing many of the old business logic routines. Also, developing a new application without the possibility of changing the database design might not be so easy either. Many technical discussions are like an argument about whether it is best to go to work by car or by bicycle. The answer is (obviously, I hope)—it depends, and techies hate the "it depends" answer.

Techies and modelers must come together. Developing the Integrated Applications Architecture is a joint exercise.

1.7   Conclusions

The Integrated Applications Architecture is the goal. Evolution is how we get there. Bringing the techies and the modelers together is how we see the traps along the way.

This book is about four topics:

- Middleware technology alternatives. This underpins much of the technology discussions.
- Distributed systems technology principles. This is the common knowledge that modelers and techies must know to do effective implementation design.
- Distributed systems implementation design. This is about splitting the application functionality into components and designing for information accessibility and accuracy. A particular difficulty is how to handle existing systems and this is discussed at length in Chapters 13 and 14.
- Guidelines on the practice of IT architecture. I will discuss an evolutionary approach to IT architecture in contrast to a rewrite approach.

The next four chapters address middleware technology alternatives.

2

A Short History of Middleware Technology— From the Stone Age to Message Queuing

The aim of this and the next two chapters is not so much to teach history but to use a historical perspective to give a short introduction to the range of middleware technologies and an insight into some of the factors that have been driving the industry. This background knowledge is vital for any implementation design exercise that uses middleware, which today is practically all of them.

But first, what is middleware? There are numerous definitions, many of them strange, for instance, "the '/' in client/server" and "the software nobody wants to pay for" (this last one was said by Christopher Stone when he was president of OMG). My definition is that middleware is software that makes it possible in practice to build distributed applications. I will discuss this definition more in Chapter 6, by which time there will be more examples. One way to look at it is that middleware is to low-level network programming what databases are to file systems.

Frankly, in the early days they didn't see a need for middleware, the awareness came later, and it is worth examining how the need for middleware came to be understood. (Actually in the 1970s many organizations didn't see much point in database systems, either.)

2.1 Early days

Distributed systems have been with us for a long time. While networking originally meant "dumb" green-screen terminals attached to mainframes, it wasn't long before, instead of having a terminal at the end of a line, organizations started putting computers there, thus creating a network of computers. The difference between attaching a terminal and talking to a computer is illustrated in Figure 2-1.

The first distributed systems were implemented by large organizations and by academia. The U.S. Department of Defense built a 4-node network, called ARPANET, in 1969. By 1972, ARPANET had grown to include approximately 50 computers (mainly universities and research sites).

An early need for middleware was for communication between companies in the same industry. Two outstanding examples of this are SWIFT (Society for Worldwide Interbank Financial Telecommunication), for international money transfers in the financial industry, and IATA (International Air Transport Association) in the airline industry. Airlines in particular were pioneers; some airlines had multi-node networks as early as the late 1960s.

During the 1970s most major IT hardware vendors came out with "network architectures" that supported large networks of distributed computers. Thus we had IBM's System Network Architecture (SNA), Sperry's Distributed Communication Architecture (DCA), Burroughs' Network Architecture (BNA), and DEC's Distributed Network Architecture (DNA). These products provided

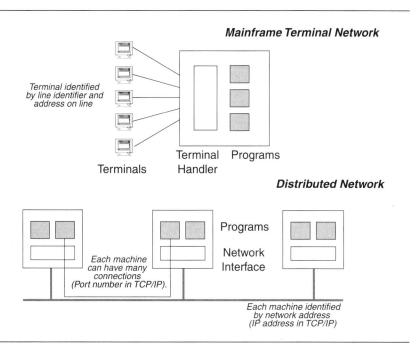

Figure 2-1   Distributed networking

facilities for programs to send and receive messages, as well as a number of basic services like:

- File transfer
- Remote printing
- Terminal transfer (logging on to any machine in the network)
- Remote file access

The vendors also developed some distributed applications of which the most prevalent by far was e-mail.

In an organization that bought all of its IT from a single vendor this worked fine, but for organizations who used or wanted to use multiple IT vendors, life was difficult. Thus arose the open systems movement.

The key idea of the open systems movement, then as now, is that if IT vendors are forced to implement the same standard, it creates competition and drives prices down. At the lower levels of networking this always worked well, perhaps because the telephone companies were involved and they have a history of developing international standardization. (The telephone companies at the time were mostly national monopolies so standards didn't hold the same threat to them as it did for IT vendors.) For instance, standards were developed for electrical interfaces (like RS232) and for networking protocols (like X.25). The chief hope of the early open systems movement was to replicate this success and widen it into all distributed computing by using the International Organization for Standardization (ISO) as the standards authority. (I did get that right, by the way. ISO does not stand for International Standards Organization and it's not IOS.) The fruit of this work was the OSI (Open Systems Interconnection) series of standards. The most influential of these was the OSI Basic Reference Model—the famous seven-layer model. The first draft of this standard came out in December 1980, but it was several more years until the standard was formally ratified. Since then, there have been numerous other OSI standards that have fleshed out the different parts of the OSI seven-layer model. The seven-layer model itself isn't so much a standard, as it is a framework in which standards can be placed. The model is illustrated in Figure 2-2.

It was apparent early on that there were problems with the OSI approach. The most obvious problem at first was simply that the standards process was too slow. Proprietary products were clearly way ahead of standards products and, the longer the delay, the more code would later need to be converted. The next problem was that the standards themselves were so complex. This is a common failing of standards organizations. Standards committees have a major problem with achieving consensus and a minor problem with the cost of implementation. The simplest way to achieve a consensus is to add every sound idea. The OSI seven-layer model probably exacerbated the situation because each committee had to look at a tiny slice of the whole problem (that is, part of one layer) and it was hard for them to make compromises on technology. However, the problem is by no means unique to networking standardization. The ISO SQL standardization effort has also

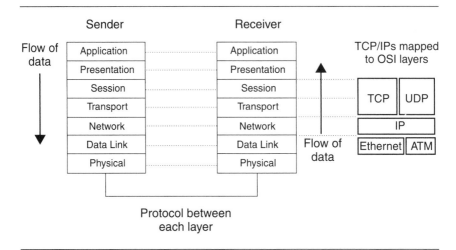

Figure 2-2   The OSI seven-layer model

suffered from runaway function creep—a function avalanche perhaps! A clear example of an OSI standard that suffered from all the problems of complexity and lateness was the OSI virtual terminal standard, which was tackling one of the simpler and, at the time, one of the most important requirements—how to connect a terminal to an application.

So the industry turned away from OSI and started looking for alternatives. Its attention turned to Unix and suddenly everyone was talking about "open systems," a new marketing buzzword for Unix-like operating systems. These products were meant to deliver cheap computing, driven by portable applications and a vigorous software market.

Unix came from the universities, and these organizations, when viewed as IT shops, have several interesting characteristics. First, they are very cost conscious—so Unix was cheap. Second, they have a nearly unlimited supply of clever people—so Unix required lots of clever people to keep it going and these clever people were quite prepared to fix the operating system. Consequently, Unix came in many different versions even then, in particular the Berkeley version and the AT&T version. Third, if the system goes down, the only people complaining are students—so Unix went down, often. Of course, given time, the IT vendors could fix all the negative points, but, being IT vendors, they all fixed them in different ways.

But this cloud had a silver lining. Along with Unix came, not SNA or OSI, but TCP/IP. TCP/IP was developed in the mid-1970s for the U.S. military and was deployed in 1983 in ARPANET. The military's influence (and money) was key to TCP/IP's success. It has been said that the resilience and flexibility of TCP/IP largely arose because of a requirement to survive nuclear war! In 1983, APRANET split into a military and nonmilitary network—the nonmilitary network being composed of academic and research establishments where Unix reigned supreme.

Over the years ARPANET evolved into the Internet and the explosion of the Internet (largely caused by the Web) has made TCP/IP the dominant networking standard. TCP/IP and the Web are examples of what standardization can do. But it will only do it if the technology works well and is relatively easy to use.

TCP/IP is a set of standards. IP (Internet Protocol) is the network standard. It ensures messages can be sent from machine to machine. TCP (Transmission Control Protocol) is a session standard for program-to-program communication over IP. If you want to write a program to use TCP/IP directly, you use Sockets in Unix and Winsock on Windows. There is a host of other stuff that is normally bracketed with TCP/IP such as Telnet (terminal interface), SNMP (Simple Network Mail Protocol—for e-mail), FTP (File Transfer Protocol), and numerous lower-level standards for network control.

Today, although Windows 2000 is threatening the Unix market from the low end and the resurgent mainframe market is pressuring Unix from the high end, all of them run TCP/IP.

So far, I have been largely discussing networking evolution. What about building applications over the network, which is, after all, the concern of middleware? Since every network architecture provides application programming interfaces (APIs) for sending messages over the network and a few basic networking services, is anything more necessary? In the early days, the need was not obvious. But when organizations started building distributed systems they found that they had to build their own middleware. There were four reasons for this: performance, control, data integrity, and ease of use. It turned out that "rolling your own" was a huge undertaking, but few of the organizations that did it regret it. It gave them a competitive advantage in the past and still allows them to integrate new applications to the existing code relatively quickly. It gave them the flexibility to change the network technology since the applications could remain unchanged. Only now is the middleware supplied by outside vendors catching up with the power of some of these in-house developments, and only now are these organizations seriously beginning to wonder whether to change. The number one priority of a large organization betting their business on distributed computing is data integrity, closely followed by performance. Migration cannot be contemplated until the middleware software vendors release products with equal data integrity and performance, and this has taken time.

2.2 Preliminaries

It will save time in describing middleware if I cover a few concepts first.

First, middleware should provide the following:

- Ease of use (compared to writing it yourself using a low-level API like Sockets).
- Location transparency—the applications should not have to know the network and application address of their opposite number. It should be possible

to move an application to a machine with a different network address without recompilation.

- Message delivery integrity—messages should not be lost or duplicated.
- Message format integrity—messages should not be corrupted.
- Language transparency—a program using the middleware should be able to communicate with another program written in a different language. If one program is rewritten in a different language, all other programs should be unaffected.

Message integrity is usually supplied by the network software, that is, by TCP/IP. All of the middleware I describe has location transparency and all, except some Java technology, has language transparency. Ease of use is usually provided by taking a program-to-program feature used within a machine (like procedure calls to a library or calls to a database), and providing a similar feature that works over a network.

Most of the middleware technology I will describe is **client/server** middleware. This means that one side (the server) provides a service for the other side (the client). If the client does not call the server, the server does not send unsolicited messages to the client. You can think of the client as the program that gives the orders and the server as the program that obeys them. Do not assume that a client always runs on a workstation. Web servers are often clients to back end servers. The concept of client/server has proved to be a straightforward and simple idea that has been enormously useful.

Since during this book I will be discussing data integrity issues, I need to ensure some consistency in the database terms I will be using. I will stick to relational databases to keep it simple. **Relational** databases are made up of **tables**, and tables have **columns** and **rows**. A row has **attributes**, or put another way, an attribute is the intersection of a row and a column. A row must be unique, that is, distinguishable from every other row in the table. One of the attributes that makes the row unique is called the **primary key**. **SQL** is a relational database language for retrieving and updating the database. The structure of the database (table name and layout) is called the database's **schema**. SQL also has commands to change the database schema.

My final preliminary is threads. When we run an application we get a **process**. The process has a memory environment (for mapping virtual memory to physical memory) and one or more threads. A **thread** has what is required for the runtime execution of code; it contains information like the position in the code file of the next executable instruction and the procedure call stack (to return to the right place when the procedure is finished). **Multi-threading** is when one process has more than one thread and makes it possible for more than one processor to work on a single process. Multi-threading is useful even when there is only one physical processor because multi-threading allows one thread to keep on going when the other thread is blocked. (A blocked thread is one waiting for something to happen: for instance, for an IO to complete.)

2.3   Remote procedure calls (RPC)

Procedure calls are a major feature of most programming languages. If you need to access a service on a machine such as a database or an operating system function you call a procedure. It seems logical therefore that the way to access a remote service should be through remote procedure calls, the idea being that the syntax in the client (the caller) and the server (the called) programs remains the same, just as if they were on the same machine.

The best-known RPC mechanisms are Open Network Computing (ONC) from SUN and Distributed Computing Environment (DCE) from the Open Software Foundation (OSF). (OSF is the group formed in the late 1980s by IBM, Hewlett Packard, and DEC, as it then was. Its rationale was to form an alternative to AT&T, who owned the Unix brand name and had formed a group—which included Unisys—called Unix International to rally around its brand. OSF was the first of the great "anti-something" alliances that have been such a dominant feature of middleware history.) The basic idea in both ONC and DCE is the same. The RPC architecture is illustrated in Figure 2-3.

If you are writing in C and you want to call a procedure in another module you include a "header file" into your program that contains the module's callable procedure declarations—that is the procedure names and the parameters but not

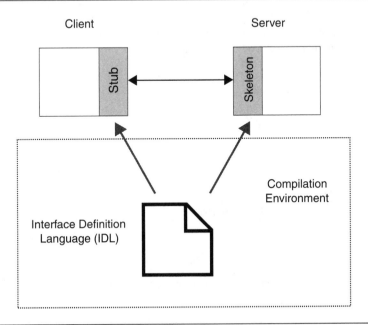

Figure 2-3   Remote procedure call (RPC)

the logic. For RPCs, instead of writing a header file you write an **IDL**—Interface Definition Language—file. Syntactically an IDL is very similar to a header file but it does more. The IDL generates client **stubs** and server **skeletons**, which are small chunks of C code that are compiled and linked into the client and server programs. The purpose of the stub is to convert parameters into a string of bits and sends the message over the network. The skeleton takes the message, converts it back into parameters, and calls the server. The process of conversion of parameters into a message is called **marshalling** and is illustrated in Figure 2-4.

The advantage of marshalling is that it handles differing data formats. For instance, if the client uses 32-bit big-endian integers and the server uses 64-bit small-endian integers, then the marshalling software does the translation. (Big-endian format integers have bits in the reverse order of small-endian format integers.)

The problem with RPCs is multi-threading. A client program is blocked when it is calling a remote procedure—just as it would be calling a local procedure. If the message is lost in the network, if the server is slow, or if the server stops while processing the request, the client is left waiting. The socially acceptable approach is to have the client program reading from the keyboard or mouse while asking the server for data, but the only way to write this code is to use two threads—one thread for processing the remote procedure call and the other thread for processing the user input.

There are similar concerns at the server end. Simple RPC requires a separate server thread for every client connection. (A more sophisticated approach would be to have a pool of server threads and to reuse threads as needed but this takes us into the realms of transaction monitors, which I shall discuss below.) Thus, for 1,000 clients there needs to be 1,000 threads. If the server threads need to share

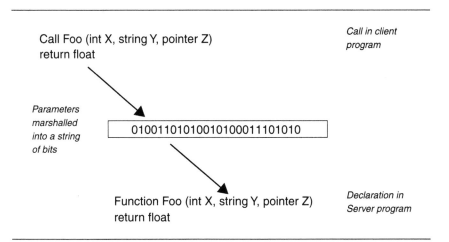

Figure 2-4   Marshalling

resources, the programmer must use locks, semaphores, or events to avoid synchronization problems.

Experienced programmers try to avoid writing multi-threading programs. The problems are not in understanding the syntax or the concepts, but in testing and finding the bugs. Every time a multi-threading program is run, the timings are a bit different and the actions on the threads are processed in a slightly different order. Bugs that depend on the order of processing are extremely hard to find. Designing tests that give you the confidence that most such order-dependent bugs will be found is nearly impossible.

RPC software dates back to the mid-1980s. RPCs were central to the thinking of the Open Software Foundation. In their DCE architecture they proposed that every other distributed service (for example, remote file access, e-mail) should use RPCs instead of sending messages directly over the network. This notion of using RPCs everywhere is no longer widely held. What has been brought forward to later technologies has been the notions of marshalling and IDL.

2.4   Remote database access

Remote database access provides the ability to read or write to a database that is physically on a different machine from the client program.

Most database vendors have their own proprietary form of remote database access. For instance, Oracle has Oracle Transparent gateway and IBM has DRDA. These standards have been available since the late 1980s.

Probably the best known remote database access technology is Microsoft's ODBC (Open Database Connectivity). ODBC is a standard programming interface for Windows, not a middleware. Either Microsoft or another software vendor provides the client and server middleware portions. ODBC is just a thin veneer on top. It does however provide the enormous advantage of forcing consistency over all databases that have an ODBC interface. Thus an ODBC compliant tool—such as Microsoft Access or Excel—will read most, if not all, ODBC compliant databases.

Microsoft is trying to move away from ODBC and have programs use OLE DB instead. OLE DB uses COM-objects (I will explain what that means in the next chapter), which makes it compliant with the Microsoft strategy. It is also more flexible than ODBC as it can run against nonrelational databases. OLE DB is rather complex, so Microsoft has a third standard, ADO—Active Data Objects—that provides a simpler COM-compliant interface. ADO uses OLE DB and OLE DB can use an ODBC data provider. The relationship between these products is illustrated in Figure 2-5.

Note you cannot take ODBC client software that is written to communicate remotely to an Oracle database and expect it to communicate to an IBM database. Anything under the ODBC layer is up to the database provider to write and control.

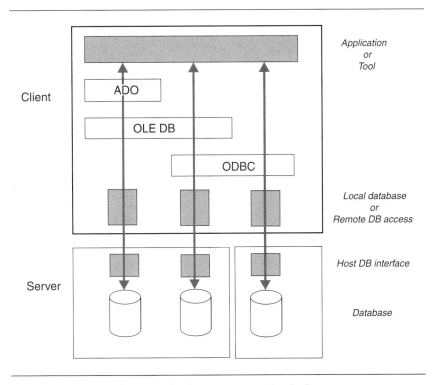

Figure 2-5   Microsoft remote database access technologies

What we have is program portability not interoperability. (Incidentally, there is an OSI standard for remote database access interoperability but I am not aware of it being used in any demonstration of interoperability between a client from one database vendor to a server from another.)

Remote database access imposes a large overhead on the network to do the simplest of commands (see SQL Parsing box). It is not a good solution for transaction processing. In fact it was this technology that was largely responsible for the bad name of first generation client/server applications. Most database vendors support a feature called stored procedures. You can use remote database access technology to call stored procedures. This turns remote database access into a form of RPC, but with a few notable differences.

- It is a runtime not a compile-time interface. There is no IDL or equivalent.
- The procedure itself is typically written in a proprietary language, though many database vendors are now allowing stored procedures to be written in Java.

In spite of using an interpreted language, remote database access calling stored procedures can be many times faster than a similar application that uses remote database access calling SQL.

SQL Parsing

To understand the strengths and weaknesses of remote database access technology, let us look into how an SQL statement is processed. There are two steps: parsing and execution. This is illustrated in Figure 2-6.

The parsing step turns the SQL command into a query plan that defines which tables are accessed using which indexes, filtered by which expression, and using which sorts. The SQL text itself also defines what the output from the query will look like—how many columns there are in the table and what is the type and size of each field. When the query is executed, there may be additional data input through parameters; for instance, if the query is an inquiry on a bank account the account number may be input as a parameter. Again the number and nature of the parameters is defined in the SQL text. Unlike RPCs where for one input there is one output, the output can be any length; one query can result in a million rows of output.

For a simple database application, remote database access technology incurs an enormous amount of work in comparison with other technologies, especially distributed transaction processing. There are optimizations. Since the host software can remember the query plan, the parse step can be done once and the execution step done many times. If the query is a call to a stored procedure then remote database access can be very efficient because the complete query plan for the stored procedure already exists.

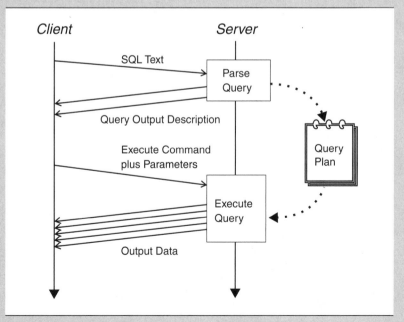

Figure 2-6   Remote database access message flow

If we turn our attention to ad-hoc queries, remote database access technology is ideal. Compare it with trying to do the same job by using RPCs. Sending the SQL command would be easy, it's just text. But writing the code to get data back when it can be any number of rows, any number of fields per row, and any data type for each field would be a complex undertaking.

2.5   Distributed transaction processing

Transactions in the old days were initiated by someone pressing the transmit key on a green-screen terminal. At the mainframe end, the input was handled by a transaction monitor like CICS on IBM MVS, TIP on Unisys 2200s, or COMS on Unisys A Series. But what did you do if you wanted to update more than one database in one transaction? What if the databases were on different machines? Distributed transaction processing was developed to solve these problems.

By way of a quick review, a transaction is a unit of work that updates a database (and/or maybe other resources). Transactions must either end up completed (the technical term is committed) or are completely undone. For instance, a transaction for taking money out of your account may include writing a record of the debit, updating the account total, and updating the bank teller record; either all of these updates are done or the transaction in its entirety is canceled.

Transactions are important because organizational tasks are transactional. If we submit an order form, we cannot tolerate the system actually submitting only half the order lines. When we put money in the bank we need both the credit to be recorded and the account total to be changed, not one without the other. From an IT perspective, the business moves forward in transactional steps. Note that this is the business perspective and not the customer's perspective. For instance, we give a bank a check to pay a bill and it seems to us as one atomic (all-or-nothing) action. But for the bank there is a complex business process ensuring that the payment is made, and several of those steps are IT transactions. If the process fails when some of the IT transactions are done, one or more reversal transactions are processed (which you might see in your next statement). From the IT point of view the original debit and the reversal are two different atomic transactions, each with a number of database update operations.

Transactions are characterized as obeying the **ACID** properties.

A is for atomic; the transaction is never half done, if there is any error, it is completely undone.

C is for consistent; the transaction changes the database from one consistent state to another consistent state. Consistency here means that database data integrity constraints hold true—in other words, the database need not be consistent within the transaction but by the time it is finished it must be. Database integrity includes not only explicit data integrity (like "Product codes must be between eight and ten digits long") but also internal integrity constraints (like "all index entries must point at valid records").

I is for isolation; data updates within a transaction are not visible to other transactions until the transaction is completed. An implication of isolation is the transactions that touch the same data are "serializable," by which I mean that from the end user's perspective it is as if they are done one at a time in sequence rather than in parallel.

D is for durable; when a transaction is done it really is done and the updates do not at some time in the future, under an unusual set of circumstances, disappear.

Distributed transaction processing is about having more than one database participate in one transaction. It requires a protocol like the **two-phase commit** protocol to ensure the two or more databases co-operate to maintain the ACID properties. (The details of this protocol are described in a box in Chapter 7.)

Interestingly, at the time the protocol was developed (in the early 1980s), people envisaged a fully distributed database that would seem to the programmer to be one database. What killed that idea off were the horrendous performance and resiliency implications of extensive distribution (which we describe in Chapters 7 and 8). Distributed database features are implemented in many databases in the sense that you can define an SQL table on one system that is actually implemented by remote access to a table on a different database. There are also products (like EDA/SQL from Information Builders Inc.) that specialize in creating a unified database view of many databases from many different vendors. In practice this technology is excellent for doing reports and decision support queries but terrible for building large-scale enterprise transaction processing systems.

A simple example of distributed transaction processing is illustrated in Figure 2-7.

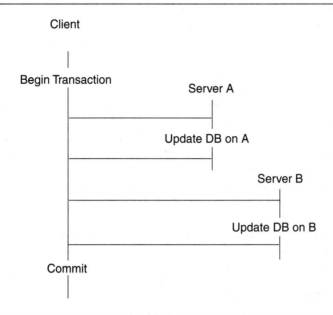

Figure 2-7   An example of distributed transaction processing

The steps are as follows:

1. The client first tells the middleware that a transaction is beginning.

2. The client then calls server A.

3. Server A updates the database.

4. The client calls server B.

5. Server B updates its database.

6. The client tells the middleware that the transaction has now ended.

If the updates to the second database failed (point 5), then the updates to the first (point 3) are rolled back. To maintain the transaction ACID properties (or more precisely the I—isolation—property) all locks acquired by the database software cannot be released until the end of the transaction (point 6).

There are an infinite number of variations. Instead of updating a database on a remote system, a local database can be updated. Any number of databases can be updated. At point (3) or (5) the server update code could act like a client to a further system. Subtransactions could also be processed in parallel instead of in series. But, whatever the variation, at the end there must be a two-phase commit to complete all subtransactions as if they are one transaction.

Looking closer at the middleware, you will see that there are at least two protocols. One is between the middleware and the database system, and the other is from the client to the server.

Distributed transaction processing was standardized by the X/Open consortium, who are now called the Open Group (www.opengroup.org). Their standard protocol between the middleware and the database is called the XA protocol (see X/Open DTB box). Thus if you see that a database is "XA compliant" it means that it can co-operate with X/Open DTP middleware in a two-phase commit protocol. All major open database systems are XA compliant.

X/Open was less successful with standardizing the client/server protocol and ended up with three protocols. From IBM they got a protocol based on SNA LU6.2 (strictly speaking this is a peer-to-peer not a client/server protocol). From Encina (who have since been taken over by IBM) they got a protocol based on DCE's remote procedure calls. From Tuxedo (originally developed by AT&T, the product now belongs to BEA Inc.) they got the XATMI protocol. (The Tuxedo ATMI protocol is slightly different from XATMI; in particular it has some additional features.) In theory, you can mix and match protocols, though most implementations do not allow it. BEA does, however, have an eLink SNA product that makes it possible to call an IBM CICS transaction through LU6.2 as part of a Tuxedo distributed transaction.

These protocols are very different. LU6.2 is a peer-to-peer protocol with no marshalling or equivalent—in other words the message is just a string of bits. Encina is an RPC, which implies parameter marshalling as described above and threads are blocked during a call. Tuxedo has its own way of defining the format

X/Open DTP

The X/Open DTP model consists of four elements, as illustrated in Figure 2-8.

I found this model very confusing when I first saw it. One source of confusion is the terminology. Resource managers—999 times out of 1,000—means databases and most of the rest are message queues. Communications resource manager sends messages to remote systems and supports the application's API (for example, XATMI and TxRPC). One reason why cRMs are called "resource manager" is that the protocol from TM to cRM is a variation of the protocol from TM to RM. Another source of confusion is that the TM, whose role is to manage the start and end of the transaction including the two-phase commit, and the cRM are often bundled into one product (a.k.a. the three-box model). The reason for four boxes is that the X/Open standards bodies were thinking of a TM controlling several different cRMs, but it rarely happens that way.

Yet another source of confusion is that no distinction is made between client and server programs. An application that is a client may or may not have local resources. An application that is a server in one dialogue may be a client in another. The reason there is no distinction in the model is because the model is completely flexible. In fact the cRM protocol does not have to be client/server at all.

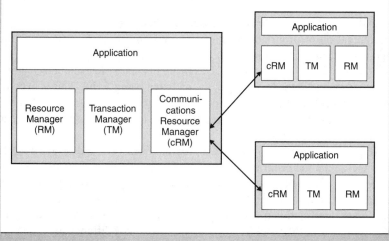

Figure 2-8   The X/Open DTP model

of the messages called View Buffers. Tuxedo supports RPC-like calls and unblocked calls (which they call asynchronous calls) where the client sends a message to the server, goes off and does something else, and then gets back to see if the server has sent a reply.

To confuse matters further, Tuxedo and Encina are also transaction monitors as well as transaction managers. A transaction monitor is software for controlling the transaction server. I noted the disadvantages of having one server thread per client in the section on RPCs. A major role of the transaction monitor is to alleviate this problem by having a pool of threads and allocating them on an as-needed basis to incoming transactions. Sharing resources this way has a startling effect on performance and many of the transaction benchmarks on Unix have used Tuxedo for precisely this reason. Transaction monitors have many additional tasks, for instance in systems management, implementing transaction security, and maybe routing by message content. Since transaction monitors are a feature of mainframe systems, mainframe transactions can often fit into a managed distributed transaction without change. For instance, the Unisys mainframe uses a product called eLink OSI Connect to link their transaction monitors with Tuxedo. There may be difficulties such as old-screen formatting and menu handling code: these are subjects I will explore later, in Chapter 13.

2.6   Message queuing

So far the middleware I have discussed has been about program-to-program communication or program-to-database communication. Message queuing is program-to-queue communication.

You can think of a message queue as being like a very fast mail box, since you can put a message in the box without the recipient being active. This is in contrast to RPC or distributed transaction processing, which are more like telephone conversations; if the recipient isn't there, then there is no conversation. The general idea is illustrated in Figure 2-9.

To put a message into the queue, a program does a Put and to take a message out of the queue the program does a Get. The middleware does the transfer of messages from queue to queue. It ensures that, whatever happens to the network, the message arrives eventually and moreover, only one copy of the message is placed in the destination queue. Superficially this looks similar to reading from and writing to a TCP/IP socket, but there are several key differences:

- Queues have names.
- The queues are independent of program; thus many programs can do Puts and many can do Gets on the same queue. A program can access multiple queues; for instance, doing Puts to one and Gets from another.
- If the network goes down, the messages can wait in the queue until the network comes up again.

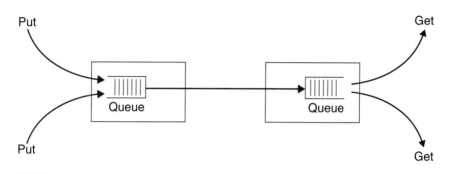

Figure 2-9   Message queuing

- The queues can be put on disk so that if the system goes down, the queue is not lost.
- The queue can be a resource manager and co-operate with a transaction manager. This means that if the message is put in a queue during a transaction and the transaction is later aborted, then not only is the database rolled back, but the message is taken out of the queue and not sent.
- Some message queue systems can cross networks of different types, for instance, to send messages over an SNA leg, then a TCP/IP leg, and finally a Novell IPX leg.

It is a powerful and simple idea. It is also efficient, and has been used for applications requiring sub-second response times. The best-known message queue software is probably MQSeries from IBM. Alternatives are MSMQ from Microsoft and Tuxedo/Q from BEA Systems. There are also products that create links between queuing systems, for instance Level 8 software integrates MQSeries with MSMQ.

A disadvantage of message queuing is that there is no IDL and no marshalling; the message is a string of bits and it is up to you to ensure the sender and the receiver know the message layout. MQSeries will do character set translation, so if you are sending messages between different platforms, it is simplest to put everything into characters. This lack of an IDL, however, has created an add-on market in message reformatting tools.

Message queuing is peer-to-peer middleware rather than client/server middleware because a queue manager can hold many queues, some of which are sending queues and some of which are receiving queues. However, you will often hear people talk about clients and servers with message queuing. What are they talking about?

Message queue clients are illustrated in Figure 2-10. A message queue server physically stores the queue. The client does Puts and Gets and a remote procedure call-like protocol to transfer the messages to the server, which does the real Puts and Gets on the queue.

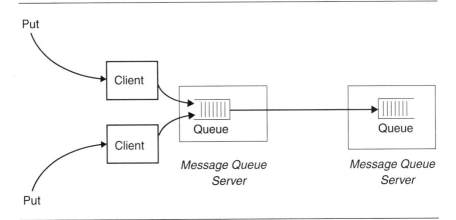

Figure 2-10   Message queuing client/server

Of course, some of the advantages of message queuing are lost for the client. If the network is down between the client and the server, messages cannot be queued.

Many message queuing products also have lightweight message queuing products targeted at mobile works using portable PCs or smaller devices. The idea is that when a mobile worker has time to sit still, he or she can log into the corporate systems and the messages in the queues will be exchanged.

2.7   Message queuing vs. distributed transaction processing

If you go to a seminar on message queuing, you will hear about users—especially large IBM users—that are, or claim to be, using message queuing for everything. Go to a Tuxedo-user meeting and you will find organizations using distributed transaction processing for everything. Since the technologies are so different, how is this possible? Let us look at an example.

Suppose we have someone moving money from account A to account B. A distributed transaction processing solution to this problem is illustrated in Figure 2-11.

In this solution, the debit on account A and the credit on account B is all done in one distributed transaction. Any failure anywhere aborts the whole transaction—as you would expect. The disadvantages of this solution are

• The performance is degraded because of the overhead of sending additional messages for the two-phase commit.

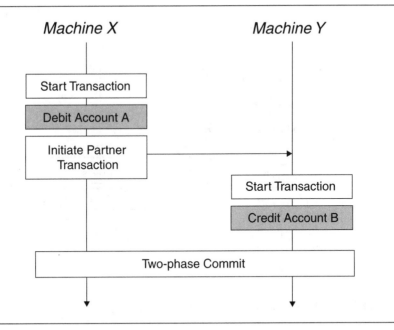

Figure 2-11   Debit/credit using distributed transaction processing

- If either of the systems is down, or the network between the systems is down, the transaction cannot take place.

Message queuing potentially solves both of these problems. The message queuing solution is illustrated in Figure 2-12. Note the vertical line dropping down from the disk. This is meant to indicate that the message cannot be allowed to reach the second machine until the first transaction has committed. The reason for this constraint is that the message queue software does not know the first transaction won't abort until the commit is successful. If there was an abort, the message must not be sent (strictly speaking this can be controlled by options—not all queues need to be transaction synchronized), therefore it cannot send the message until it knows there won't be an abort.

But this scheme has a fatal flaw; if the destination transaction fails, money is taken out of one account and disappears. In the jargon of transactions, this schema fails the A in ACID—it is not atomic, it can be partly done.

The solution is to have a reversal transaction; we can reverse the failed debit transaction by having a credit transaction for the same amount. This is illustrated in Figure 2-13.

But this fails if account A is deleted before the reversal takes effect. In the jargon of transactions, this scheme fails the I in ACID—it is not isolated; other transactions can get in the way and mess it up. Is this likely? Well, actually, yes; the reason for the debit and the account deletion could be for closing account A and

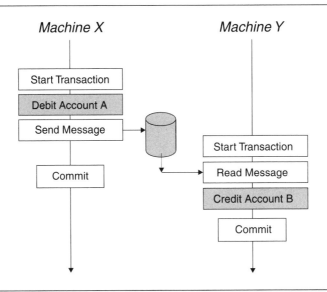

Figure 2-12   Debit/credit using message queuing

unfortunately there was a mistake in specifying the account number for B. It is not going to happen very often, but it may well happen.

In a real business situation, many organizations will throw up their hands and say, we will wait for a complaint and then do a manual adjustment. Airlines are a case in point; if the computer loses the record of a passenger checking-in they will rectify the ensuing chaos at the gate. There is already enough chaos caused by passengers not turning up at the gate, standby, canceled flights, and so on, that any additional errors caused by the computer are a minor inconvenience.

Often an application programming solution exists, at the cost of additional complexity. In our example it is possible to anticipate the problem and ensure that the accounts are not deleted until all monetary flows have been completed. This has the business impact of there being an "in the process of being deleted" type of account.

Thus the choice between what seems to be two esoteric technologies is actually a business issue. In fact, it has to be. Transactions are the steps that business processes take. If we change one step into two smaller steps we change the business process. This is a point I will be returning to again and again.

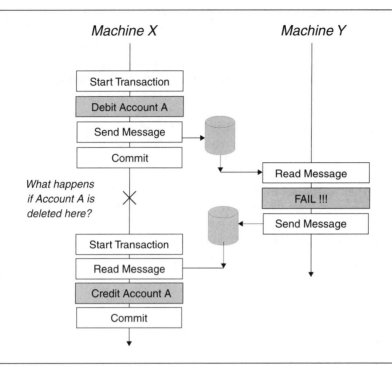

Figure 2-13   Debit/credit with reversal

2.8   What happened to all this technology?

With remote database access, remote procedure calls, distributed transaction processing, and message queuing you have a flexible set of middleware that can do most of what you need to do to build a successful distributed application. All of the technologies described above are being widely used and most are being actively developed and promoted by their respective vendors. But the market for middleware is still wide open. Many organizations haven't really started on the middleware trail and, as noted in the first section, many large organizations have developed their own middleware. Both of these are potential candidates for the middleware technologies described in this chapter. In short, none of this technology is going to die and much of it has great potential to grow.

Yet most pundits would claim that when we build distributed applications in the 21st century we will not be using the technology discussed above. Why?

The main answer is component middleware. It is generally believed that component middleware will replace RPCs and all the different flavors of distributed transaction middleware. Component middleware will be discussed in Chapter 4.

The future development of message queuing is less clear. MSMQ (Microsoft Message Queuing) provides a component interface to message queuing and provides for some ability to send objects instead of a string of bytes. For instance, it can send a Microsoft Word document or an ADO recordset (the output from a database query) so long as they are not too large. But IBM's MQSeries is the dominant message queuing technology and it is not going to be pushed off of its perch easily. Some form of message queuing will always be around.

Remote database access looks like it will always fit a niche. In some ways it is less attractive than it used to be because database replication technology will develop and take away some of the tasks currently undertaken by remote database access. But new standards for remote database access will probably arise and existing ones will be extended.

In summary, while we may not see these specific technologies, we will see technologies of these three types—real-time transaction oriented middleware, message queuing, and remote database access—playing a large part in our middleware discussions for the foreseeable future.

3

A Short History
of Middleware Technology—
Object Middleware

All of the technologies described in the previous chapter have their roots in the 1980s. At the end of that decade, however, there was a resurgence of interest in object-oriented systems, in particular object-oriented programming languages. To do effective implementation design today, you have to understand object-oriented concepts fully.

In many ways the resurgence in interest in all things object-oriented was strange since object-oriented programming languages had been around for many years. In fact, the original object-oriented language, Simula, was invented in the late 1960s. One reason for the change in perception within the industry was the easy fit between object-oriented programming and developing Windows or Apple Macintosh applications. Hard on the heels of this change in perception (perhaps part of the reason for the change in perception) was the arrival of familiar languages in object-oriented guise, namely C++, Visual Basic, and Object Pascal. Not long after this was the publication of object-oriented design and analysis methodologies, work that has revolutionized application modeling.

"Object-oriented" is an adjective, not a noun. Furthermore, it is an adjective that can be applied to an enormous number of things. There are object-oriented programming languages, object-oriented middleware, object-oriented databases, object-oriented GUI interfaces, object-oriented system management systems, object-oriented analysis, and so on. In addition, the languages range from Lisp and Smalltalk to C++ and Cobol. The words "object-oriented" tell us that the product follows a set of concepts. But it would be impossible to apply the concepts to so many things if the concepts weren't so loose. This can be seen as object-oriented's biggest strength but, when it comes to interoperability, an area where precision is paramount, it will at times trip us up.

3.1   Object-oriented concepts

I will start by reviewing object-oriented concepts. If you understand O-O you might want to skip this section. On the other hand, you might want to check that what you understand by O-O is the same as what I understand by O-O.

An object has a **state** and is **encapsulated**. State means a collection of data attributes and references to other objects. Encapsulation means that the object's state is only changed by calling one of the object's **operations**. Calling an operation is like calling a procedure or function, except that it is associated with an object. Like procedures, operations have parameters and maybe a return value. The implementation of an operation is called a **method**. The term "operation" applies to the external view of a piece of code while the term "method" applies to the internal view. When I come to discuss polymorphism you will see that this distinction is useful. Sometimes you will hear people talking about passing messages to an object rather than calling an operation. This is terminology that comes from Smalltalk and messages in Smalltalk have a looser syntax (that is, less type checking) than a function call in a language like C or Pascal. The strictness of encapsulation varies from language to language. C++ allows you to define an attribute that is directly accessible outside the object; other languages like Eiffel insist that all access to the object is through its operations.

Encapsulation has a superficial resemblance to modules in older computing languages. The difference is that objects can be created and deleted at runtime while modules are a compile-time construct—variables declared in the module are just added to the global variables. The compile-time definition of an object is called a **class** and for each class you can have any number of runtime objects. The class defines everything about the object—its attributes, its operations, and its methods. If you want to put objects into older programming terminology, the nearest equivalents are records in Pascal or structures in C in that they can be created and deleted at runtime. The difference is that objects have operations, methods, and encapsulation.

The visible part of an object is called its **interface**. Classes, objects, and interfaces are illustrated in Figure 3-1.

Let us take a real example. Products like Microsoft Word or Excel have the concept of multiple documents and multiple views on a document (go to the Window menu and select New Window and you get a new view on an existing document). Microsoft provides a class library called MFC (Microsoft Foundation classes), which is used by C++ programmers for building Windows programs, and in there you will find a class called CDocument and a class called CView. The CDocument has operations for opening, saving, and closing documents. The CView has operations for displaying the document on the screen. You have to write the method code for these operations to implement your application, but they provide some standard code that will create and delete the CDocument and CView objects for you and hook them up to the File menu and Window menu

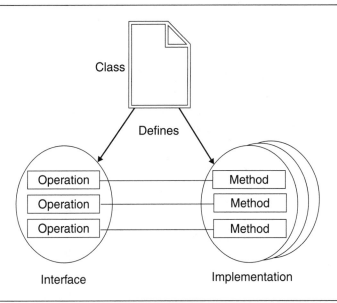

Class

Defines

Operation — Method
Operation — Method
Operation — Method

Interface   Implementation

Figure 3-1   Objects and classes

commands. By using objects, the programmer has a one-to-one correspondence between what the user sees and what the programmer implements. This correspondence goes very deep: buttons, drop-down lists, menus, forms all have corresponding classes in MFC.

The second main feature of object-oriented systems is **inheritance**. Inheritance allows you to define a new class by adding to an existing class rather than starting from scratch. For example, in a payroll system you might have a class that describes employee objects but then you might define a class called full-time employees that is inherited from the employee class. You might then further define classes for managers, technicians, and sales staff that are inherited from full-time employees. Thus, we have a class hierarchy. Inheritance is illustrated in Figure 3-2.

Getting your class hierarchy right turns out to be both important and difficult. The trivial example of employees already shows a few of the problems. How do we handle part-time managers? We cannot, of course. We got the class hierarchy wrong—the full-time/part-time distinction should be handled as attributes of any employee object, not by inheritance. How do we handle sales managers? We have to form a new class that inherits from sales staff and from managers. Inheriting from more than one class is called **multiple inheritance**. (It's not really a "class hierarchy," it's a "class graph," a DAG—Directed Acyclic Graph—to be precise.) Programmers tend to think of inheritance as a reuse mechanism, a technique for writing less code. Modelers and designers tend to think of inheritance as a classification hierarchy. These views can conflict. For instance, in a drawing

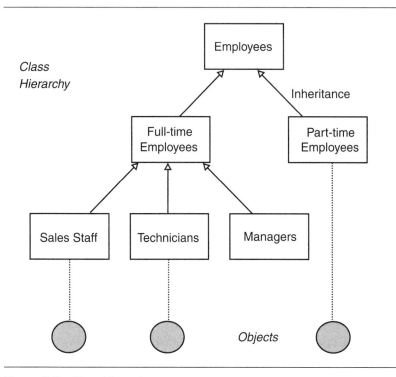

Class Hierarchy

Inheritance

Objects

Figure 3-2   Class hierarchy

program you might be tempted for reuse purposes to define a polygon class as a subclass of (that is, inherited from) a rectangle class. However, the mathematical classification of these terms makes the rectangle a subclass of polygon. What's the answer? It depends on what you are doing. There is a good chance that the best solution for a program turns out to make them both peers, both inheriting from an abstract class called something like "drawable thing."

The final feature of object-oriented systems I want to discuss is **polymorphism**. This is illustrated in Figure 3-3. With inheritance you can add attributes, operations, and methods. With polymorphism you add a new method in a subclass for an operation that has been already declared in the superclass. In our payroll example, `CalculatePay` may be an operation on all employees, but the algorithm will be different for part-time and full-time, not to mention managers and sales.

Polymorphism should also be handled with care, especially in conjunction with multiple inheritance. For instance, if you create a sales manager class you must create a new method for `CalculatePay`, otherwise you have ambiguity.

As you no doubt have noticed, I have been pointing out some of the difficulties with object-oriented systems along the way. This is not because object-oriented ideas are flawed: The ideas are extremely powerful but you have to start

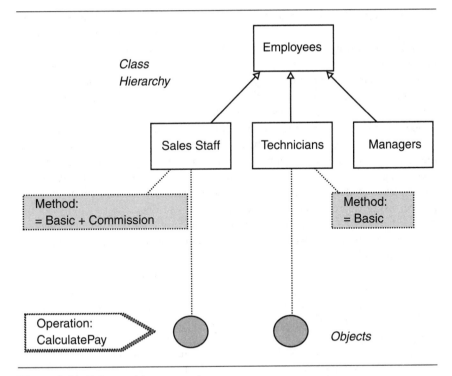

Figure 3-3   Polymorphism

thinking in object-oriented terms to get your design right. Once you have got your mind into object-oriented thinking, you will find that identifying objects is basically easy. For both a programmer and a designer, an object is essentially anything you want to keep track of in your program or design. What is hard is designing the class hierarchy. I said designers think of class hierarchies as classification, but zoologists still can't agree about species classification after two hundred years. And just as an experiment, ask a librarian why the books are placed where they are and whether there isn't a better way. You might just find that librarians aren't quite so sure how to classify books in a library. But, just because it is difficult, it does not make it any less important or useful.

On the other hand, the arguments of whether inheritance is a reuse mechanism or a classification mechanism are almost entirely bogus. Let us take an example; I have seen a textbook explain inheritance by using the example of a circle inheriting from a point and a cylinder inheriting from a circle. The justification is obviously reuse. But this is poor design. There are two issues that must be considered. First, the designer must think of the users of the objects at least as much as they think of the implementers of the object. In my example, the code for DrawLine (with parameters start point, end point) is likely to need to behave differently according to whether the points turn out to be circles! The poor design raises questions that should not be there. Second, you can reuse code by simply copying and pasting the bits you want. What is different about reuse in a class hierarchy is that, when you change the class implementation, all the subclasses pick up the changes automatically. In our example, you must ask yourself the question—if I change the code for the point class, do I want the implementation of circle class to change? If the answer is no, then the class hierarchy is wrong. What happens in practice is that programmers often don't find this out until they come to make the change. On the other hand, programmers often find they are making the same changes in two or more disparate parts of the system and this tells the good programmer that perhaps they should share a common superclass. A strange consequence of changing the class hierarchy is that the actual amount of code in a project using object-oriented languages may even decrease as time goes on. A classification view of class hierarchies and a "single point of change" view of class hierarchies are pretty close. There are not many examples of a class that isn't one without being the other.

It is not only programmers that get it wrong. Some design methodologies in the past have had the concept that a subclass does not need to have all the properties of its superclass. For instance, they might have a class called "flying things" with a subclass of birds and then add a subclass of penguins and exclude everything about flight. This is wrong. The rule programmers and designers must obey is that if X is a subclass of Y then every object that is an instance of X is also an instance of Y—without exception. (Technically, in program language jargon, X is a subtype of Y, meaning that an instance of X can be used in a parameter of type Y but not vice versa.) In our example, if you don't do that then you have to handle cases where the "flying things" don't fly! If you disobey this rule, you cannot treat an object interface as a black box interface; you have to worry about what subclass the object belongs to. Obey this rule, and you start simplifying the structure of the whole program or system, which makes it far less likely that changes in the future will disrupt the interface, causing changes to cascade throughout the program.

Object-oriented ideas are now pervasive everywhere. Interestingly, the group that has been particularly wary of the wholesale adoption of object ideas and has incorporated them only in "controlled" fashion has been the relational database vendors (see OODB box).

OODB

The one area where object-oriented concepts met with serious resistance was the database community. The situation now (end of 1999) is that there are a small number of fully object-oriented database products sold (like Versant, O2, and Gemstone) and a large number of relational database systems with object-oriented extensions. Ten years ago, when the object-oriented database vendors marched onto the stage and told everyone that relational databases were dead, they met with hostile and effective resistance. For a while there was the battle of the manifestos. On one side was "The Object-Oriented Database System Manifesto" (Atkinson, M., et al. in *Deductive and Object-Oriented Databases.* Amsterdam: Elsevere, 1990) and on the other, "Third-Generation Database System Manifesto" (The Committee for Advanced DBMS Function (sic) in *Object-Oriented Databases: Analysis, Design & Construction.* Amsterdam: North Holland, 1990).

The original idea of object-oriented databases was that you take C++ objects (or other O-O programming languages) and make them persistent and sharable. This made them look rather like the earlier network database systems, as the data was packed full of pointers. This idea was strongly and effectively criticized since it destroyed much of what databases stood for, such as:

- Powerful query languages based on relational calculus and relational algebra
- Simple tabular data structures
- Selective data hiding through views

The attention then turned to how object-oriented ideas could be used to extend relational functionality.

Relational databases consist of tables of rows and rows of attributes. Which of these are objects (see Figure 3-4)?

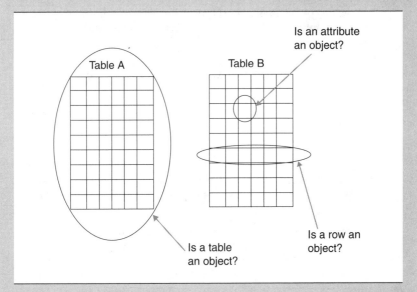

Figure 3-4   What is an object?   *(continued)*

OODB   *(cont.)*

The object-oriented aficionado's answer is "everything." Object-oriented concepts can easily be applied to attributes. Instead of simple attributes of integers or strings, you can have complex attributes like GridReference, Map, and DateAndTime, each of which is an object. Object-oriented concepts can be applied to rows. Say the table is AccountSet and the rows are accounts; an account is an object. But tables are sets of accounts and they can be objects too. There is no reason why you can't have many sets of accounts, each an instance of an AccountSet object.

The database row is the nearest element in a relational database to a modeler's notion of an object. But modelers see objects as possibly complex things. An account object may include not only an account row but also multiple debit and credit records. Furthermore, there is inheritance, so different account objects may have a different structure.

Relational database experts are happy with attributes as objects and some of them will tolerate the notion of rows supporting inheritance. But there they stop. There are several reasons:

- Rows might belong to multiple objects. I suspect this is in theory only. For instance, for all practical purposes an order line is part of an order and not part of a product object. You can tell the difference by asking yourself the question, If an order line changed, has the order changed? Yes—therefore it is part of the order. Has the product changed? No—it is not part of the product.
- Query languages are based on relational tables.
- Queries rely on the data being visible—it contradicts the spirit of encapsulation. Database technology uses views to restrict data visibility.
- Relational database constraints are specified in rules (the SQL check clause). Object-oriented technology uses encapsulation to force all updates through method code and relies on the method code to do the relevant checks.

But the most significant two reasons why O-O databases have made so little headway are probably factors that have nothing to do with the data model:

- Inertia—there is a lot of existing data in relational databases.
- Maturity—there are a lot of reasons for choosing a database system besides the data model, like scalability, resiliency, and design tools; building a database product is a huge investment.

Personally, I think there is much more that the database system could do to support objects more explicitly. While it is true that the naïve application of object-oriented principles, especially encapsulation, does not work for database systems, SQL is not the perfect answer either. It does not support recursive queries. For instance, on a database of family trees you cannot ask the query—list all dukes who are descended from Queen Victoria.

SQL muddles up object identity with primary keys. For instance, give an order a new order number and all its order line rows must be updated because the order line rows hold a copy of the order number to use as a foreign key. SQL does not allow you to model additional relationship semantics. For instance, if you want to implement version control you will want to ensure that a change to an object's subpart (e.g., an order line) will create for you a new version of the object (e.g., the order). In relational databases you can't make general rules like this; you must handle each relationship explicitly.

3.2   Object middleware concepts

Object middleware is built on the simple concept of calling an operation in an object that resides in another system. Instead of client and server there is client and object.

To access an object in another machine, a program must have a reference pointing at the object. Programmers are used to writing code that accesses objects through pointers, where the pointer holds the memory address of the object. A reference is syntactically the same as using a pointer; calling a local object through a pointer and calling a remote object through a reference are made to look identical. The complexities of using references instead of pointers and sending messages over the network are hidden from the programmer by the middleware.

But, compared to earlier forms of middleware, it does mean that calling an operation on a remote object requires two steps: getting a reference to an object and calling an operation on the object, though once you have gotten a reference you can call the object any number of times.

I will illustrate the difference between simple RPC calls and object-oriented calls with an example. Suppose you wanted to write code to debit an account. Using RPCs, you might write something like this (I've used a pseudo language rather than C++ or Java because I hope it will be clearer):

```
Call Debit(012345678, 100) ;   // where 012345678 is the
                               // account number and 100
                               // is the amount
```

In an object-oriented system you might write:

```
Call AccountSet.GetAccount(012345678) return AccoutRef;
                               // get a reference to
                               // the account object
Call AccoutRef.Debit(100);     // call debit
```

What I am doing here is using an AccountSet object to get a reference to a particular account. (AccountSet is an object that represents the collection of all accounts.) I then call the debit operation on that account. On the face of it this looks like more work but in practice there usually isn't much to it. What the client is more likely to do is:

```
Call AccountSet.GetAccount(X) return AccountRef;
Call AccoutRef.GetNameAndBalence(....);
... display information to user
... get action to call—if it's a debit action then
Call AccountRef.Debit(Amt);
```

What this code segment does not explain is how I get a reference to the AccountSet object in the first place.

In general there are four ways to get an object reference:

- A special object reference is returned to the client when it first attaches to the middleware.
- The client calls a special "naming" service that takes a name provided by the client and looks it up in a directory. The directory returns the location of an object and the naming service converts this to a reference to that object.
- The client requests that a new object of a certain class is created and gets back its reference.
- An operation on one object returns a reference to another object. This is what the operation `GetAccount` in `AccountSet` did.

Which of these four ways can be used in which circumstances depends on the choice of middleware and on the server code. I shall return to this subject after I have discussed the technology.

There are similarities between object-oriented middleware and RPCs. In particular, the operations are declared in an Interface Definition Language (IDL) file, like it is with RPCs. This is illustrated in Figure 3-5.

Like RPCs, the IDL generates a stub that converts operation calls into messages (this is marshalling again) and a skeleton that converts messages into operation calls. It's not quite like RPCs since each message must contain an object reference and may return an object reference. There needs to be a way of converting an object reference into a binary string and this is different with every object middleware.

Unlike existing RPC middleware, the operations may also be called through an interpretative interface such as a macro language. There is no reason why RPCs shouldn't implement this feature, it's just that they haven't. An interpretative interface requires some way of finding out about the operations at runtime and a way of building the parameter list. In CORBA (discussed below) the information about an interface is stored in the interface repository (which looks like another object to the client program).

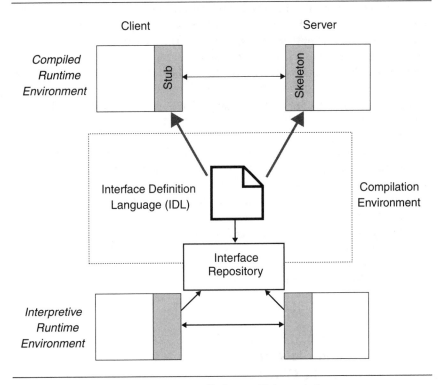

Figure 3-5   Object middleware compilation and interpretation

In object middleware the concept of an interface is more explicit than in object-oriented languages like C++. Interfaces give enormous flexibility and strong encapsulation. With interfaces you really don't know the implementation because an interface is not the same as a class. One interface can be used in many classes. One interface can be implemented by many different programs. One object can support many interfaces.

So why would you think of using an object middleware instead of, say, RPCs? There are three main reasons.

The first is simply that object middleware fits naturally with object-oriented languages. If you are writing a server in C++ or Visual Basic almost all your data and logic will (or at least should) be in objects. If you are writing your server in Java, all your data and code must be in objects. To design good object-oriented programs you start by identifying your objects and then you figure out how they interact. Many good programmers now always think in objects. Exposing an object interface through middleware is more natural and simpler to them than exposing a non-object interface.

The second reason is that object middleware is more flexible. The fact that the interface is de-linked from the server program is a great tool for simplification. For instance, suppose there is a single interface for security checking. Any number of servers can use exactly the same interface even though the underlying implementation is completely different. If there is a change to the interface, this can be handled in an incremental fashion by adding a new interface to the same object rather than by changing the existing interface. Having both the old and new interfaces concurrently allows the clients to be moved gradually, not all at once.

A third but more subtle reason for having an object interface is that it forces the programmer writing the client side to think about the state in the server. In an interface defined in procedures (such as a C header file or an RPC IDL) you frequently see parameters called something like Handle or Id, which are used to identify a resource, like a file, a network connection, or a database. This is how programmers worked with objects before they realized objects existed! No one thought too deeply then about the ramifications of what they were doing, such as what happened if the client went away without deallocating the resource. Now when you do the same thing with objects it is that much more obvious.

3.3 Object middleware technologies— DCOM and CORBA

There are three major object middleware standards: CORBA, COM/DCOM, and Java RMI (Remote Method Invocation). COM/DCOM underpins the Microsoft strategy. Java RMI can only be used for Java to Java communication. (If you want Java to talk to non-Java you are meant to use CORBA.)

I have moved more detailed descriptions of CORBA and COM into the following boxes (see CORBA box and COM/DCOM box). By explaining the notion of object middleware I have explained the basics of both, but there are some significant differences.

An important difference is that a COM object is pinned to a memory location and belongs to an active process. If the memory becomes invalid by the machine powering off or the object's controlling program dying, then the COM object disappears. In CORBA, by contrast, the object can last for ages. In theory you can convert a CORBA object reference to a string, write the string on a piece of paper, send the paper to someone else (one article I read had the suggestion of putting it into a bottle and throwing it into the sea), and the recipient can write a program that converts the string back into an object reference and calls the object.

Another key difference between the technologies is that in COM each object has a count of the number of references pointing to the object and if all the clients stop using the object, the object is automatically deleted. In CORBA this is not the

CORBA

CORBA is a standard, not a product. The initials stand for Common Object Request Broker Architecture. It was developed by OMG, the Object Management Group, which is a consortium of almost all the important software vendors as well as a large number of user organizations. Well-known implementations are VisiBroker from Inprise, Orbix from Iona, Weblogic from BEA Systems, and Component Broker from IBM.

The structure of CORBA is illustrated in Figure 3-6.

At the bottom is IIOP. The CORBA standard defines GIOP—General Inter-ORB Protocol—and IIOP, which is GIOP over TCP/IP. Vendors can choose to implement their own protocol but must support IIOP as well. You will hear people use the words CORBA and IIOP interchangeably. This is at best misleading. There are some IIOP implementations for embedded systems that don't use the upper layers of CORBA at all and you need the upper layers to build client programs and supply naming services.

Syntactically client programming for CORBA is straightforward. Except for initialization, everything is achieved by calling operations on object references. The only way to get another object reference is to call an operation that returns the object reference you want (as I did in the earlier example by using the AccountSet object to get an AccountRef reference). Even the Orb itself is an object or at least looks like an object to the client programmer. All the low-level calls, which are implementation specific, are hidden by the stubs.

There are both compiled and interpretative interfaces for client and server. For compiled access the CORBA IDL is used to created the IDL Stub for the client side and the Static IDL Skeleton for the object implementation side. As with RPCs the Stub marshals the parameters (puts them into a string of bits) and the Skeleton un-marshals the message and calls the object implementation. For interpretative access, the client can use the "Interface Repository" to find out about the interface (of course the Interface Repository also looks like a CORBA object and has an IDL and a stub). The object implementation can also be interpretative, in which case it uses the (wonderfully named) Dynamic Skeleton. Whether an object is implemented statically or dynamically is transparent to the client.

The purpose of the Object Adapter is to provide the environment for running the server objects. In particular it looks after

- mapping object reference to object implementation.
- threading—the server may have many threads and needs to allocate the object calls to a thread.
- object life cycle—creating new objects and deleting objects.

CORBA takes a wide view of object life cycle. It allows objects to exist even when the program that instantiates them is NOT running. What this means in practice is that when a client calls an object reference for an object

(continued)

CORBA (*cont.*)

that is "inactive," the Object Adapter must first activate the object before handling the call. Activating an object brings the object into memory, which in turn means running some code that supports objects of this class. How the code is packaged and gets started is an implementation issue. This code—known as a servant—creates a runtime object. This notion of long-lived object references has all sorts of ramifications:

- Object references for long-lived objects do not rely on memory addresses because every time the servant program creates the activated object in memory it will run in a different memory location.
- If the object has additional state, the servant program will have to find it. The only information it has to find this state is data in the object reference itself.
- The CORBA client can turn an object reference into a string, store it away somewhere, and turn it back into an object reference later, possibly months later.
- There must be an implementation repository for converting strings to object references and vice versa.
- The servant must be able to deactivate an object because there is no way that the server knows when the client has finished using the object.

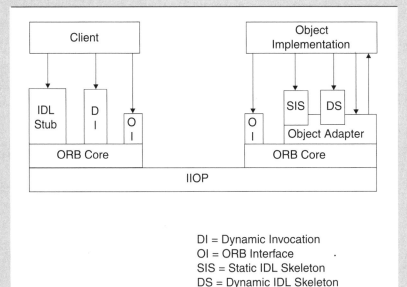

DI = Dynamic Invocation
OI = ORB Interface
SIS = Static IDL Skeleton
DS = Dynamic IDL Skeleton

Figure 3-6 The CORBA model

The overhead of doing all this is considerable, so CORBA also supports short-lived objects that disappear when the servant is finished. Note however that from the client's perspective short-lived and long-lived objects are indistinguishable. Unfortunately, unless the programmer implements some extra code, the server will not know when a short-term object is no longer being used.

But basic CORBA is just a start. There are a large number of additional services, namely: life cycle, naming, event notification, persistence, relationship, transaction, concurrency control, externalization, query, licensing, security, collection, and trader. Of these, probably naming, transaction, event notification, and security services are the ones most used. All of these services have standard CORBA object interfaces. The complete CORBA standard with all its services runs to over 142 interfaces and 488 operations (so I'm told) and numerous constants, structure definitions, and typedef definitions. Furthermore, CORBA is just the underpinnings to OMG's Object Management Architecture (OMA).

COM/DCOM

COM—Component Object Model—comes from Microsoft and underpins almost everything it does. COM was designed from the beginning to be a standard for components. In particular it was designed to underpin OLE—Microsoft's Object Linking and Embedding technology.

In a later chapter I will discuss the wider meanings of the word *component*. A COM component, however, is a separate code file that has one or more object interfaces. Since it is code and not source, the COM component can be written in a wide variety of languages, such as C++, Visual Basic, Object Pascal, and Java.

To start up a COM component a client supplies two bits of information—a CLSID and an Interface ID (IID). Both of these are unique 128-bit numbers, which fortunately the system can invent for you.

The letters CLSID hints that it stands for "Class Identifier" but it is sufficiently different from O-O classes to be confusing. I find it easiest to think of a CLSID as doing two things. First, CLSID is a Component ID because what happens is that the CLSID is used to search the registry for the component's code file and initiates it if needed. (The registry is the file that contains most of the configuration information in Windows. On Windows 2000 its role is taken by the Active Directory.)

Second, think of the CLSID as an object creator because when the component gets going it looks at the CLSID and creates an object. While a CLSID can point at only one code file, one code file can support more than one CLSID; in other words, it can create different objects with different interfaces for different users.

(continued)

COM/DCOM   *(cont.)*

Once an object is created it returns an interface pointer of the type requested by the Interface ID. However, one object can support multiple interface pointers, which is why you need an Interface ID to tell it which one the client wants. This is a useful feature; for instance, it allows one object to support both an old and new version of the same interface by giving them a different Interface ID.

Objects can also be created by the component behind the client's back, so to speak. In this case an interface pointer may be returned to the client by an operation—just like you saw in the earlier example with AccountSet returning the AccountRef reference.

Components can run in the same address space as the client (fast), or in a separate address space (not so fast), or over a network (comparatively not fast at all). The latter case, COM over a network, is called DCOM, Distributed COM. It is the registry that holds all the information about how and where the components run.

COM objects are runtime things and they have a memory address. They exist in the address space of the executable code and, when the component finishes running, the COM object disappears. Each COM object has a reference count that keeps track of how many interface pointers are currently pointing at the object. When the reference count goes to zero the object is deleted. When the component has no active objects, it is terminated.

As well as a compile-time interface, COM optionally supports an interpretative interface. A COM object with such an interface is usable from Visual Basic, Java, and macro languages like Excel, Access, or Word macros. One component can support both a compile-time and interpretative interface.

case; there is no count and all object deletion can only be done by explicit programmatic command.

One reason for these differences is that the original COM developers were trying to solve a systems problem, namely a robust implementation for OLE, Object Linking and Embedding (for example, embedding an Excel spreadsheet in a Word document). CORBA was developed from the ground up, by committee, as an object middleware.

3.4   Using object interfaces

So we have these objects and object interfaces. How do we use them? Middleware objects mostly fall into the following categories:

- Proxy objects
- Agent objects
- Service objects

- Singletons
- Call-back objects

(These are my own terms. I had to invent them because at the time I was writing this book I could find very little substantive discussion on how distributed object technology should be used.)

A proxy object stands in for something else. The AccountRef object above is an example of this since it stands in for the account object in the database and associated account processing. Another example is objects that are there on behalf of a hardware resource like a printer.

A proxy object can be a constructed thing, meaning that it is pretending that such and such object exists, but in actual fact the object is derived from other information. For instance, the account information can be dispersed over several database tables but the proxy object might gather all the information together in one place. Another example might be a printer proxy object. The client thinks it is a printer but actually it is just an interface into an e-mail system.

Agent objects are there to make the client's life easier by providing an agent on the server that acts on the client's behalf. An important subcategory of agent objects are cursors used to navigate around a database, such as might be used with OLE DB (described in the previous chapter). A cursor represents a current position in a table or list, such as the output from a database query, and the cursor supports operations like MoveFirst (move to the first row in the output set) and MoveNext (move to the next output row). Similarly, agent objects are required for serial files access. In fact, cursors or similar objects are required for most large-scale data structures to avoid passing all the data over the network when you may only need a small portion of it. Other examples of agent objects are objects that store security information or hold temporary calculated results.

One key difference between a proxy object and an agent object is that a proxy object can be shared among different clients. (It need not be shared but then you must have some code to ensure the two or more copies of the same proxy are kept in sync.) Agent objects, on the other hand, are never shared.

A service object is an entrypoint into a system. In my earlier example, the AccountSet object could be a service object.

Note, I have used the term "service" not "server" because there is not necessarily a simple mapping between entrypoint and server program. The service object is what the client uses; a server is about how the objects are implemented at runtime. It would be possible for a server to have two service objects for two different views of the same set of underlying objects.

Singletons are the objects of which only one exists—it is a class with one object instance. Actually (I add, sotto voce), singletons are what you use when you want an object system to deliver a traditional RPC service. Examples would be a service that needs no state, like a set of arithmetic or interest calculation routines.

Call-back objects implement a reverse interface, an interface from server to client. The purpose is for the server to send the client unsolicited data. Call-back mechanisms are widely used in COM. For instance, GUI Buttons, Lists, and Text input field are all types of Windows control(s) and control fire events. Events are implemented by COM call-back objects.

With these kinds of objects in mind, let us look at how COM and CORBA compare.

Recall that the objects in COM don't exist for any longer than either the component or the client is running. CORBA on the other hand has a dual notion of object lifetime. The actual object reference may exist for only as long as the server or client are running but object references can be converted back and forth into strings and the strings can exist for as long as you like. Superficially, this idea of strings for objects looks ideal for proxy objects. In practice it isn't, for two reasons:

1. The number of proxy objects can be very large. Have a million accounts and you have a million proxy objects. Have a proxy object for every debit and credit record and you have orders of even more magnitude. You don't want to have to be converting strings to object references for all of these.

2. How do you synchronize the creation and deletion of the object string with the actual object? In theory you should probably use a two-phase commit transaction to synchronize the CORBA implementation repository (which stores the object strings) with the database. I am not aware of any CORBA implementations that support this.

What the object string might be useful for is for service objects. However there is a CORBA service—CORBA naming services—specifically designed for these kind of objects so it is unclear whether there really is a role for object strings.

COM has reference counting, which implies that server objects are removed when they are no longer used. This is ideal for agent objects but it is also fine for other objects. The disadvantage of reference counting is that it is easy to forget to do it, in particular to forget to decrement the reference count. But having no reference count is not a solution. Consider the scenario of a server, which is up for weeks, connected to workstations that are restarted at least once a day. If the system does not support reference counting, you must write your own system for deactivating unused agent objects because every time the workstation application is started it creates some more.

3.5 Conclusions

There is much in common between using COM and using CORBA. Both have an IDL. The language of the IDL is very similar since both were based on C. Interfaces can be inherited from other interfaces. Both have a notion of object reference and, in both, an operation can return a reference to an object created by the server. There are bridges between COM and CORBA so some level of interoperability is possible.

COM/DCOM and CORBA were designed with very different goals in mind. In broad terms, CORBA was designed to implement long-lived objects and COM was designed to implement short-term objects.

In any case, this book is not about doing point-by-point product comparison. Point-by-point comparisons can be very dangerous; it implies that the best product is the one stuffed with the most features, which can lead to ridiculous conclusions like saying that the car with a cigarette lighter is better than a car that does not break down.

Object-oriented ideas have had an enormous impact everywhere and middleware is no exception. There are many advantages to object-oriented middleware:

- It is more flexible.
- It is a natural fit with object-oriented languages.
- It makes you think about state held in the server on behalf of the client.

But there are two traps.

First, reuse is a dangerous allure. Inheritance can be used to simplify the client's life (polymorphism) or to simplify the object implementer's life (reuse) and these two goals can conflict. Simplifying the client's life is far more important than simplifying the object implementer's life because it is key to simplifying the structure of the system.

Second, the notion of an object to a programmer, a modeler, and a database guru are not necessarily the same thing. By and large, the objects defined by the modelers end up stored in databases. But still there are issues (see OODB box). With regard to the object exposed over the middleware, many of these will bear no resemblance to the modeler's objects because they will be agent objects. Even proxy objects can be constructed out of many database objects.

4

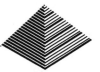

A Short History
of Middleware Technology—
Components and the Web

Object middleware technology became available in the early 1990s. Since then there have been three great changes: the introduction and rise of Java; the introduction of transactional component middleware; and, most important of all, the rise of the Internet. All three have changed our thinking in implementation design.

In retrospect, the Internet and the introduction of transactional component middleware have an aura of inevitability about them, but the rise of Java was unforeseen and in some ways bizarre. Java as a language is essentially a cleaned up version of C++. Its great advantage is that it is highly portable (for instance an integer is always 32 bits irrespective of the platform) and it is relatively safe (for instance, there are no pointers and there are bounds checks on all array indexing). But Java is not only a programming language; it is also an environment. Java is usually interpreted; the development tool translates Java source code to bytecode, which is interpreted by what is called the Java Virtual Machine (JVM). The JVM may translate Java bytecode to machine code on the fly. The JVM assures a consistent interface to external resources, albeit with platform specific extensions, and this consistency further enhances Java portability. The flip side of all of this is that Java is comparatively slow and not suitable for those applications that need to be close to the machine. In practice, this means that Java is a hopeless language for writing system software but a great language for writing application code.

I find it extraordinary that Java has risen from nowhere to be an important language in such a short period of time. If you had announced in the mid-1990s that you had a great language that was going to compete with Cobol, everyone would have thought you were mad; there have been many great programming languages developed over the years and without exception they have gone nowhere. An important reason for Java's prominence is that large powerful organizations are behind it, in particular, Sun, IBM, and Oracle, organizations not normally noted for their cooperativeness. Why? Is it possibly to use Java as a stick for beating Microsoft?

In this chapter, I look at two competing middleware standards. On one side is the Java crowd and their middleware standard bearer is EJB—Enterprise Java Beans. On the other side is Microsoft and its middleware standard bearer is COM+. Both these products are in a category I am calling transactional component middleware.

But before I describe these products, I feel impelled to make a few comments about the Internet. I am not going to describe Internet technology, it is now too large a subject to describe in a few swift paragraphs and it is changing too fast. But I must address the question that directly pertains to this book, which is, how does the Internet change our approach to building applications?

4.1 Internet applications

The Internet was a people's revolution and no vendor has been able to dominate the technology. Within IT, the Internet has changed many things, for instance:

- It has hastened (or perhaps caused) the dominance of TCP/IP as a universal network standard.
- It has led to the development of a large amount of free Internet software at the workstation.
- It inspired the concept of thin client—a client program that could be downloaded over the network.
- It led to a new fashion for data to be formatted as text (e.g., HTML, XML, and SOAP). The good thing about text is that it can be read easily and edited by a simple editor (like Notepad). The bad thing is that it is wasteful of space and requires parsing by the recipient.
- It has changed the way we think about security.
- It has liberated us from the notion that specific terminals are of a specific size.
- It has led to a return to centralizing computer applications.
- It has led to a better realization of the power of directories, in particular DNS—Domain Name Servers—for translating Web names (that is, URLs) into network (that is, IP) addresses.
- It has led to the rise of intranets—Internet technology used in-house—and extranets—private networks between organizations using Internet technology.
- It has, to some extent, made people realize that an effective solution does not have to be complex.

As I write this book, it looks like we are on the verge of another revolution, the rise of mobile phone access to computer systems (the so called m-commerce). How much this will end up using existing Internet technology is an open issue (to me, writing in early 2000), but it does seem that there will be some kind of Internet integration. On the horizon is access to computer systems from the TV (couch-potato-commerce).

When we come to consider how Internet (and telephony) applications differ from traditional applications, four points stand out.

First, the user is in command. In the early days, computer input was by command strings and the user was in command. The user typed and the computer answered. Then we went to menus and forms interfaces, where the computer application was in command. The menus guided the user by giving them restricted options. Menus and forms together ensure work is done only in one prescribed order. With the Internet, the user is back in command in the sense that they can use Links, Back commands, Favorites, and explicit URL addresses to skip around from screen to screen and application to application. This makes a big difference in how applications are structured and is largely the reason why putting on a Web interface to an existing menu and forms application does not work well in practice.

Second, when writing a Web application you should be sensitive to the fact that not all users are equal. They don't all have high resolution, 17-inch monitors attached to 100Mbit Ethernet LANs. Screens are improving in quality but new portable devices will be smaller again. Slow telephone-quality lines are, and will continue to be, the dominant connection medium for the underprivileged (like me, when I work from home).

Third, you cannot rely on the network address to identify the user, except over a short period of time. On the Internet, the IP address is assigned by the Internet provider when someone logs on. Even in-house on a LAN, many organizations use dynamic address allocation (the DHCP protocol) and every time a person connects to the network they are liable to get a different IP address.

Fourth, the Internet is a public medium and security is a major concern. Many organizations have built a security policy on the basis that (a) every user can be allocated a usercode and password centrally (typically the user is given the opportunity to change the password) and (b) every network address is in a known location. Someone logging on with a particular usercode at a particular location is given a set of access rights. The same user at a different location may not have the same access rights. I have already noted that point (b) does not hold on the Internet, at least not to the same precision. Point (a) is also suspect as it is much more likely that usercode security will come under sustained attack. I will discuss these points later, in Chapter 9.

To these four points, at some stage in the near future, we should add a fifth. It makes much more sense on the Internet to load a chunk of data, do some local processing on it, and send the results back. This would be ideal for filling in big forms (for example, tax forms). At the moment these kinds of applications are handled by many short interactions with the server, often with frustratingly slow response times. What is holding up this method of work is the lack of a standard tool (and a catchy buzzword—I vote for "Big Internet Messaging").

Most nontrivial Web applications are implemented in a hardware configuration that looks something like Figure 4-1.

You can of course amalgamate the transaction and database server with the Web servers and cut out the network between them. However, most organizations don't do this. This is partly due to organizational issues—the Web server belongs to a different department—but there are good technical reasons for making the split, for instance:

- You can put a firewall between the Web server and the transaction and database server, thus giving an added level of protection to your enterprise data.
- It gives you more flexibility to choose different platforms and technology from the backend servers.
- A Web server often needs to access many backend servers, so there is no obvious combination of servers to bring together.
- Web servers are easily scalable by using load balancing across multiple servers (so long as they don't hold session data). Transaction and database servers are hard to load balance. By splitting them we have the opportunity to use load balancing for one and not the other. I discuss this issue in the chapter on performance (Chapter 8).

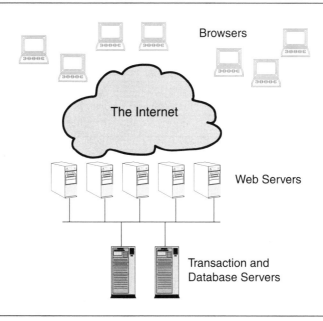

Figure 4-1 Web hardware configuration

The transactional component middleware, which will be discussed later in this chapter, is designed to be the middleware between front- and back-end servers.

Many applications require some kind of session concept to be workable. A session makes the user's life easier by:

- Providing a log on at the start, so authentication need only be done once.
- Providing for traversal from screen to screen.
- Making it possible for the server to collect data over several screens before processing.
- Making it easier for the server to tailor the interface for a given user, giving different users different functionality.

In old-style applications these were implemented by menu and forms code back in the server. Workstation GUI applications are also typically session-based; the session starts when the program starts and stops when it stops. But the Web is stateless, by which I mean that it has no in-built session concept—it does not remember any state (i.e., data) from one request to another. (Technically, each Web page is retrieved by a separate TCP/IP session.) Sessions are so useful that there needs to be a way of simulating them.

One way is to use applets. This essentially uses the Web as a way of downloading a GUI application. But there are problems, for instance:

- If the client code is complex, the applet is large and it is time-consuming to load the applet over a slow line.
- The applet opens a separate session over the network back to the server. If the application is at all complex we will need additional middleware over this link.
- A simple sockets connection has the specific problem that it can run afoul of a firewall, since firewalls may restrict traffic to specific TCP port numbers (such as for HTTP, SMTP, and FTP communication).
- The applet has very restricted functionality on the browser (to prevent malicious applets from mucking up the workstation).

Java applets have been successful in terminal emulation and other relatively straightforward work, but in general, this approach is not greatly favored. It's easier to stick to standard HTML or dynamic HTML features where possible.

An alternative strategy is for the server to remember the client's IP address. This limits the session to the length of time that the browser is connected to the network since on any reconnect it might be assigned a different IP address. There is also a danger that a user could disconnect and another user could be assigned their IP address and therefore pick up their session!

The best approach for session management is to use cookies. Cookies are small amounts of data the server can send to the browser and request that it is loaded on the browser's disk. (If you use Windows, look in the Windows/Cookies directory. You can have a look at any text in the cookies with Notepad.) When the browser sends a message to the same server the cookie goes with it. The server can store enough information to resume the session (usually just a simple session number). The cookie may also contain a security token and a timeout date.

Neither using cookies nor using IP addresses for sessions is quite the same as traditional sessions. For example, one crucial difference is that the server cannot detect that the browser's workstation is switched off.

I will return to the subject of sessions later in this chapter, but before I do, let us examine the next layer down—transactional component middleware.

4.2   Transactional component middleware

Transactional component middleware (TCM) currently covers two technologies: Microsoft Transaction Server (MTS), which has now become part of COM+, from Microsoft, and Enterprise Java Beans (EJB) from the anti-Microsoft camp. OMG has released a CORBA-based standard for transactional component middleware, which is meant to be compatible with EJB but extends the ideas into other languages. I will not describe this standard further since at the time of writing its importance in the marketplace is uncertain.

Transactional component middleware is my term. I discussed distributed transaction processing and transaction monitors in Chapter 2. TCM is about taking components and running them in a distributed transaction processing environment. There are other terms being used, such as *COMWare* and *Object Transaction Managers* (*OTM*). I don't like *COMWare* for two reasons. First, it isn't exactly an EJB-friendly term. Second, I can see that components could be used in a non-transactional environment in a manner that is very different from a transactional form of use, so having something about transactions in the title is important. I don't like *OTM* because components are too important and distinctive not to be included in the name. Fussy, aren't I?

So what about the word *component*? *Component* is sometimes used to mean any asset that can be lifted from one context and reused in another, even source code. More commonly a component is defined as runtime code that can be taken from one context and run in another. In other words, any program is a component and so are Windows DLLs (dynamic linked libraries). However, to be able to use the component in another environment you must know what its interface is to the rest of the system. In batch Cobol programs this would mean knowing what switches it used and the format of the external files. In a program run by a transaction monitor it would mean knowing about the program's database connections and the format of its input and output messages. When I come to discuss component development in Chapter 10, I shall resurrect and refine this definition of a component because it is useful.

But in this chapter I am talking about a more restrictive definition of components: Components are runtime code with an object interface that can be taken out of one context and run in another. By this definition, COM code files are components and so are Java Beans. (Java Beans are one or more Java classes and support files brought together and put into a special file, called a JAR file, for distribution.) As with any runtime code, you need to know enough about the component to be able to use it in its new environment. Many pundits in this area talk about "introspection" and give the impression that you can find out all you need to know to use a component from the component itself. Of course for this to be true you would need a complete formal spec, a list of the bugs where it deviates from the spec, and performance and platform characteristics. Introspection in practice means that many components provide a description of their interface and perhaps a bit of comment, which, to be fair, is a useful first step in understanding a component.

Java Beans can run in any Java Virtual Machine and COM components can run in any Windows operating system. Furthermore Java provides RMI for calling remote Java Beans and Microsoft provides DCOM for calling remote COM objects. Both Java Beans and COM objects can call database systems and do transactions. So why do we need transactional component middleware?

Transactional component middleware fits the same niche in object middleware systems that transaction monitors fit in traditional systems. It is there to make transaction processing systems easier to implement and more scalable. The magic it uses to do this is known as a container. The container provides many useful features, the most notable of which are transaction support and resource pooling. The general idea is that standard facilities can be implemented by the container rather than by forcing the component implementer to write lots of ugly system calls.

One of the advantages of transactional component middleware is that the components can be deployed with different settings to behave in different ways. Changing the security environment is a case in point where it is clearly beneficial to be able to change the configuration at deployment time. But there is some information that must be passed from developer to deployer, in particular the transactional requirements. For instance, in COM+ the developer must define that the component supports one of four transactional environments, namely:

- Requires a transaction—either the client is in transaction state (i.e., within the scope of a transaction) or COM+ will start a new transaction when the component's object is created.
- Requires a new transaction—COM+ will always start a new transaction when the component's object is created, even if the caller is in transaction state.
- Supports transactions—the client may or may not be in transaction state, the component's object does not care.
- Does not support transactions—the object will not run in transaction state, even if the client is in transaction state.

In general it is the first or third of these transactional environments that are commonly used. Note the client can be an external program (perhaps on another system) or another component working within COM+. EJB has a similar set of features. Because the container delineates the transaction start and end point, the program code needs to do no more than commit or abort the transaction. The notion of a little code and a few attribute settings makes COM+ and EJB much easier to use than, for instance, the CORBA Object Transaction Service.

Microsoft COM+ is illustrated in Figure 4-2 and Enterprise Java Beans is illustrated in Figure 4-3. You will see they both have a similar structure.

When a component is placed in a container (that is, moved to a file directory where the container can access it and registered with the container), the administrator provides additional information to tell the container how to run the component. This additional information tells the system about the component's transactional and security requirements. How the information is provided depends on the product. In Microsoft COM+ it is provided by a GUI interface—the COM+ Explorer. In the EJB standard, the information is supplied in XML.

A client uses the server by calling an operation in the IClassFactory (COM+) or MyHomeInterface (EJB) interface to create a new object. The object's interface is then used directly, just as if it were a local object.

If you look at Figures 4-2 and 4-3 you see that the client reference does not point at the user-written component but at an object wrapper. This is a structure provided by the container that provides a barrier between the client and the component. One use of this barrier is security checking. Since every operation call is intercepted it is possible to define security down to a low level of granularity.

The other reason for the object wrapper is for performance. The object wrapper makes it possible to deactivate the component objects without the client knowing. When the client next tries to use an object, the wrapper reactivates the objects again, behind the client's back so to speak. The purpose of this is to save resources. Suppose there are thousands of clients, as you would expect if the application supports thousands of end users. Without the ability to deactivate

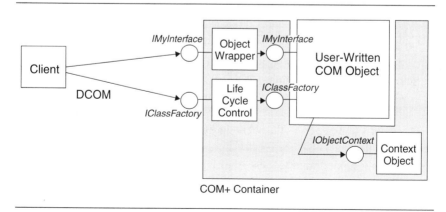

Figure 4-2   COM+

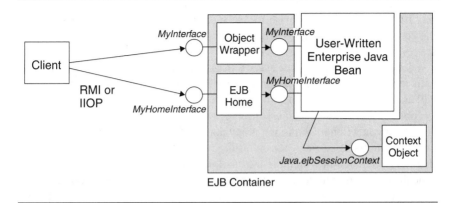

Figure 4-3   Enterprise Java Beans

objects, there would be thousands of objects, probably many thousands of objects because objects invoke other objects. Each object takes memory, so deactivating unused objects makes an enormous difference to memory utilization.

Given that objects come and go with great rapidity, all the savings made from the efficient utilization of memory would be lost by creating and breaking database connections, because building and breaking down database connections is a heavy user of system resources. The solution is connection pooling. There is a pool of database connections and, when the object is deactivated, the connection is returned to the pool. When a new object is reactivated, it reuses an inactive connection from the pool. Connection pooling is also managed by the container.

The next obvious question is—when are objects deactivated? Simply deleting objects at any time (when the resources are a bit stretched for instance) could be dangerous because the client might be relying on the component to store some information. This is where COM+ and EJB differ.

4.2.1   COM+

COM+ is an extension of the original COM model mainly done by merging MTS—Microsoft Transaction Server—into the core COM implementation. The underlying protocol is DCOM. It is likely that there will be an alternative network protocol called SOAP—Simple Object Access Protocol—which uses XML data streams. SOAP is a proposed Internet standard that could potentially make it a great deal easier for a client running on a non-Microsoft platform to call a COM+ server.

In COM+ you can declare that the object can be deactivated after every operation or at the end of a transaction. Deactivation in COM means elimination; the next time the client uses the object it is recreated from scratch.

Deactivating after every operation frankly brings the system back to the level of a traditional transaction monitor because at the beginning of every operation the code will find that all the data attributes in the object are reset to their initial state.

Deactivating at the end of every transaction allows the client to make several calls to the same object, for instance, searching for a record in the database in one call and updating the database in another call. After the transaction has finished, the object is deactivated.

What you will notice missing is any notion of the traditional features in transaction monitors of storing data on a session basis. In most transaction monitors there is a data area in which the transaction code can stash away data. The next time the same terminal runs a transaction, the (possibly different) transaction code can read the stash. This feature is typically used for storing temporary data, like remembering the account number the user is working on. Its omission in COM+ is a cause of much argument in the industry, and I will return to the subject in a later section.

4.2.2   EJB

Enterprise Java Beans is a standard not a product. There are EJB products from BEA, IBM, Oracle, and many others. The network connection to EJB is RMI— the Java-only Remote Method Invocation—and IIOP—the CORBA interface. IIOP makes it possible to call an EJB server from a CORBA client.

EJB has two flavors of component, session beans and entity beans. Both have two sub-flavors.

Session beans are private beans, that is, they cannot be shared across clients. They correspond roughly to what I described in the previous chapter as agent objects. The two sub-flavors are:

- Stateless session beans—these are like the COM components that are deactivated after every operation.
- Stateful session beans—these hold state for their entire life.

Exactly when the stateful session bean is "passivated" (the EJB term for deactivated, ugh!) is entirely up to the container. The container reads the object attributes and writes them to disk. The stateful bean implementer can add their own code, which is called by the passivate and activate operations. This might be needed to attach or release some external resource.

The EJB container must be cautious about when it passivates a bean because, if a transaction aborts, the client will want the state to be like it was before the transaction started rather than what it came to look like in the middle of the aborted transaction. That in turn means that the object state must be saved during the transaction commit. In fact, to be really safe, the EJB container has got to do a two-phase commit to synchronize the EJB commit with the database commit.

(Alternatively it would be possible to implement the EJB container as part of the database software and share the database log.)

Entity beans are rather like the proxy objects I described in the previous chapter. They were designed to be a bean that represents a row in a database. Normally the client does not explicitly create an entity bean but finds it by using a primary key data value. Entity beans can be shared.

The EJB specification allows implementers to cache the database data values in the entity bean to improve performance. If this is done, and it is done in many major implementations, it is possible for another application to update the database directly, behind the entity bean's back so to speak, leaving the entity bean cache holding out-of-date information. This would destroy transaction integrity. One answer is to only allow updates through the EJBs, but this is unlikely to be acceptable in any large-scale enterprise application. A better solution is for the entity bean not to do any caching, but you must ensure your EJB vendor supports this solution.

There are sub-flavors of entity beans:

- Container managed persistence—the EJB automatically maps the database row to the entity bean.
- Bean managed persistence—the user writes the bean code.

Bean managed persistence can be viewed as a kind of fourth generation language since it saves a great deal of coding.

4.3   The issues of state

Clearly EJB has a richer model of component types than COM+. The controversial question is whether this is necessary.

Let us take a specific example—Web shopping-cart applications. The user browses around an on-line catalogue and selects items he or she wishes to purchase by pressing an icon in the shape of a shopping cart. The basic configuration is illustrated in Figure 4-1. We have:

- A browser on a Web site
- A Web server, possibly a Web server farm implemented using Microsoft ASP (Active Server Pages) or Java JSP (Java Server pages) or other Web server products
- A backend transaction server implemented using COM+ or EJB

The session is implemented by using cookies. That means that when the shopping cart icon is pressed the server reads the cookie to identify the user and displays the existing contents of the shopping cart. When a new item is added to the shopping cart the cookie is read again to identify the user so the item is added to the right shopping cart. The basic problem becomes converting cookie data to the primary key of the user's shopping cart record in the database. Where do you do this?

There are several options:

- Do it in the Web server.
- Hold the shopping-cart information in a session bean.
- Put the user's primary key data in the cookie and pass it to the transaction server.

The Web server solution requires holding a lookup table in the Web server to convert cookie data value to shopping-cart primary key. The main problem is that, if you want to use a Web server farm for scalability or resiliency, the lookup table must be shared across all the Web servers. This is possible, but it is not simple. (The details are discussed in more detail in Chapter 7.)

Holding the shopping-cart information in a session bean suffers from the same problem, but in this case the session bean cannot be shared. This is not an insurmountable problem because in EJB you can read what is called a Handle from the object, store it on disk, and the other server can read the Handle and get access to the object. But you would have to ensure the two Web servers don't access the same object at the same time, and probably the simplest way to do this would be to convert the Handle into an object reference every time the shopping-cart icon is pressed. Note that a consequence of this approach is that with 1,000 concurrent users you would need 1,000 concurrent session beans. A problem with the Web is that you don't know when the real end user has gone away, so deleting a session requires detecting a period of time with no activity. A further problem is that, if the server goes down, the session bean is lost.

The simplest solution is to store the shopping-cart information in the database and put the primary key of the user's shopping carts directly in the cookie. The cookie data is then passed through to the transaction server. This way, both the Web server and the transaction server are stateless, all these complex recovery problems disappear, and the application is more scalable and efficient.

So have I been unfair in choosing my example? It is the example chosen in the document "Sun Blueprints Design Guidelines for J2EE" (found on the Sunsoft Web site) to illustrate stateful session beans. I can see stateful session beans being useful for applications that are not transactional, such as querying a database. I can envisage situations where it would be useful to keep state that has nothing to do with transaction recovery, for instance for performance monitoring. But as a general principle, if you want to keep transactional state, put it in the database.

On the other hand, keeping state during a transaction has no problems as long as it is reinitialized if the transaction aborts, so the COM model is a good one. To do the same in EJB requires using a stateful session bean but explicitly reinitializing the bean at the start of every transaction.

But you needed session state for old transaction monitors, so why not now? Old transaction monitors needed them because they were dealing with dumb terminals that didn't have cookies. Also, old applications were typically much more ruthless about removing session state if there was a recovery and forcing users to log on again. For instance, if the network died, the old mainframe applications would log off all the terminals and remove session state; this simplified recovery. In contrast, if the network dies somewhere between the Web server and the browser, there is a good chance the Web server won't even notice. Even if it does, the Web server can't remove the cookie. In the old days, the session was between workstation and application, now it is between cookie and transaction server. Stateful session beans support a session between the Web server and the transaction server, which is only part of the path between cookie and transaction server. In this case, having part of an implementation just gets in the way.

Entity beans on the other hand have no such problems. They have been criticized for forcing the programmer to do too many primary key look-up operations on the database, but I am doubtful whether this performance hit is significant.

4.4 Conclusions

So which is better—COM+ or EJB? I refuse to answer this question for two reasons. At the time I am writing (early 2000) this technology is immature and it is easy to pick holes in it. If I had to make a decision today I would be more confident in implementing a large scalable application using COM+ rather than EJB mainly because there is more evidence that COM+ is more scalable (for example, Published TpcC benchmarks). But over the next few years EJB implementations will improve enormously. The key issue for developers is whether these technologies can live up to their promises, and the answer is probably yes for both of them. That does not mean that everyone using the technology will be successful. There are pitfalls, one of which is understanding the recovery requirements described above. I hope in the course of this book to explain how you can be successful with this technology, at least at the design level.

The second reason for not answering the "what's best" question is that the major reasons for liking or disliking both of the technologies are not technical. The anti-Microsoft camp will not accept any solution that only runs on the Windows 2000 operating system. And on the other side, there are many who will never accept a major middleware element that only runs with Java. As I said earlier, OMG has developed a component model in CORBA version 3, which could potentially be a third way, that suffers from neither of these negatives. But the CORBA component model is late and has possibly missed the window of opportunity; only time will tell.

Transaction component middleware is likely to become the dominant transaction server technology at the start of the 21st century. While the details will change, the basic notions of component and container will not.

5

Middleware Classification and Middleware Architectures

The previous three chapters have described in outline a vast array of different technologies. This chapter and the next are about the question, what middleware technologies do we need? This is a key question for implementation design and IT architecture. In this chapter I will approach this question from a technical angle. First, I discuss the different constituent parts of middleware technology. Second, I explore whether a middleware classification is possible from basic principles. Third, I examine vendor architectures like Microsoft's DNA—Distributed inter-Net Applications Architecture—and Sun's J2EE—Java 2 Enterprise Environment—to see how they answer the question. In the next chapter, I look at the same question from the application developer's point of view.

5.1   Middleware elements

Middleware is more complex than most IT people recognize (and certainly a good deal more complex than most middleware vendors would have you believe). For a complete solution you need to consider at least eight elements, though many of these elements are considered part of the network infrastructure and not middleware. (It is a hard line to draw between networking software and middleware software so I will consider it in its totality.) The total picture is illustrated in the Figure 5-1.

A and B are different machines. The box around both is meant to indicate the complete systems environment. The eight elements fall into four categories.

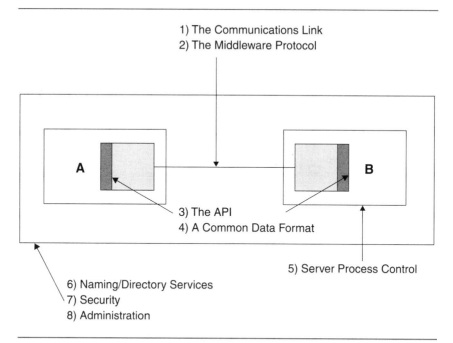

1) The Communications Link
2) The Middleware Protocol

A   B

3) The API
4) A Common Data Format

5) Server Process Control

6) Naming/Directory Services
7) Security
8) Administration

Figure 5-1   Middleware elements

5.1.1   Networking and interoperability

1. The communications link. Most middleware is restricted to using one or a few networking standards, the dominant standards at the moment being TCP/IP and SNA. The network protocol itself offers a set of value-added features, which may or may not be useful. TCP/IP, for instance, offers reliable delivery of messages and DNS (Domain Name Services) for converting names into IP addresses.

2. The middleware protocol, often called the "wire protocol." The protocol is the definition of the rules that make it possible for the two processes to communicate effectively. Formally, middleware protocols, like all protocols, are defined by

• The format of the messages over the communications link and
• The state transition diagrams of the entities at each end

Informally the protocol defines who starts the conversation, how to stop both ends speaking at once, how to ensure both sides are talking about the same subject, and how to get out of trouble.

There are many products, such as SMTP and FTP, which communicate over the network and have protocols, that aren't normally considered to be middleware. The distinguishing characteristic of middleware is the fact that middleware allows programs to communicate.

5.1.2   The programmatic interface

3. The application programmatic interface (API). An API is a set of proce-dure calls used by the programs to drive the middleware. Huge variation is possible:

- The API can be object-oriented or traditional.
- The API can be fixed (like ODBC) or it can be compiled for a specific application. In the latter case, there needs to be an Interface Definition Lan-guage (IDL) or equivalent.
- The API can be operations-based or language-based. For instance, the CORBA interpretative interface is operations-based while remote database access is language-based (the language typically being SQL).
- The API calls may or may not block the processing thread until the server replies.

4. A common data format. A message has some structure and the receiver of the message will split the message out into separate fields and will be convert-ing the data values for each field into something the recipient understands. Both sender and receiver must clearly know the structure of the message. Dif-ferent machines have different data representation standards. One might use ASCII, the other EBCDIC or UNICODE. One might have 16-bit, little-endian integers, the other might use 32-bit, big-endian integers. Sender and/or receiver may need to convert the data values. Many, but not all, mid-dleware products do this message assembly/disassembly and data format conversion for you. Where there is an IDL, this is called marshalling. But assistance with reformatting does not need an IDL. Remote database access also reformats data values. XML is being used more and more as a universal data presentation standard.

5.1.3   Server control

5. Server process control breaks down into three main tasks.

Process and thread control. When the first client program sends its first message something must run the server process. When the load is heavy, additional processes or threads may be started. Something must route the server request to (a) a process that is capable of processing it and (b) an avail-able thread. When the load lightens, it may be desirable to lessen the number of processes and/or threads. Finally, when processes or threads are inactive, they need to be terminated.

Resource management. For instance, database connection pooling.

Object management. Objects may be activated or deactivated. Clearly this only applies to object-oriented systems.

5.1.4   System administration infrastructure

6. **Naming/directory services.** The network access point to a middleware server is typically a 32-bit number defining the network address (IP address) and a port number that allows the operating system to route the message to the right program. Naming services map these numbers to names we can all understand. The best-known naming service is Domain Name Service (DNS) used by the Internet. Directory services go one step further and provide a general facility for looking things up; a middleware equivalent to the telephone directory. Directory services tend to be separate products that the middleware hooks into. Example directories are the Microsoft Active Directory and Netware Directory Services (NDS).

7. **Security.** Only valid users may be allowed to use the server resources and when they are connected they may be given access to only a limited selection of the possible services. Security permeates all parts of the system. Encryption needs support at the protocol level. Access control needs support from the server control functions, and authentication may need support from a dedicated security manager system.

8. **Administration.** Finally, we need a human interface to all this software for operational control, debugging, monitoring, and configuration control.

5.2   A technical classification of middleware?

Why is there such a great variety of middleware? What is the scope for middleware? What are the really crucial differences between different middleware technologies? Is there some important middleware missing? A middleware classification would go a long way toward answering these questions. But is it possible to devise such a classification? Let us look at some of the elements identified above and see if they could be used as the basis of a classification hierarchy.

5.2.1   What is communicating?

The first dimension is a classification according to what entities are communicating. We can see an evolution here. In the early days, terminals communicated with mainframes—the entities were hardware boxes. Later, process communicated with process. Now client programs and/or objects communicate with objects, or message queues communicate with message queues. The evolution is for communicating entities to become smaller and smaller, more and more abstract, and more and more numerous.

Observe that this is layering. Objects reside (at runtime at least) in processes. Processes reside in hardware boxes. Underpinning the whole edifice is hardware-to-hardware level communication. This is reflected in the network protocols: IP is for hardware-to-hardware communication, TCP is for process-to-process communication, and IIOP is for object-to-object communication (see Layering box).

Layering

Layering is a fundamental concept for building distributed systems. The notion of layering is old and dates back to at least the early 1960s; for instance, it features in Dijkstra's 1963 paper "The Structure of the Multi-programming System." Layering became prominent when the original ISO seven-layer model was published. The seven-layer model itself and the role of ISO in pushing through international standards has diminished, but the concept of layering is as powerful and as obvious as ever. I will illustrate it using TCP/IP but also using some ISO terminology. There are basically four layers:

1. Physical layer—the wire, radio waves, and pieces of wet string that join two hardware boxes in a network.
2. Data link layer—the protocol between neighboring boxes in the network (for example, Ethernet and Frame relay).
3. Network layer—the protocol that allows messages to be sent through multiple hardware boxes to reach any machine in the network. In TCP/IP this is IP—Internet Protocol.
4. Transport layer—the protocol that allows a process in one hardware box to create and use a network session with a process in another hardware box. In TCP/IP this is TCP—Transmission Control Protocol.

The fundamental notion of layering is that each layer uses the layer below it to send and receive messages. Thus TCP uses IP to send the messages, and IP uses Ethernet or Frame relay or whatever to send messages. Each layer has a protocol. The system works because each layer has a (very) well-defined behavior. For instance, when TCP gives IP a message, it expects that the receiving TCP node will be given the message with exactly the same size and content. This might sound trivial but it isn't when the lower-level protocols might have message length restrictions that cause the message to be segmented. When a user program uses TCP it expects that the receiver will receive the messages in the same order the sender sent them. This too sounds trivial until you realize that IP obeys no such restriction. IP might send two messages in a sequence by an entirely different route and so getting them out of order is quite possible.

(continued)

Layering   (*cont.*)

Middleware software typically starts above the TCP/IP layer and typically takes all these issues of message segmentation and ordering for granted.

Layering is not confined to the network layer. First, it is important as a thinking tool; it is a wonderful technique for structuring complex problems so we can solve them. Second, people are forever layering one technology on another to get around some specific problem. The networking specialists have a special term for this—tunneling. For instance, SNA can be used as a data link layer in a TCP/IP network and (not at the same time hopefully) IP can be used as a data link layer in SNA networking. Note that if we do this, all the advantages of the underlying network are lost and there are additional network management challenges. It is not an ideal solution but sometimes it is a useful tactical solution. In the middleware context, people rarely talk about tunneling, but the idea comes up often enough, for instance, layering a real-time client/server application over a message queuing infrastructure.

Some people have invented additional layers above the OSI seven layers. Many of these layered architectures take a very loose notion of layering. They don't, for instance, insist that a layer only talks to the layer above and beneath it. They don't insist each layer has a protocol for communication with its peers in other nodes. Personally, I hate this; I feel that either an attempt has been made to deceive me or the speaker does not know what he or she is talking about. But I have discovered that many people aren't so picky.

In this book I have used terms like "presentation layer" and "transaction server layer." These are being used in a systems context, not a network context, and have no relationship to the seven-layer model. Since it is not about network node to network node communication, there is no implication that for a presentation entity to talk to a presentation entity, it must send messages down to the database layer and back up the other side. But the implication that the presentation layer cannot jump around the transaction server (or whatever the box is called in the middle) is correct. Basically, the message and the flow of control can move around the layers like a king in chess—one box at a time—and not like a knight. If I do want to allow layers to be missed, I will either draw non-rectangular shapes, to create touching sides, or I will draw a line to indicate the flows. Strictly speaking, when this is done, it stops being a layered architecture.

5.2.2   How they communicate

Each layer has a protocol. The essence of middleware functionality is its protocol. It is also the essence of networking, so is there any difference between middleware protocols and network protocols? I will start with a general discussion on protocols before discussing what is distinctive about middleware protocols.

Protocols fall into two major categories: session protocols and sessionless protocols. Sessionless protocols are like sending a letter. You chuck the message into the ether with the address on it and hope it reaches its destination. In networking, UDP (User Datagram Protocol) is a sessionless alternative to TCP that also runs above the IP network layer. IP is sessionless, and so are most LAN protocols.

By far the greater number of middleware protocols are session protocols. Session protocols can be classified by who starts the session. We can identify three situations analogous to many-to-one, one-to-one, or one-to-many. These are illustrated in Figure 5-2.

The first situation is client/server. The client initiates the dialogue and there can be many clients to one server. Normally speaking, the client continues in control of the dialogue. The client will send a message and get back one or more replies. The server does nothing (in the context of the client/server dialogue) until the next client message arrives. It is the client asking the questions and the server giving the answers.

Note client/server is not a hardware configuration or an era in the mid-1990s during the evolution of middleware. The names client and server simply refer to roles in a dialogue. A process that is a server in one dialogue can be a client in another. There is no theoretical limit to the number of dialogues one process can belong to.

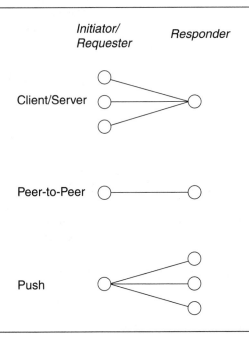

Figure 5-2   Protocol categories

In peer-to-peer protocols, both sides are equal, and either one initiates a conversation. TCP is a peer-to-peer protocol. Peer-to-peer is also used by e-mail and directory servers to communicate with each other.

Push protocol is a bit like client/server except that the server initiates the messages. (It could be called server/client technology I suppose, but the word "push" has more zip. When talking about push protocols people commonly call client/server technology "pull" technology.) The best-known instances of push protocols are within publish and subscribe tools. The actual subscribe process is standard client/server; a client indicates to the server that they want to subscribe to a certain information delivery, for instance to track stock movements. The publish process is a push mechanism, which means that the message is sent to the client without any prompting from the client. Push is ideal for reacting to server events. At the moment, there is no commonly accepted standard for push. In fact, most so-called push technology is actually regularly scheduled pull technology. This means the client wakes up every *n* minutes and checks to see if it has any messages. In Internet Explorer, for instance, you can subscribe to a "channel" and you will get regular updates of information. This works by using periodically scheduled inquiries to check whether there is more information available. Alternatively the information will be sent by e-mail. To find a real example of a push protocol in action, you need to turn to something like Webcasting and video on demand. These technologies are a form of multicast (messages sent simultaneously to multiple clients) and are used in collaboration software rather than business processing.

Classifying protocols along the lines of one-to-many, one-to-one, and many-to-one muddles up transactional middleware with networking and collaboration software, which makes one wonder whether we are missing some essential dimension here. We are; it is integrity.

At the base level are the sessionless network protocols, like IP, which have minimal integrity. These protocols are just meant to be fast. They rely on the upper layers to provide integrity.

For voice and video communication, timeliness is more important than data quality. Think of a telephone call. A little crackle on the line (that is, lost or altered bits) is not too bad, but delays in the voice, especially irregular delays, are difficult to cope with. With data transfers, exactly the opposite is true; integrity is everything. We cannot tolerate any corruption to the message but short delays are perfectly acceptable. This trade-off between quality and delay, as well as the necessity to prioritize some traffic in preference to others, is taxing the minds of the network vendors at the moment because of the trend for data and voice to share the same physical network.

More specifically for transactional and information retrieval middleware, there must be

- No messages lost
- No messages received in the wrong order
- No message corruption and
- No message duplication

Actually, TCP handles all of these without any help from the middleware. Note: you can't actually detect messages lost or duplicated without some kind of session concept, which implies middleware protocols are almost certainly session-based. Some network technologies are not so obliging, in which case the middleware must step in to fill the gap.

But the network protocol cannot cater to transactional integrity on the client or server side. For this we need additional protocols like two-phase commit or message queuing.

The real characteristic of middleware protocols is that the protocol is integrated with the applications. This means two things:

- The middleware should have a protocol that is convenient for the structure of the application—for instance, client/server or queuing.
- The middleware can implement additional application-level integrity like two-phase commit.

Interestingly, publish and subscribe tools show applications being built on top of middleware. I suppose the reason that push is not an established middleware style like client/server is that we are prepared to control a server to ensure it is ready to receive messages but there is no practical way to control clients.

5.2.3   What is the interface?

Clearly classifying middleware by the protocol is a complex undertaking, so perhaps looking at the programming interface would be a simpler and better approach.

As I noted earlier, interfaces fall into two basic categories, let us call them API-based and IDL-based. An API—Application Programming Interface—is a fixed set of procedure calls for using the middleware. IDL—Interface Definition Language—is a separate language that defines the interface independently from the rest of the programming. IDL-based applications have compile-time flexibility; API-based middleware have runtime flexibility.

Within API-based middleware there are many different styles of interface. A possible classification is

- Message-based: the API has a message and a message type. The server looks at the message type to decide where to route the message. Examples are Tuxedo distributed transaction processing and MQSeries (where the message type is the queue name).
- Command language-based: the command is encoded into a language. The classic example is remote database access for which the command language is SQL.
- Operation call-based: the operation call—the name of the server operation and its parameters—is built up by a series of middleware procedure calls. This is what happens in interpretative interfaces for CORBA and COM. In

many cases, the considerable complexity of building the operation call is disguised from the end user (for example, it is implemented behind the scenes in Visual Basic).

There is another way of classifying the interface; another dimension of classification if you will. This is a classification according to the impact on process thread control. The classification is

- Blocked (also known as synchronous)—the thread stops until the reply arrives.
- Unblocked (also known as asynchronous)—the client every now and then has a look to see if the reply has arrived.
- Event-based—when the reply comes, an event is caused, which wakes up the client.

To further muddy the water, the trend is for middleware to support many different styles of interface. Thus we see CORBA and COM supporting both interpretive and IDL-based interfaces.

5.2.4   Classifying middleware from technological principles

There are two conclusions from the proceeding three subsections.

The first is that there are many ways of classifying middleware, none of which is entirely satisfactory. What we have is a multi-dimensional classification with almost complete independence between the dimensions.

The second conclusion is that there are many possible middlewares, many of which we don't exploit. Somewhere in a parallel universe, programs send objects, not messages. They have just discovered peer-to-peer communication (a revolution from the traditional server/client—also known as the master/slave—model), and event-based programming is the order of the day.

5.3   Vendor architectures

In the previous section I was unable to bring order to the middleware chaos. How do vendors do it? The answer is that they publish vendor architectures.

The word "architecture" seems to be a continual source of controversy in the IT industry. Part of the problem is that the word is so widely used. Thus there are IT Application Architectures, IT Technical Architectures, Business Architectures, and numerous subcategories—Component Architectures, Network Architectures, Storage Architectures, and so on. You also see terms like Physical Architecture and Logical Architecture.

Software vendors often have architectures, for instance Microsoft DNA and SunSoft J2EE, which are described below. The purpose of these is to position products and help market their products. In particular, it is a means to tell clients how to develop with their products.

IT departments often talk about an IT architecture meaning the IT infrastructure design and the rules and guidelines for IT implementation (for example, choice of platform).

Consulting organizations, for a lot of money, will develop business models, application models, information models, and technology models—any of which may be called an architecture.

Hardware vendors talk about architecture (for example, the Intel chip architecture) and even have employees called architecture consultants.

About all these have in common is a desire to look at the forest not the trees.

The other problem is the word itself. Architecture for buildings is about design. In IT, architecture also often means a high-level description of a design, but not always. Some very high-level architectures are more akin to zoning regulations than they are to individual building design. Vendor architectures are more like abstract patterns than explicit designs.

Most of this book is about IT architecture in the sense of generic implementation design (see IT Architecture box in Chapter 1). But in this section I want to discuss vendor architectures as they implicitly are about positioning middleware in a grander scheme of things, which is this chapter's subject matter.

Historically, vendor architectures have been around for many years. The early architectures were restricted to the network, like SNA from IBM. Later they became more inclusive. Examples are: System Application Architecture (SAA) from IBM, Distributed Computing Environment (DCE) from the Open Software Foundation (OSF), and Object Management Architecture (OMA) from the Object Management Group (OMG). However, times have changed and of the above examples only OMA is being actively developed. The two architectures that are grabbing the attention now are

- Microsoft Windows' Distributed interNet Applications Architecture (DNA)
- Java 2 Enterprise Edition (J2EE)—developed by Sun

DNA consists of

- Presentation services—includes HTML, DHTML, scripting, ActiveX COM components
- Application services—includes Internet Information Server (IIS), COM+, MSMQ
- Data services—includes ADO and OLE DB
- System services—includes directory, security, management, and networking

The common building blocks everywhere—the unifying thread—are COM components.

DNA has now been subsumed into Microsoft's .NET strategy.

The DNA architecture is illustrated in Figure 5-3.

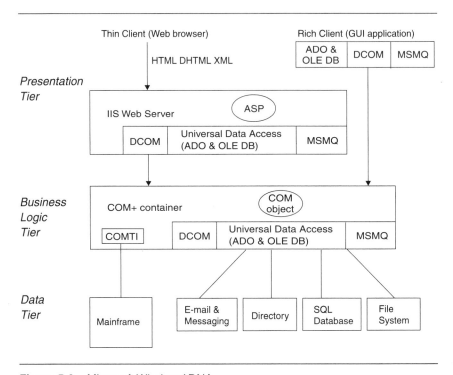

Figure 5-3   Microsoft Windows' DNA

J2EE consists of

- The client tier—either browser, possibly with Java Applets, or a standalone Java program.
- The Web tier—a Web server running Java Server Pages (JSP) and Java Servlets.
- The Enterprise Java Beans tier—an EJB container.
- The Enterprise Information Systems tier—a database or a mainframe application

Each tier supports a set of platform APIs. For instance, JMS (Java Messaging Services), which supports message queuing, and JDBC (Java Database Connectivity), which supports remote database access, are supported everywhere except in Java Applets.

The J2EE is illustrated in Figure 5-4.

The common building blocks everywhere are Java components.

Both of these architectures are likely to change in detail with the addition of other elements. Certainly, in the past the architectures have not stood still. (In fact, since I drew the diagrams some time before the publishing date, they are probably out of date already.)

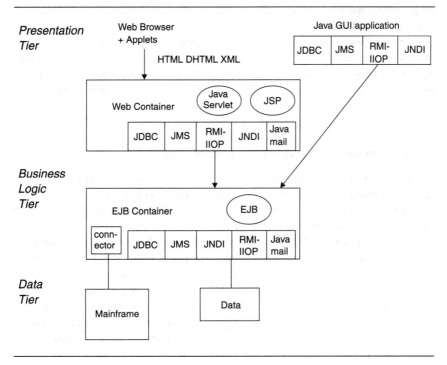

Figure 5-4   J2EE

Vendor architectures serve a number of different related functions: positioning, strawman for user architectures, and marketing. I will explore each of these in turn.

5.3.1   Positioning

At the beginning of this chapter, I described how complex middleware is and how varied the functions are that middleware serves. All of those functions are not necessarily implemented by one product. A function of the architecture is to show how different products from the vendor co-operate. For instance, the implication of J2EE is that JSP, Servlets, and Enterprise Java Bean co-operate together and users should expect to build applications that use at least two of the three.

Some products offer alternatives. DNA has a number of alternative presentation technologies, ranging from "rich clients" (their expression) to "thin clients."

A well-presented architecture should let you see at a glance what elements you need to select to make a working system. Positioning helps both the vendor and the user identify what's missing in the current product portfolio, and architectures usually lead to vendors ensuring that either they or someone else is ready to fill in the gaps.

In many ways the DNA and J2EE architectures are similar. They both have Web servers in which Web page scripting languages (ASP and JSP) play a prominent role. They both have transactional component middleware engines in the middle and relational databases at the back end. But of course one is COM-based and the other is Java-based.

5.3.2   Strawman for user target architecture

Architectures are used to tell users how functionality should be split. DNA, for instance, describes three layers—presentation, business logic, and data. The purpose of this kind of layering is to tell developers how they should partition up application functionality between the layers.

Both the DNA and J2EE architectures also offer both message queuing and transaction services, but they aren't given equal prominence. In J2EE, for instance, the EJB is a container while JMS is just a service. The implication is that EJB is essential while JMS might be useful if you happen to need it. But perhaps I am drawing too many conclusions from a picture! I have seen other pictures of J2EE where both transactions and messaging are services and EJB is just a container. That is the problem with pictures, they can kind of hint at things without saying them outright, rather like a politician giving a non-attributable quote.

More pertinently, the implication of architectures is that the set of tools from the DNA bag will work together, and the set of tools from the J2EE bag will work together, but, if you mix and match from both bags, you are on your own.

Both DNA and J2EE are silent on the subject of batch processing. You should not expect architectures to be comprehensive—none have been in the past.

5.3.3   Marketing

An architecture can provide a vision of the future. The architecture is saying: This is how we (the vendor) believe applications should be built and our tools are the best for the job. Using an architecture the vendor can show that they (possibly with partners) have a rich set of tools, they have thought of the development issues, they have a strategy they are working toward and, above all, they are forward looking.

But there are dangers for a vendor in marketing architectures. The biggest problem is bafflement—by its very nature when explaining an architecture you have to explain a range of very complex software. If the architecture is too complex, it's hard to explain. If it's too simple, the vision can seem to have no substance. Unfortunately, the people whom marketing most wants to hear the strategic message are probably senior executives who haven't had the pleasure of reading a book like this to explain what it is all about. Bafflement is only one problem. There are also some fine lines to be drawn between having an architecture that is too futuristic, too far ahead of the implementation, and so cautious that it's boring. Then there are the dangers of change. You can guarantee that, if the architecture changes, most people will have the wrong version.

I often think that the most important audience for the architectures are the vendor's own software developers. It helps them understand where they stand in the wider scheme of things.

5.4   Implicit architectures

Arguably every software vendor has an architecture, it's just that many of them don't give it a name. I described the dangers of too aggressive an approach to marketing architectures and many vendors will choose to talk instead about software strategies and roadmaps. What all vendors need is the positioning, the view on application development, and the visioning.

In practical terms this means that if your organization buys an application product like SAP, Baan, or PeopleSoft then like it or not, your organization has bought into the SAP, Baan, or Peoplesoft architecture, at least in part. For instance, PeopleSoft uses Tuxedo from BEA as their middleware glue. In theory, this enables close integration with other applications that also use Tuxedo or are capable of bridging to Tuxedo.

Another example is Enterprise Application Integration (EAI) products. (I won't mention products because Murphy's Law tells me the product will be extinct by the time this book is published.) These products provide an approach to application integration. If you go with these products, it pushes you along a certain direction that impacts how you develop applications in the future, a vendor architecture in all but name.

A way of accessing the architectural implication of products is to ask yourself three questions:

1. What impact does this product have on the positioning of existing applications? For instance, the product might communicate with your backend mainframe application by pretending to be a 3270 terminal. This is positioning the back end as a transaction server but one with a load of superfluous formatting code.

2. What impact does this product have on future development? What tools do I use and where? How do I partition the functionality between the tiers?

3. What is the vendor's vision for the future?

A further consequence of this discussion is that large organizations are likely to implement many vendor architectures. If we further consider that new architectures will come and old ones will fade away, we can conclude that the words "are likely" in the previous sentence should be changed to "will inevitably."

5.5   Conclusions

In this chapter I have tried to widen the perspective from point technologies to the larger picture. I have described how middleware is part of a wider set of software that supports distributed processing. I tried to make a technical classification to bring order to the chaos and could not find a classification that was very meaningful. I looked at vendor's attempts to bring order and found similar visions but conflicting technologies.

We have also noted that large organizations will have a bit of everything.

Furthermore, it is clear this is not the end of the road. Middleware technology has transformed over the last ten years. My bet, for what it is worth, is that it will transform again over the next ten years.

What on earth should IT organizations do? Do they choose an architecture and hope it solves all their problems? Do they forget about a strategy and just make tactical day-to-day decisions and hope it turns out okay? I believe IT departments can do better than that. They need an architecture and a vision, but the big mistake is to try and emulate the vendors. In broad terms, users should aim for an architecture strong on application partitioning and neutral on technology. The starting point is to ask, what is middleware for? This is the subject of the next chapter.

6

What Is
Middleware For?

Middleware is the key piece of technology for building distributed systems, and understanding middleware is essential for implementation design and IT architecture. This chapter is about choosing which middleware to use.

But middleware is a slippery concept. We have already seen in the last chapter how difficult it is to classify the different kinds of middleware and how difficult it is to draw the line where networking software ends and middleware begins. To resolve these difficulties, I will return to my definition of middleware.

A simple definition of middleware is: Middleware is software that makes it possible in practice to build distributed applications.

Why do I say "in practice"? You can, of course, build a distributed application without buying any middleware products. Many large organizations have indeed done so, usually because when they started out there were no appropriate middleware products on the market. But if you take this approach you are likely to find that a major part of the project will be building your own middleware and it turns out that building resilient, scalable, and secure middleware is a lengthy and skilled undertaking.

But why in my definition does the application have to be distributed? It does not; the middleware could easily be used to integrate applications in one machine. In fact, it is important that middleware software can integrate two applications in one machine; first for testing purposes and second because it is sometimes a convenient way of implementing an application you anticipate may later be distributed. However I don't want to widen the definition to include every piece of integration software that cannot operate over a network. I think it is an important characteristic of middleware software that it is capable of operating over a network.

This definition of middleware is very broad and other authorities have used definitions that are more restrictive. For instance, some would add a third point restricting middleware to off-the-shelf products. Others may insist that middleware should run over several different kinds of network, in other words, be network independent. If that pleases you, that's fine by me. No one in IT is the keeper of the definitions so it's okay if we agree to differ.

The point about middleware is that it should make life easier for the distributed systems implementer and that brings us back to the original question posed at the top of this chapter—what is middleware for?

From a user's perspective there are four large groups of distributed processing technology.

1. Transaction technology, or more generally, technology for supporting business processes.

2. Information retrieval technology, or more generally, technology for supporting process management and process review.

3. Collaborative technology, like e-mail, for helping people work together.

4. Internal IT distributed technology.

I will not discuss the internal IT needs in this chapter. It is covered to some degree in Chapter 9.

6.1   Support for business processes

Imagine yourself sitting behind a counter and someone comes up and asks you to do something. (Imagine you are a check-in clerk in an airport if you like.) There are three kinds of actions:

1. Inquiries

2. Action by me, now—I am responsible for seeing it through now (for instance, giving them a boarding pass).

3. Action by others (or by me later)—I am not responsible for seeing it through now (for instance, ensuring their loyalty card is correctly updated with the right miles).

Action by me, now, is required when the person on the other side of the counter is waiting for the action to be done. The desire from both sides of the counter is that the action will be done to completion. Failing that, life is much simpler if it is not done at all; the person in front of the counter goes away unsatisfied but clear about the status. What gets really complicated is if the action is partially done (for instance, in the airport check-in example if they took the baggage but they couldn't give you a boarding pass).

Action by others usually means giving them a form to fill in and, when it is done, giving them a broad smile and putting it on a pile of paper. The person on the other side of the counter will not wait for the action to be processed, they just want to see that it is in for processing. You, as the clerk, are responsible for having the document sent but not responsible for any errors in its later processing.

It is a similar story when computers call computers. Instead of two people, one on each side of a counter, there are clients and servers. Instead of an action, we have a transaction. From the client's perspective the transaction must be atomic: if there is failure, nothing is updated on the database and no external device does anything (for example, no invoices are printed).

I will call the message from a client to a server in the case of inquires or action now requests, **real-time** messages. I will call the "action by the server now" processing, real-time transactions.

In the case of action by others, the client fills in the request and, instead of giving it to a server to process, they put it into a queue. I will call these kinds of messages, **deferrable** messages, and, the "action by another" transactions, deferrable transactions.

Observe that I called it deferrable, not deferred. The key difference between real-time and deferrable is what happens if the message cannot be sent now, not how fast it takes. If a real-time message cannot be sent immediately the client must be told; it is an error condition. On the other hand, if a deferrable message cannot be sent immediately it hangs about in a queue until it can be sent. The distinction between real-time and deferrable are business process distinctions not technology distinctions. There are some people who will be reading this saying: I call real-time message, synchronous messages, and deferrable messages, asynchronous messages. But these terms asynchronous and synchronous are viewing this issue from the programmer's perspective. With synchronous messages the client program waits for the reply. With asynchronous messages, the program goes off and does something else. But you can build real-time transaction calls with asynchronous calls. The client program goes off and does something else, but then checks for the reply (typically in another queue). If the reply does not come, the client reports the problem. The important characteristic of deferrable messages is that they can be deferred. If they cannot be deferred then the messages are real-time.

There are situations where you want to say if the action can be done now, I want it done now, but if it cannot, do it later. From a computer perspective it is best not to think of this as a strange hybrid somewhere between real-time and deferrable messages. It is simpler to think of it as a two-step action by the client; the client requests a real-time transaction and, if that fails, it requests a deferrable transaction. With any transaction someone must be told whether the transaction failed. With a real-time transaction that someone is always the client. With a deferrable transaction life is not so simple, it may be impossible for the client to handle the errors, since the client might not be active. You cannot just turn a real-time transaction into a deferrable transaction without a lot of thought.

What about transactions calling transactions? The distinction between inquiry, real-time, and deferrable transactions applies here also. Inquires are very common; for instance, reading a common customer or product database. Real-time transaction-to-transaction calls are less common, actually they are quite rare.

An example might be a delivery system asking a warehouse system to reserve some parts for a particular delivery. If the warehouse system cannot reserve the parts, the delivery must be rescheduled. Calling a real-time transaction from within a transaction means using distributed transaction processing technology (in other words, usually using two-phase commits). Many organizations go to great lengths to avoid distributed transaction processing, and you can often do so. For instance, the delivery system might do an inquiry on the warehouse system but only send the actual "reserve" update as a deferrable message. The consequence of this is that it is just possible that there is a run on certain parts and when the "reserve" update message is processed the part is no longer there. You can handle these errors by building additional business processes, and actually, in this case, the business processes probably already exist as the warehouse computer system is not 100 percent accurate in any case.

So what middleware fits these categories?

6.1.1   Transactional, real-time

Middleware choices include RPC, CORBA, EJB, MTS/COM+, and Tuxedo. In some cases, the application must support distributed transaction processing, but in general, as I shall discuss in later chapters, we try and avoid two-phase commits where possible.

Many organizations are using message queuing for real-time processing. You can do this by having one queue for input messages and another queue for output messages. I don't recommend this approach for the following reasons:

- If two transaction servers communicate by message queuing, they can't support distributed transaction processing across them (see Figures 2-10 and 2-11).

- Remember with real-time calls there is an end user waiting for the reply but if there is no reply they eventually give up and go away. With message queuing, if the end user goes away, the message stills goes in the return queue because message queuing guarantees to send the message. This is called a "dead message," and is often put into the "dead letter box." The administrator now has to look at the message and figure out what to do with it.

- There could be an enormous number of queues. If there are 1,000 users, logically you need 1,000 output queues. You probably don't want that and therefore you end up writing some code to share queues.

- Queues have no IDL and no control of the message format.

- For high performance you will need to write your own scheduler. Imagine again the 1,000 users hammering the same transactions. You need multiple programs to empty the input queue and therefore something to initiate the programs and stop them when they are no longer needed.

In short, it is operationally difficult.

6.1.2   Transactional, deferrable

But message queuing is the ideal technology for deferrable messages. You can use simple file transfer, but then you have to build the controls to ensure data is sent once and only once, and not sent if the transaction is aborted.

Alternatively, you can take the view that instead of deferring the transaction, why not process it immediately and use real-time transactional software for deferrable transactions? There are two reasons why not to do this:

1. It's slower—messages cannot be buffered and there is overhead in two-phase commit processing.

2. If the destination server is down, then the calling server cannot operate. Having the flexibility to bring a transaction server off-line without bringing down all other applications is a great bonus.

In practice our architecture will probably look something like Figure 6-1.

That is, use real-time for end-user messages and deferrable messages for server-to-server messaging. However, there are many exceptions. I described one earlier: a bank accepting an inter-bank financial transaction from the SWIFT network. This does not have to be processed in real time but it must capture the transaction on a secure medium—it is a classic deferrable transaction but this time from the outside world. Another example mentioned earlier is that if the presentation

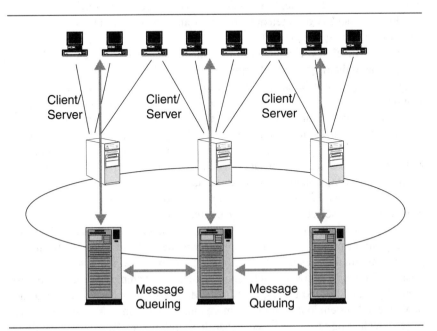

Figure 6-1   Typical use of transactional middleware

device is a portable PC, queues are useful for storing data for later processing. All the same, Figure 6-1 covers the vast majority of cases.

6.2 Information retrieval

While transactions are about business operations, information retrieval is about management and customer information.

Information retrieval requirements are positioned along four dimensions. One dimension is timeliness—the extent to which the users require the data to be current. Some users, for instance a production manager trying to find out what has happened to a particular order, need to view data that is 100 percent up-to-date. Other users, for instance a strategic analyst looking at historic trends, will work happily with data that is days, weeks, even months behind.

The second dimension is usability. Raw data tends to be cryptic. Information is held as numeric codes instead of easily understood text. Data about one object is fragmented among many tables or even many databases. Minor inconsistencies—like the spelling of a company's name—abound. Indexing is geared to the requirements of the production system, not for searching. You can think of this dimension as going from data to information. It is easy to assume that the further you go along the information dimension the better, but people close to the business process and, of course, IT programmers, need access to the raw data.

Putting these two dimensions together and positioning users on the chart gives us something like Figure 6-2.

Clearly timeliness is a matter of toleration rather than an actual requirement. The people to the right of this diagram would probably prefer timely information but are willing to sacrifice some delay for the benefit of more understandable information. I am noticing more and more intolerance to delay and it's probably only a matter of time before any delay is perceived as undynamic and unacceptable.

The third dimension is the degree of flexibility to the query. Some users want canned queries like—I'll give you an order number and you show me what the order looks like. Some users want complete flexibility, the privilege to write arbitrarily complex SQL statements to extract data from the database. There are gradations in between, like the user who wants to see orders but wants to use a simple search criteria to select the orders they are interested in.

The final dimension has (luckily) only three values: time-based push, event-based push, or pull. It is the dimension of whether the users want to be able to get the data themselves or whether they want to be informed when something changes. The old-fashioned batch report is a classic example of time-based push technology. Put the report in a spreadsheet and use e-mail for distribution, and suddenly the old system looks altogether more impressive. A more sophisticated style of push technology is event-based rather than time-based. An example would be to send an e-mail to the CEO automatically when a large order comes in.

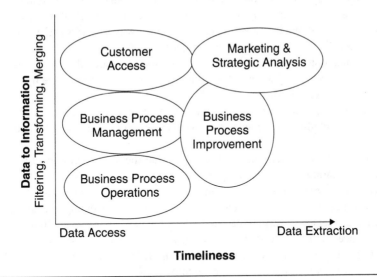

Figure 6-2   Information vs. timeliness

With four dimensions we clearly have the potential for defining a vast range of possible technologies and there certainly is a vast range of technology, though not all of the combinations make much sense; untimely raw data is not of much interest to anybody.

There is a good deal of technology that creates canned inquires and reports and a good deal for ad-hoc queries. Ad-hoc queries can be implemented with remote database access middleware.

There are products available for data replication, but they tend to be database vendor specific. There are many data warehouse and data mart tools for creating a data warehouse and analyzing the data.

There are also products available for subscribe and push. Microsoft is trying to have the CDF (Channel Definition Format) become a standard for Internet-based push. Strictly speaking, this standard is actually "regularly scheduled pull" rather than genuine push. The options for genuine push to an end user are e-mail or a programmatic interface to send pager messages. For push messages to other computers, message queuing may be an option.

6.3   Collaboration

There is a great deal of distributed system software that is about helping workers communicate with each other. This includes office software like e-mail, newsgroups, and scheduling systems and direct communications technology like online meetings, Webcasts, online training, and video conferencing. Whether this fits into the category of middleware is a moot point, but we are slowly seeing convergence, first at the technical level and second at the user interface level.

Technical convergence includes shared networks, shared directory services, and common security systems. The driving force is a common desire to use the common Internet infrastructure.

User interface convergence includes using e-mail as a report distribution mechanism, including multimedia data in databases and using your TV set to pay your bills.

It is hard to see where this will end and what the long-term impact will be. While at the moment these developments are not important to most IT business applications, in the future that may not be true. Meetings are commonly part of business processes, and one can envisage an IT system scheduling a meeting and providing an electronic form to be filled out by the participants that will be immediately processed by the next stage in the process. For example, suppose an order cannot be fulfilled because a part is in short supply. The system could schedule a meeting between manufacturing representatives and sales, and then immediately act on the decisions made.

This book concentrates on transactional and information retrieval systems so I will not explore this area further.

6.4   The presentation layer

Having decided what middleware can do, the next question is how can it be used to assemble large systems? I will start this investigation by looking at the user.

Originally, online access was through terminals. Later there were workstations. As a variant on the theme, there were branch networks with small LANs in each branch and a WAN connection to the central system. Processing in the branch was split between the branch server and the branch workstations. Now of course there is the Internet.

This is only part of the picture.

We have telephone access and call centers.

We have self-service terminals (like bank automatic teller machines and airline check-in machines).

We have EDI or XML transfers for inter-business communication.

We have specialized networks like the bank SWIFT network and the inter-airline networks.

The banking industry is probably furthest along the path to what they call multi-channel access. You can now do a banking transaction by using a check, by using a credit card, by direct inter-bank transfer, through an ATM, over the Web, on a specialized banking PC product, by using a bank clerk, or over a telephone. I've probably missed a few options. It's only a question of time before other industries follow. The Internet is often seen as a consolidating technology but it is unlikely that one Web application will be appropriate for PC access, intelligent mobile phone access, and television set access, for instance. There will also be an increasing number of Internet intermediaries demanding that transactions are done their way. What this all comes down to is that the Internet itself is a multi-channel interface.

This has profound implications on how applications should be built.

The banking example has shown how we want one service to be used from multiple channels. Traditional terminals were 20 lines or 80 characters or something similar. Web pages can be much bigger than traditional terminal screens. Telephone communication is much smaller. In many existing applications the number and size of the transaction messages is designed to satisfy the original channel. To support a new channel either a new interface must be built or some intermediary software must map the new messages into the old messages.

We have finally reached our first architectural stake in the ground. We want an architecture to support multiple channels. This defines what is in the presentation layer, namely:

- All end user formatting (or building voice messages)
- All navigation on the system (for example, menus or Web links)
- Security authentication (prove the users are who they say they are)
- Build and transmit the messages to the backend systems

The reason the security is there is because authentication depends on the channel. Usercodes and passwords might be fine internally, something more secure might be appropriate for the Internet, and, over the telephone, identification might be completely different.

The presentation layer may be nothing more than a GUI application in a workstation. It may be a Web server and Web browsers. It may be a voice server. It may be a SWIFT network connection box. It may be some old mainframe code handling dumb terminals. It is a logical layer, not a physical thing. It is illustrated in Figure 6-3.

However, whatever the channel, for business processing and business intelligence there are only a few types of messages for the backend server, namely:

- Real-time
- Deferrable
- Ad-hoc queries

And the backend has two types of unsolicited messages for the presentation layer:

- Simple push messages
- Reports

The simple push message normally acts as a wake-up call because the backend system cannot guarantee that the user is connected.

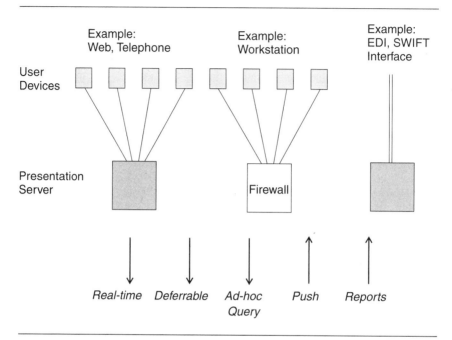

Figure 6-3   The presentation layer

6.5   The transaction server layer

While it is a requirement of the multi-channel presentation layer that the channel servers should be able to handle mismatches in the size between the user interface and the transaction interface, that does not mean that the transaction server should be designed oblivious to the presentation layer requirements. There are ways of designing the transaction server interfaces that also make it easier for the presentation layer.

First, the transaction servers should ideally not give the presentation layer the problems of dealing with old screen formats, menus, and such.

Second, the transaction servers should be constructed for reuse so new channels can be implemented as fast as possible with minimal changes at the back end. This is easier said than done. It does not mean breaking the transaction services up into tiny code chunks because that way business logic will creep into the presentation layer. The last thing we want is dispersed business logic. This is discussed at length in later chapters.

Third, the presentation layer should be able to demarcate transaction boundaries. In many cases this will be unnecessary, but sometimes it is the only way to recover the dialogue satisfactorily. Suppose a large Web form has been split into five transaction calls on the transaction server. Suppose further that the third transaction call fails. How does the Web server undo the work of the first two completed transactions? If the Web server code has been able to call a start transaction command before doing other processing on the form, all the transactions can become sub-transactions in a global transaction. The roll out of the updates is then handled automatically.

A final point is that the transaction server is more likely to be reusable if it is stateless between transactions. If we design a transaction server with a sophisticated set of session objects it is highly likely we will need to totally redesign the session objects when we add a new channel. Session objects are fine if their function is to help get the transaction done. Session objects are a hindrance if their purpose is a prop to the original user interface. It is very important to design the transaction interface with the thought in mind that a completely different kind of user interface might be implemented some time in the future.

A new concept of user/application interaction is developing. Before, a user did one task, in one place, at one time. For instance, to submit an order the old way was to type in the order form details by filling in a series of screen forms all at once. Now we can envisage the same work being split among different presentation devices. There can be delays. For instance, the order form could be started on the Internet and completed by a voice interface a few days later. Input could be while the user is on the move. Shortcuts can be taken because information is read from smart cards or picked up from loyalty card systems. This is a revolutionary change, and in later chapters we shall look more into what this means for the application.

6.6   The data layer

Most vendor architectures today are three-tier or multi-tier and split out a data layer from the business logic. The data layer is basically the database software. The purpose of splitting the data out into a separate layer is meant to point out that one database can be shared by multiple applications.

The notion of a separate data layer is fine insofar as it expresses a technology point; each layer has a different set of tools for developing that layer and each layer interacts with the layer above or below it. But in considering the structure from an application point of view there is a higher concern: splitting the system into its major functional services. There is no magic here. It is just a question of applying the same techniques you apply within a program to split it up into modules. There are two considerations:

1. Do all parts of the functional service stick together, in other words, are there many interdependencies within the service? If not we can split it further.

2. Does the service have strong dependencies, especially cross-dependencies (that is, A depends on B and B depends on A), with another service? If it does, then perhaps the services should be merged.

Transaction service routines have a very strong dependency on their database. The database and the transactions must be designed hand in hand. By all the rules above, they belong together. This is illustrated in Figure 6-4.

The implication of Figure 6-4 is that if a transaction needs information from another database it should call another transaction server rather than get the data directly. This implication is precisely what I mean. If the transaction logic in one transaction server can access another database directly then changes to the database design can have an unraveling effect on the whole system design. A programmatic interface also allows us to implement controlled duplication across multiple systems, a point that will be discussed in Chapter 12. Finally, the interface allows us to give the database an object look and feel.

The dotted lines in Figure 6-4 from the transaction servers to the business intelligence server are for data extraction. I have used business intelligence server as a generic term for data warehouse, data mart, decision support system, management information system, or whatever else you call a system used for retrieval and searching. A generic business intelligence server is illustrated in Figure 6-5.

In general terms, data taken from a production database will need to be filtered and reformatted before being loaded into the business intelligence server. The filtering takes out irrelevant data and the reformatting turns cryptic codes into

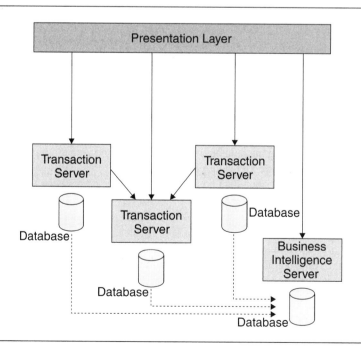

Figure 6-4 Transaction and database servers

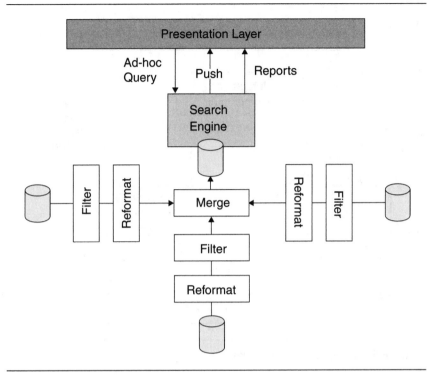

Figure 6-5   Business intelligence servers

meaningful character strings. In the merging phase inconsistencies between the many databases must be ironed out.

There could be multiple levels of business intelligence servers, for instance a data warehouse could feed data to many data marts.

Middleware like remote database access is useful for accessing the business intelligence server. But let's not be too dogmatic about this. Sometimes it is fine to use business intelligence software on the production transaction server databases.

6.7   A generic functional architecture

To complete the picture we will put these elements together. This gives us Figure 6-6. This architecture is broadly equivalent to what others have called a "service-oriented architecture."

Three boxes have been added. At the top is batch. Batch is still important and will never go away because many business processes are run in daily, weekly,

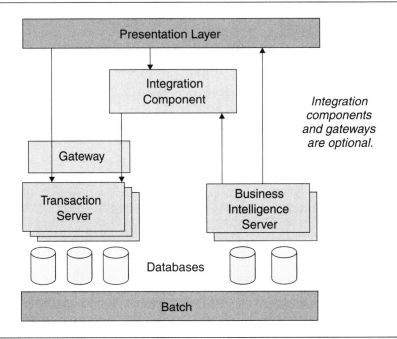

Figure 6-6   The generic architecture

monthly, quarterly, or yearly cycles. Two examples are payroll and interest accrual for bank accounts. Interest accrual is an interesting case in point. It is clearly possible to calculate the interest on an as-needed basis; in other words, when the customer next asks for a balance inquiry. However, the bank itself wants to know how much money is in all of its accounts and what their interest payment obligations are, so it is the bank itself that wants interest payments to be calculated immediately when payment is due. Thus the requirement for (some) batch comes from the business.

The gateway component is in there to indicate the necessity of translating from one technology to another.

The integration component is sometimes required when a number of services need to be made to look like one service. A classic example is an airline reservation system where there is a necessity to provide an integration component between the front end and multiple backend servers that belong to the individual airlines, in order to handle tickets for multi-leg journeys across more than one carrier.

So whatever happened to the business logic? I will discuss this subject at length in later chapters. Most of the business logic is in the transaction server. This makes sense, business processing is heavily dependent on data and, as I observed earlier, business moves in transaction steps—transactions are the lowest processing unit of the business process. But sometimes, additional business logic is elsewhere. The integration component is an obvious place for business logic that spans multiple backend systems. Some business process logic might be in the presentation layer if it is only applicable to a particular channel. For instance, a self-service terminal may only be usable if the user possesses an intelligent card, and the procedures might be different from doing the same transaction through a clerk.

The boxes in Figure 6-6 are meant to indicate the major functional elements of the integrated architecture. A real life example would have many transaction servers, business intelligent servers, and presentation servers and devices.

The two criteria for dividing the functionality among the elements are:

1. A recoverable unit—if one element fails the rest of the system is unaffected as far as possible
2. A development unit—programmers can change one element without impacting the rest of the system as far as possible.

Between the elements should be middleware.

6.8   Mediators

Clearly, technology is changing fast. However you don't have to be stuck with a particular middleware technology. Instead you can use mediator components to form a barrier between your business code and the middleware. This is illustrated in Figure 6-7.

Mediators provide a place you can put code to handle:

- Load balancing—routing messages to multiple backend servers
- Switching to backup servers in the event of a failure
- System management interfaces, for instance to trace message flows
- Security code

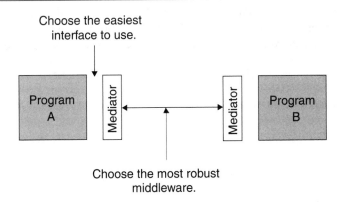

Figure 6-7   Mediators

Mediators also provide a place to overcome limitations in the software. Earlier I gave an example of a client calling begin and end transaction to simplify its recovery code. That may not be possible with some middleware technology, so the actual begin and end transaction calls might need to be done by the mediator located on the server machine. The performance cost of using mediators is nearly nothing (an extra procedure call) and sometime in the future, the benefits might be enormous.

6.9   Conclusions

In this chapter I set out to answer the question, what is middleware for? The simple answer is that middleware is there to link together the major functional elements in the integrated application we are trying to build. We have spent most of this chapter discussing what kinds of functional elements there should be and how we should partition the application across the functional elements. The major functional elements are:

- Transaction servers
- Presentation layer
- Business intelligence servers
- Batch

There may also be a need for additional glue elements—gateways, integration components, and mediators. The logic for dividing the functional elements this way is the same as the logic for dividing applications into modules.

This chapter is actually about building an integrated application, which, as Chapter 1 indicated, is my approach to building application architectures. A major task in building an integrated application is identifying the functional elements and the relationships between them. We will discuss the process more in a later chapter. However, before we turn away from technological issues and look at design we need to understand better how these functional elements can be made scalable, resilient, and manageable. These are the topics for the next three chapters.

7

Resiliency

In this chapter and the next three, I turn away from discussing specific technology and look at the underlying principles of building resilient, scalable, and manageable distributed systems. This chapter tackles resiliency.

There are many aspects to resiliency. The most obvious ones are:

- How do we reduce the number of visible stoppages?
- How do we reduce the length of time the system is down if there is a failure?

But perhaps more important than either of the above is, how do we ensure that there is no data loss and no message loss?

There is also disaster recovery to take into account—recovery from fire, floods, earthquakes, things falling out of the sky, bombs, and other acts of God and man.

Finally, the biggest single cause of downtime in most organizations is scheduled downtime. How can we turn an application into a true 7 by 24 by 365 application?

In this chapter I am going to concentrate on what an IT department can do, not what an IT vendor can do. Thus, this chapter has little discussion on hardware resiliency, partitioning, clustering, and system software resiliency. These are all good features, but accidents happen, and this chapter is about what to do when they do, and taking steps to avoid turning an accident into a catastrophe.

Some highly respectable authorities have expressed platform resiliency in terms of NT 4.0 provides X percent uptime, Unix provides Y percent, OS/390 provides Z percent, and Parallel Sysplex provides P percent. What they neglect to mention is that if you manage an NT 4.0 box like a mainframe you can get outstanding reliability, and if you manage a mainframe like most people manage NT 4.0 servers you will get appalling reliability. I am always curious how said respected authorities take this into account. If you take an application and run it on any of the major platforms, test it well, fix the problems you find, and ensure you have good (and followed) operational procedures, you can achieve a high level of reliability. While there is a difference between the theoretical best level of resiliency you can achieve with each platform, the most important difference is in the time and effort it takes to get there.

I am going to assume that the processes required to run an application reliably on a server are known. But even if the servers are totally reliable that does not deliver a totally reliable end-user service. Hardware faults on a server typically correspond to about 20 percent of the total downtime. Other big factors in total downtime are planned downtime (for instance, backing up a database), application problems, and operational problems. Total server reliability is of no use in a disaster when the whole building is down. It is also of no use in a distributed environment if the network is down.

More can go wrong in a distributed application than in a centralized application, but there are new ways of tackling resiliency. In particular, take the notion of backup systems. If the system uses subsystems A, B, and C in series, it is no more reliable than the least reliable of A, B, and C. For a complex distributed environment using workstations, local servers, wide area networks, internal backbone networks, and perhaps a couple of backend servers, that is a lot to go wrong. But if you can do processing in parallel, reliability is greatly enhanced. If one server is down on average for 1 day in every 100, then two parallel servers will both be down together on average for 1 day every 10,000 days. Two unreliable servers can theoretically give a remarkably high level of service.

Turning theory into practice is not easy, and this is largely what this chapter is about. In particular, my interest is in exploring how distributed systems can be used to our advantage and what difference this makes to the application structure.

7.1 Using backup servers

The obvious way to build a resiliency is to have a backup system. Let us consider the simple configuration shown in Figure 7-1.

When the production system fails, the work is taken over by the backup system. Recovery consists of four steps:

1. Detecting the failure

2. Cleaning up work in progress

3. Activating the application on the backup system

4. Reprocessing "lost" messages

I will look at each of these steps in turn.

7.1.1 Detecting failure

Many vendors offer a heartbeat feature whereby the backup system sends the primary system a message on a regular basis. The backup system says, "Are you there?" The primary system replies, "Yes I am."

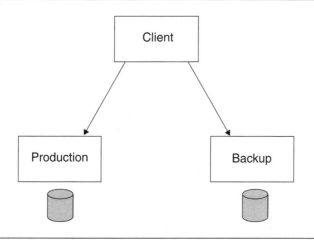

Figure 7-1   Simple backup configuration

There are many difficulties with heartbeats; it is a very coarse mechanism. For instance, it only checks whether the heartbeat program is running, not whether the production application is running. If the heartbeat does report a failure, the backup system can't tell whether the primary is inactive or whether there is a difficulty with the heartbeats. For instance, if the network between the systems goes down, the heartbeat may report an error whereas in fact the production system is working fine. This problem can be overcome by using a backup network connection. If the network is fine and there definitely is an error, then the heartbeat cannot tell you whether the failure is a temporary glitch or a long stoppage.

In practice, the heartbeat must be supplemented by a range of other tests. The most important test is for the client program to give regular reports on its progress. Simple information like, what are the response times of the last ten transactions, is really helpful.

Having detected a failure, but before analyzing the failure, a simple question must be posed and answered. Do we stick to the current system and fix it in place or do we switch to the backup?

There are two alternative strategies:

Strategy One: On any failure, switch to backup, then think.

Strategy Two: Stop, think, and switch to backup as the last resort.

Really resiliency-conscious sites often take the first strategy. Most sites take the second. To be brutally frank, most organizations do not regularly test their backup-switching procedures. If they are forced to switch they run into a bunch of problems like incorrect network configurations, incorrect software configurations, or, in the worst case, a system too small to run their production load. And there are good reasons not to switch automatically to backup; many problems are not corrected by switching to backup. Many software and operational problems are not cured by a switch. Switching to backup may not cure a network problem. Disk failures may be fixed more easily locally.

The reason really resiliency-conscious sites will take a switch first strategy is that they have already tried to eliminate all these local problems. This means anticipating all possible causes of failure and building a plan to detect and correct the failure. This is a massive effort and if you don't want to make the effort don't even think about taking a switch first strategy. For instance, all operator commands should be analyzed to check whether they can cause a system stop, and then procedures should be put into place to ensure unqualified operators don't do them.

Building such plans is configuration specific. The best a vendor can provide is a stable hardware and software platform and assistance.

For the rest of this section I assume that the decision has been made to switch to backup.

7.1.2   Clean-up work in progress

Clearly switching to backup requires all the data updated on the production system is copied to the backup system. Two techniques used today are:

1. Copying the database logs and applying them against a copy of the database, like a continual roll forward (this assumes non-database data is copied across some other way).

2. Having the disk subsystem keeping a mirror copy of the disk on the backup system by duplicating all writes on the backup system.

The second approach is easier to operate since non-database disk is catered to. The first approach is more efficient. The network bandwidth required to send all writes to the remote backup machine might be considerable and the cost excessive. (But like disk and processor costs, network costs are coming down.)

As an aside, regular database backups should still be taken even if the data is mirrored locally and remotely. Some failures need the backup; for instance, the operator might accidentally (or deliberately) delete the database's entire disk directory.

Simply having the latest copy of the data is not sufficient; incomplete transactions must be rolled out. Doing this on the backup machine should be the same as doing it on the production machine and the database system should handle the transaction clean-up automatically. For non-database files, you are on your own and have to synchronize the state of the file with the last completed transaction. My recommendation would be to put all important data in the database or in secured message queues.

7.1.3   Activating the application

Having tidied up the database and the message queues, the next task is to restart the complete running environment and put it into a state ready to accept more

After the switch the client must send its input to the backup machine rather than the primary machine. There is a fundamental choice to be made here. Will the client be able to resume their session where they left off or will they have to restart the session, possibly having to log on again?

I will consider TCP/IP networks only. Since the TCP/IP sessions for Web traffic are so short, it is rarely worth worrying about keeping browser sessions open across a switch to the backup Web server. But you may want to resume current TCP/IP sessions in other cases, like between a Web server and a transaction server. Some techniques are:

- The backup machine can come up with the same IP address as the production machine. This is typically only possible if the IP address of the production and backup machine are on the same LAN segment.
- There are intelligent routers on the market that will redirect the traffic meant for one IP address to another IP address.
- There could be special protocol written between the client and the server for the client to resume a user session over a new TCP/IP session. Put another way, a new session is started without telling the end user.

The first two will only work if the recovery is quick enough to complete before the TCP session times out. If it does time out, the client will need to start another session.

If we accept that a new session is going to be started then there are other options for fixing the network. For instance, the Domain Named Server (DNS) can be changed to make the server name map to a new IP address. This is how it is possible to switch a Web server to backup. There are routers on the market that can give several Web servers the same domain name. This is mainly sold as a load balancing feature (the so called Web farms we mentioned in Chapter 4) but it can also be used as a resiliency feature.

What about restarting the programs?

Before looking at online programs, let us look at batch. Batch programs that update a database are almost always reading either an external input file or a table in the database. To restart successfully they must reposition the input data on the next record to be processed and must rebuild any internal data, like totals, they are holding in memory. This can only be done by having the database system hold the program restart data, such as a count of the number of input records already processed and the current value of all total variables. This means there must be some data in the database whose only purpose is for recovering a running program. Typically it will be a row in a table with a large field that the program then uses any way it sees fit. If there are no special features in the database system for restart information then you will have to add a table into the database schema yourself.

In many ways batch recovery is more difficult than online. The first hurdle is finding out what job control deck is running and restarting that at the right place.

Good mainframe operating systems do this for you. Even then there is an issue; consider the case where the job control thinks program A was running at the time of the failure and there is no restart information for program A. There are two alternatives; at the time of the failure the program was just starting, and hadn't created a restart area, or second, the program was finishing and had deleted the restart area. Which one is it? So there needs to be work done to synchronize the job control with the restart area and to manage the restart data itself (so for instance, your program does not inadvertently recover from a restart point left over from a failure one month previously).

If all else fails with batch, you can reload the database (or roll it back if your database software supports that) and restart the batch processing from the beginning. This option is typically not available for online applications—the equivalent of reprocessing for them is to have end users retype all their online transactions, which is useless for customers over the Web.

In a distributed environment there are three scenarios we should examine: the client failing, the server failing, and both the client and the server failing.

If the client fails, then when it restarts it must recover itself. Suppose the client is a workstation program that is reading data from a file and for each record processing a transaction on the server. This is identical to the batch case and there must be restart information in the database. If the client is servicing a human then it is likely that for security reasons the end user will be forced to log on again after a failure. It could be that the session will then be restarted where it left off, but clearly the program cannot reposition itself in the right place in the dialogue without having some restart information somewhere. In most instances that "somewhere" does not need to be the database. But remember that even if repositioning the client dialogue is desirable in the general cases, there will be times where it is undesirable, such as when the client has been off-line for 24 hours and the end user can't remember what they were doing. You need, therefore, to design sessions that are helpful for the end user but not so rigid that they make recovery of half-completed sessions difficult.

If the server fails, it simply recovers to the last transaction. The client must now figure out which of the transactions in progress failed and which succeeded. I discuss this point in the next subsection. Also note that in most (maybe all) object middleware, the object references in the client pointing at the server are broken, which is particularly a problem if you are using stateful session beans.

We also have to handle the case of both the client and the server failing at the same time. The best solution is to ensure that there is one recovery routine in the client that handles all the scenarios—client failure, server failure, and both client and server failure. It is important not to try to be too clever in recovery code and the simplest and most effective strategy is to ensure all the state is kept in the database and both client and server applications themselves are stateless.

7.1.4   Reprocessing "lost" messages

If you read the white papers and listen to the presentations you would be forgiven for thinking that database recovery is enough. Look however at Figure 7-2.

Let us take the client program perspective. Suppose the client sent a message to the server and then the server failed. The client does not know whether the failure was before the transaction was committed or after the transaction was committed. In some cases it is satisfactory to tell the end user that there is uncertainty and let the end user interrogate the database with another transaction if they think it is important. But many end users will simply retransmit the message when the server recovers. If the last transaction was "Debit $1,000,000 from Mr. Big's account" this might not be such a smart idea.

There are two questions to ask during a recovery:

1. How does the client know the server completed the last message input?

2. If it did complete, what was the last output message?

You can have the client emulate the sort of discovery process the end users would go through. Alternatively, you can implement a recovery protocol along the lines of the following. The client can put a sequence number in one of the fields in the message to the server. The server stores the sequence number in a special row reserved for client recovery. The client increments the sequence number every transaction. On recovery the client sends a special message to interrogate the last

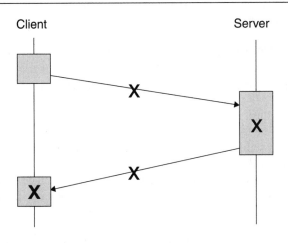

X = Failure points to consider

Figure 7-2   Lost messages

sequence number captured. This tells the client if the last input, or the one before, was the last processed transaction.

This special recovery row can also be used to store the last output message, but it is simpler if update transactions do not return data, except for errors. For instance, if you wanted to update a bank account and tell the user the new balance, it could be coded as an update transaction followed by an account enquiry transaction. This is not more code to implement because if you save the last output somewhere you still have to write code to retrieve it.

This is a situation where the techies must sit down with the application designers and talk through the consequences of failure on the end user.

7.2   Dual active

The recovery process to switch to backup has the potential for major delay. Having the backup application active waiting for the data to start the recovery process eliminates some delay. Even better is to implement a dual active strategy by having the client logged onto both systems. This avoids the time needed to switch the network (the major delay of which is starting the client sessions, especially if there are thousands of them, each with a log-on security check). If no delay is allowed, dual active is the only solution.

In a dual active strategy, both systems are equal, both do work. This may have load-balancing advantages as well as resiliency advantages.

I shall discuss two approaches:

1. Clustering—the database (which should be mirrored) is shared by both systems.

2. Two-database approach—each system has its own database.

Clustering is illustrated in Figure 7-3. (Note: clustering is a fuzzy word and I am talking about one form of clustering that might not be the one your friendly hardware vendor is selling you.) The basic principle is that both systems can read and write to all the disks.

Clustering is complex technology and this is not the place to describe it in detail. What I will do, however, is list some of the problems that need to be overcome:

- Buffer management: if one system has updated a buffer and the other system now wants the same data, either the buffer must be written to disk or the buffer data must be sent directly to the other machine.
- Lock management: both systems must see all the database locks. In Figure 7-3 I have drawn the lock manager as a separate box.

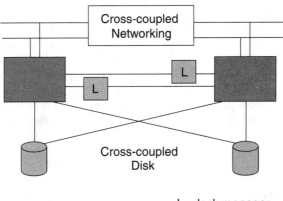

L = lock manager

Figure 7-3   Clustered servers

- Lock manager duplication: the lock manager is potentially a single point of failure so it must be duplicated.
- Log file: Normally databases have a single log file. Performance will be terrible if both systems are trying to write to the same file, so in a clustered configuration each system should have its own log file. You then need to implement an algorithm that ensures that during a roll forward the transactions are processed in the right order.

These problems are all solvable, but at the cost of lower performance. It is impossible to predict the cost without a detailed analysis of the application. For instance, there is a considerable overhead incurred by writing lock information over a network connection. To alleviate this, one technique is to have less locking by locking out more at one time; for instance, by using block locks instead of record locks. But this increases lock contention. To make matters worse, everything takes longer because of the time taken to send messages to the other system, which increases elapse time and therefore increases the likelihood of contention. (By the way, delay is inevitable: if the systems are 100 kilometers apart the speed of light ensures a minimum of 0.67 milliseconds to travel from one system to another and back again, which is a significant overhead for a lock.)

As an aside, you might be wondering how clustered systems improve performance like the marketing blurb insists. The answer is: It can, but only if the number of reads far exceeds the number of writes.

An alternative is the two-database approach. Each system has its own database, each transaction is processed twice, once on each database, and two-phase commit (see Two-Phase Commit box) ensures the systems are kept in sync. If one of the systems is down then the other system simply stops sending it subtransactions.

Two-Phase Commit

The two-phase commit protocol is the most widely used protocol for ensuring two transactions are synchronized. The protocol is illustrated in Figure 7-4.

In this diagram B is the coordinator. In the first phase, the coordinator finds out whether all subtransactions are ready to commit or not. In the second phase, the coordinator tells all subtransactions to either commit or abort. A commit will only be done if all subtransactions want to commit.

So what happens if one of the machines fails during this process? If it is in the first or "prepare" phase then the transaction can time out. If A or C failed the coordinator will take the time out and abort the transaction. If B failed, A and C will take a time out and will mark the transaction as aborted. The failure could be in the second or "commit" phase of the protocol. If A and C fail after sending an "OK" message, but before processing the commit, then they must be able to interrogate B when they come back up again to see whether the transaction has to be aborted or not. This means the final state of the transaction must be captured somewhere in non-volatile storage before the commit or abort messages are sent out. But what if B fails? A and C are left waiting with all their locks held. This could have a bad performance impact so some systems have a heuristic commit or heuristic abort. "Heuristic" here is computer jargon for "good guess." In this case, you might think that since many more transactions commit than abort the good guess would be heuristic commit. But on the other hand, since B failed, there is a good chance that the failure happened before the commit message was sent, so a heuristic abort makes more sense. Neither are very satisfactory.

A feature of the protocol is that A and C can be coordinators of their own and can have subtransactions. This is called a transaction tree. The total prepare phase of the protocol—that is, propagated down all branches—must be completed before the commit phase starts.

There are performance issues with two-phase commit. There are clearly more network messages. As I noted as well, the subtransaction status must be captured on non-volatile media before sending an "OK" message and again at transaction completion so there is an extra disk write. Since the commit processing takes some time, locks are held for longer. There are also more opportunities for deadlock because subtransactions can become entangled. Subtransaction C could be waiting on a lock owned by another distributed transaction that itself is waiting for subtransaction B to complete. Deadlocks are handled by one of the transactions timing out.

As you can see, there are many reasons to avoid two-phase commit transactions and in general that is precisely what you should do. But, sometimes they are just so useful, they are worth using.

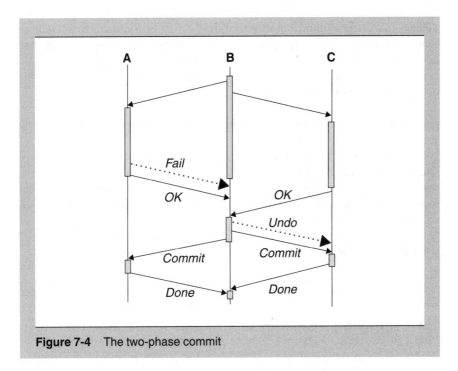

Figure 7-4   The two-phase commit

It is not quite as simple as that of course. There are two problems to overcome.

1. If a system was down and is now mended, then before bringing it online, it must catch up with all the missed transactions. This is more difficult than it looks. The obvious solution is to capture the information that would have been input to the subtransactions and to reprocess this information for catch-up purposes. The wrinkle, though, is that you have to reprocess the subtransactions in the same order the transactions were processed on the live system. This order is not the input order but the order the commits were processed.

2. The system needs to handle the situation where the client connection to both systems is working just fine but the connection between the two systems is broken. This is not easy either. A possible solution is for each system to contact a third system when it finds it can't send a message to its partner. The third system would then kill one of the systems since it is better to have one consistent system than two inconsistent systems.

What this comes down to is that you are on your own. Standard software out of the box does not have facilities such as these. (Okay, someone, somewhere is going to point to some unknown, 15-year-old software that does it all.) Actually, software has been going in the opposite direction. Coding the above is far easier if, for each transaction, one message contains all the data necessary to do the updates in the transaction. But there is a big temptation with object software to send the update data in many small chunks by calling many methods to make one update. (If this is the case and you want to take the two-database approach, you probably need to have an expert devise a method of rolling forward one of the databases by using information from the other database's log.)

Processing the transactions on both machines incurs a considerable performance penalty. How serious this is depends again on the proportion of read-only transactions to write transactions.

The clustering solution has potentially less processor overhead than the two-database solution. The two-database solution has less networking overhead than the clustering solution. Clustering is less work for the applications developer (but more for the vendor). The two-database solution is better at handling new versions of software or the database schema.

The bottom line, however, is that both dual-active solutions only work well when the volume of update transactions is low relative to the volume of reads.

7.3 Applying resiliency techniques in practice

So far I have only considered one client and two servers. Our architecture is unlikely to be that simple. Let us consider the configuration discussed in an earlier chapter but redrawn in Figure 7-5. It consists of:

- Client–Web browser
- Web server
- Transaction server with database

I want maximum resiliency, but I also want to cater to disaster recovery, so I have decided that the two sites are 100 kilometers apart.

The box and network configuration is shown in Figure 7-5.

The general idea is to try and push back all the tough, resiliency issues to the transaction servers (since this way we solve the problem only once and don't introduce additional synchronization problems).

I noted in an earlier chapter that network routers exist to balance the Web traffic across multiple servers. The router itself is a single point of failure and there would need to be a backup router.

Ideally, since the Web servers hold mainly static data, they could be dual active (or multiple active). Thus the more state I can take off the Web servers and put on the transaction servers the better the dual-active strategy works. If we manage to put all the session state in the back end I won't have to worry about a clustering or a two-database strategy to implement common Web server state.

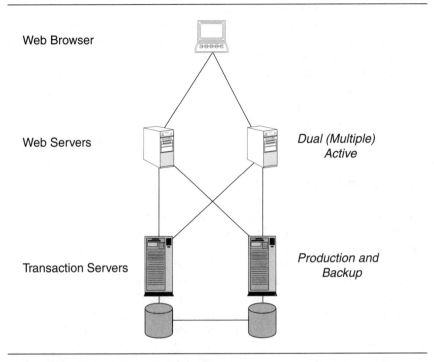

Web Browser

Web Servers

Dual (Multiple)
Active

Transaction Servers

Production and
Backup

Figure 7-5   Web configuration for resiliency

I would like to cater to switching to a backup transaction server without the end user knowing about it. This can be done by having the Web servers open connections to both transaction servers, but only using the active one. The transaction server recovery is as described in the previous section. There is no need for a heartbeat between the transaction servers since the Web servers themselves will immediately notice if the production system goes down and can either inform the operator that something is wrong or automatically trigger the switch to backup.

It is clear that with some thought, very high levels of resiliency are possible.

7.4   System software failures

While system software failures are alarming, they are often less dangerous than application errors simply because many are timing errors or memory leakage errors, and can be fixed by a reboot. The worst errors are database or operating system errors that corrupt data on disk. Some of these can be corrected by doing database reorganizations such as a garbage collection or a rebuild of an index. However, they provide another reason for making database backups and keeping a log of afterimages since it may be necessary to rebuild the database using a corrected version of the database software.

You might think that there is little point in switching to backup for system errors because the backup system should have the same software installed. But if the problem is a timing problem, there is indeed a good chance that the system will recover and continue.

7.5   Planned downtime

One of the major causes of downtime is planned downtime.

Planned downtime is used for housekeeping functions, preventive maintenance, and changing the hardware and software configuration.

The major factor in housekeeping is making a backup copy of the database. There are two techniques: use online backup copies or use special disk mirroring features to copy the database onto another machine. The principle of taking an online copy is that, to recover from the copy, you must apply afterimages from the log to bring the database back to a consistent state. This is true even if the database is not doing anything while the copy is taking place, because it could still have modified buffers in memory that it never got around to writing to disk. Many organizations are loath to move to online dumps; offline database copies somehow feel more reassuring. An online dump is only good if the database log is good. But many large and safety conscious database users have been using this technique for years, albeit on mainframes.

Many of the large-scale enterprise disk subsystems have a feature that allows you to make a mirror copy of some disks and then (logically) break the disks from one machine and attach them to another. If you do this with a database that is up and running, then the database will be in an inconsistent state just like it is after a machine stop. Taking a copy of the database in that state is the same as taking an online copy of the database—you need the log to effect a recovery of the data. It is probably operationally more useful to stop the database before breaking the mirror and giving the database copy to another machine. The copy of the database is then an offline copy and the database not only can be used to make an offline backup copy but can also be used for queries without having to apply any log afterimages to make it consistent.

Preventive maintenance is not an issue on platforms that have features such as hot replacement and dynamic hardware partitioning. If the platform does not support these features you can handle preventive maintenance as if it were a hardware reconfiguration.

It is possible to handle many reconfiguration changes in hardware and software by the intelligent use of backup systems. The steps are as follows:

1. Take the backup machine off line.

2. Change the software or hardware.

3. Bring the backup machine up-to-date.

4. Switch to backup.

5. Repeat process on the other machine.

This strategy calls for one system stop in step 4 and some organizations will want an additional system stop after step 5 to switch back to the original primary machine.

The number one reason why organizations so rarely use this technique in practice is that organizations don't have a symmetrical backup configuration and do not regularly move the load from one machine to another. They are not prepared to risk running the production load on the backup machine except in the case of a disaster.

That said, there are technical issues as well. The difficult step is the third one— bringing the backup machine up-to-date. We have observed three techniques for keeping data in the backup in sync with the production system, namely remote disk mirroring, reapplying the database log, and reprocessing transactions. The first two of these techniques do not work if the database schema is different on primary and backup. The solution therefore is to make the database schema change online on both the primary and backup simultaneously before step 1. How easy or practical this is will depend crucially on the capabilities of your favorite database product.

If you can't handle software and hardware changes as described here, it looks like you're going to have to work over Christmas.

7.6   Application software failure

In many ways application software failure is the worst kind of error. It cannot be emphasized enough that programmers must write code that:

- Prevents bad data from getting to the database—check all the input data and if anything is awry at any stage don't commit the transaction to the database.
- Looks for corruption in the database as it is being read.
- Displays as much information as possible about any errors detected.

They should also write policing programs that scan the database checking the data's integrity and, of course, everything should be tested thoroughly.

But in spite of everything, applications will go wrong. The best case is that the program fails. The worst case is that the program does not fail but the database is corrupted. Failing programs usually have to be fixed and restarted, although sometimes problems can be worked around. If the database is corrupted two strategies can be applied. Go back to a state before the corruption and rerun the work, or fix the database in situ by writing a program that fixes the corruption.

Some database systems have a roll-back facility whereby log beforeimages on the database can be applied, taking the database back to the state it was in earlier in the day or week. This is typically faster than reloading the database and applying log afterimages until the database is in the state it was before the corruption started. (This assumes you can find the point the corruption started—as you see, I'm discussing a nightmare scenario and nightmares can often get worse.) When the database is in its earlier non-corrupted state, the transactions can be reapplied. In theory, if the input data is captured then the transactions can be replayed in exactly the same order the transactions were originally committed. (This is exactly the same point I discussed in the two-database strategy for dual active.) In practice this kind of input audit trail was possible with traditional mainframe transactions but is virtually impossible with object middleware. The reason is that, while mainframes often had a log of input messages, it is hard to have the same when the objects are being updated in one transaction by a large number of small operation calls. It's this kind of point that keeps some large users wedded to their home-grown middleware!

The alternative to an automated reprocessing of transactions is a manual reprocessing of transactions. Don't throw away all that paper yet!

But even a manual reprocessing is difficult if multiple databases are involved. In theory I suspect it is possible to roll back two databases to a point before the corruption started and roll them forward together in sync. In practice no software exists to do this. If there is a message queue between two systems it should be possible to roll back one database without the other and throw away the messages regenerated on the rerun. This assumes that all messages on the rerun are generated in the same order as in the original, which will only start to be possible if order-dependent messages are in the same queue.

Roll back was a really good idea for batch, but now it's hard and it's getting harder. So what about writing a program to fix up the data? To do that you need to know the transaction type in error, the effect of the error—obtainable from the database before and after images on the log—and what the input data was for that transaction—perhaps a log of the Web browser input. With that information you can work out the effects on the database the input should have had. Unfortunately, trying to change the database using this information does not take into account second order effects. A program or a user could have seen the corrupt data and acted wrongly. Eventually this becomes a business decision. For instance, you've accidentally put $2,000 in someone's account and they've spent it. Do you: Forget it? Write them a nasty letter? Take the money out of their account without telling them? As I said, it's a business decision.

In a distributed system you must rethink your strategy for error reporting. In particular you need:

- An input log of all important input transactions: you need to know who the user was, what transaction they were doing, and the data they input.
- A record in the database (or the database log) that is sufficient to tie the information captured in the input log to the transaction on the database.

- Good error reporting—displaying the nature of the error and enough information to be able to track back to the input log.

Of course if you do all this you are much less likely to have application errors in the first place because your testing will be so much more effective.

7.7   Developing a resiliency strategy

There is a line of thinking in IT that resiliency is entirely a technical issue, that you can take any design and turn it into a resilient application. What this view misses is two points:

1. Error recovery is a business issue.
2. The designers must set the resiliency goals; adding resiliency is a cost and you can't do a cost/benefit analysis without understanding the business benefits and risks.

Resiliency analysis requires the designer and implementer sitting down together and discussing the business process. Let us take a simple example—submitting expenses. At the top level, this is a four-stage process:

1. Submitting the expenses
2. Sign off
3. Payment
4. Auditing

Each stage is a self-contained chunk of work, with one or more transactions. The first two stages could be real-time, on-line processes, the third stage might be a batch process. Between each stage will be a delay because different people are involved.

Resiliency is clearly not going to be the only concern (security comes to mind). Resiliency analysis is part of the wider process of implementation design.

There are three parts to resiliency analysis: data safety analysis, uptime analysis, and error handling analysis. Data safety analysis starts early on in implementation design when deciding on the data distribution structure for the application. There are numerous alternatives even for a simple process like this, such as:

- Completely distributed. The submit process could run on a workstation and send a message directly to the manager's workstation through a queue (perhaps even e-mail).
- Two central databases, one for expenses and sign off, and the other for payment.
- Departmental databases.
- One database. The expense handling could be a module of the financial systems.

I started the resiliency analysis by considering the safety and integrity of the data. The main resiliency requirements are:

- Each expense claim must be captured securely, once and only once.
- There must be a reference so the paper receipts can be tied to the payment (and the taxman or taxwoman is happy).
- There must be no possibility of paying the same expense report twice.

Note that data is of paramount importance; the system being down for a few hours is a nuisance but nowhere near as important. In fact, response time is probably more important than uptime. This kind of resiliency requirement is completely different from, say, an airline check-in process where the paramount requirement is for the system to be up and running with good response times, and if a little bit of data is lost every now and then that is a real shame, but not a disaster because the passenger has the information on his or her ticket.

But not every piece of data is of equal importance, for instance, the table mapping department codes to managers can be re-input from information in the personnel system.

In our expenses example, these requirements led us strongly in the direction of a centralized secure server with, ideally, a resilient backup. There I can ensure high data integrity. The system does not have such a high uptime requirement that I have to take special precautions if the network is down. Instead of actually duplicating the key parts of the database I might consider a special audit trail of expenses either on a separate database or even a non-database file that could be kept in a remote location.

The other aspect of data safety is the reliable transport of messages from stage to stage. These messages are what I called in the previous chapter deferrable messages. We have already noted that message queuing is an ideal technology for this requirement.

Having considered the data safety requirements, the next step is to look at uptime requirements. The impact of the system being down is that it wastes people's time. It is hard to put a cost to this, the main factor is poor perception of the IT systems. In this application, it is probably more important to have good response times than 365 times 24 uptime. It is also more important for the manager's sign-off to be up and running, partly because they have more work to do, partly because they have less incentive to try again, and partly because their time is more valuable (I generalize here).

The third part of resiliency analysis is to look at error handling. This is done during the detailed part of implementation design. It is worth looking at errors caused by external factors (for example, a department that temporarily has no manager), errors caused by IT infrastructure breakdown, errors caused by users doing the wrong thing, and even errors caused by wrong or malicious programming.

Suppose the message to the manager for sign-off uses e-mail; this is notoriously unreliable. The resiliency strategy should be to recreate the message at any time, perhaps with a message saying "This is a possible duplicate." Suppose the manager is away for four weeks. There should be a time limit on the sign off and then the messages are sent to the next level of manager. Perhaps the next-level manager signs off, but when the manager gets back he or she rejects the expenses. A better solution would be to use e-mail as a reminder, not as a carrier of data, so the manager would actually sign-off the expenses by running a program or using a Web application. Note that these are all business process issues as well as technical issues; techies and modelers must work together.

A good resiliency analysis has many benefits:

- Helps prevent over-engineering.
- Helps prevent under-engineering.
- Helps test the integrity of the business process model.

The key is a discussion of the business processes. Noting that business processes go across departments, I would suggest the modelers come to the techies with a business process diagram (also called an activity diagram) as the starting point for the discussions. It is easy to assume everybody knows what needs to be done but, especially when it comes to error handling, they don't.

7.8 Conclusions

Building resilient systems is largely a matter of attitude. Remember the resiliency designer's motto—"Just because I'm paranoid, doesn't mean that they are not out to get me."

There are a few simple points that keep on coming up again and again:

- Keep the application simple.
- Have minimal session state.
- Test programs thoroughly.
- Catch errors early and report them in full.
- Make sure the errors are traceable to end input.
- Have a backup system.
- Practice switching to the backup system.
- Anticipate errors—you're going to get them.
- Understand the business impact of different failures.

There are some obvious extra costs in building a resilient system such as paying for backup hardware and software. Many organizations are prepared to pay a bit extra for much better resiliency. But building resilient systems is not just a matter of cost. It needs a commitment to developing tight operational procedures, extensive testing, and a willingness to anticipate problems before they occur, even unlikely ones. Building resiliency into an existing application is usually possible (with application changes), but it is much better to design for resiliency from the beginning.

Techies and modelers must work together on a resiliency strategy for an application. I suggest a three step process for analyzing resiliency requirements:

1. Analyze which data and which messages have special integrity requirements.

2. Analyze uptime requirements.

3. Analyze error handling.

The first two steps are important for developing a data distribution strategy for the application. The discussion should be centered around the business process diagram of the application.

8

Performance
and Scalability

This is the second chapter about distributed systems principles. This time it is about the principles that govern high performance and scalability in the context of commercial systems, especially transaction processing applications.

One of the extraordinary features of the modern IT industry is the ability of vendors to produce benchmark performance figures that seem to be in another dimension. For instance, in 1999 a Unisys Aquanta ES2085R Intel server (eight Intel Pentium 550 MHz procs) was rated at 37,757.23 TpmC. If you sustain that over five hours that's roughly 11 million transactions, which is enough for a major bank! But banks have massive mainframe systems and gut feeling tells us that, resiliency aside, they would not be able to sustain such a throughput. Clearly something funny is going on.

One way of looking at this is by analogy. The TpcC benchmark is like riding a car around a racing circuit, while running a commercial application is like driving a car over a ploughed field. The fact that a formula one racing car is extremely quick on a track is of little relevance on the ploughed field. This is a rhetorical argument, of course, and not very insightful. A closer analogy would be to compare computer hardware to a car engine and the software to a car's body, wheels, brakes—all the rest that is needed to turn a power unit into something that can be used to move people. The TpcC benchmark is a measure of the speed of the engine by looking at how effectively it performs when the vendor puts it into a racing car. What we need to understand is how to take the same engine and build the car body around it for going shopping or clambering around fields. This analogy is not bad because when vendors do TpcCs they use different development tools from what you and I would use (they won't be using interpretive Visual Basic or Java for instance), they don't add anything for backups or fast recovery, and they have teams of experts nursing it along.

For at least twenty years, people in the IT industry have been looking at Moore's law (processor power increases by a factor of two every 18 months), or at disk performance projections or network performance projections, and have been saying: don't worry about the performance of the software, the hardware will fix it. And for twenty years they have been wrong. What's happening? And will they be wrong for the next twenty years?

One thing that has gone wrong is encapsulated in the saying—"What Intel giveth, Microsoft taketh away." Software has been getting fatter. It uses up much more memory than its predecessor did five years ago, and it requires enormous amounts of processing power simply to keep the screen looking pretty. As 3D effects, voice processing, and natural language understanding become more common there will be an ever-increasing requirement for power at the desktop. But the chief concern of this book is backend systems, so I won't concern us with these front-end challenges.

8.1   The un-slippery slope

A more pertinent reason for the difference between benchmarks and reality is the hardware architecture. Look at Figure 8-1. I call this the un-slippery slope.

What this diagram is meant to show is that there is a gap between what the processor could do and what it actually does do. This gap I call the HW architecture gap. The reason for the gap is simple—the processor is faster than the memory, and every now and then must wait. Another old IT proverb is "All processors wait at the same speed." Of course these days, every system has cache. But every now and then

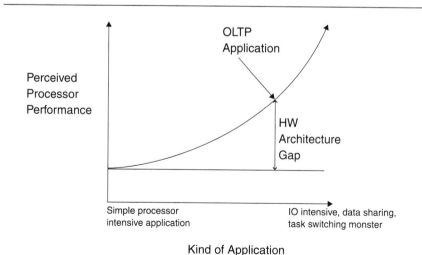

Figure 8-1   The un-slippery slope

there is a cache miss—the data is not in the cache and it must be fetched from main memory. Processors these days go at 300, 500, 1000 Mhz or higher. This means one cycle takes 3.3, 2, or 1 nsecs. A PCI bus on the other hand goes at 33Mhz—one cycle every 30 nsecs. Fast main memory goes at 50 nsecs. Then we must allow time for the fact that the clocks aren't synchronized, bus and memory handling logic must be processed, the fact that we will be reading, say, four words into cache at one time not one word, and so on. In other words, every cache miss means at least 20 cycles of doing nothing. This is in the best case. It can get really bad. The cache might need to write old updated data to memory to make room for the new data. It might be impossible to read the data from memory for a while because another processor or some IO is writing to memory at the same time and got there first. The latest version of the data might be in the cache belonging to another processor.

There are sophisticated ways of handling these problems, sophisticated hardware architectures in fact. Probably the least sophisticated is a simple PC using a PCI bus to memory. At the other end of the scale are machines like the Unisys CMP hardware that has cross-bar memory interconnects, third-level cache shared between processors, separate IO processors, and other facilities. The effect of a sophisticated hardware architecture is to change the slope of the un-slippery curve, as illustrated in Figure 8-2.

This analysis implies that there are three ways to improve the performance:

1. Have a faster processor.

2. Improve the hardware architecture.

3. Push the application leftward, down the slope.

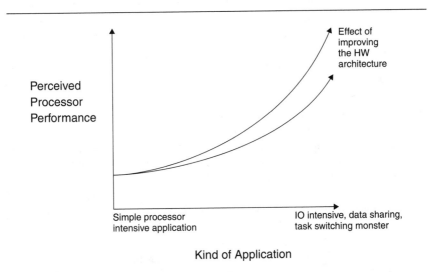

Figure 8-2   The effect of improving the hardware architecture

So how do we push the application down the slope? Here are some ways:

- Reduce the active memory footprint. By active memory footprint I mean the memory used for the main path processing. If the active memory footprint is greater than the cache size then cache is being continually recycled.
- Reduce the number of task switches. Task switching is slow at the best of times because it means saving away one set of register values and reloading another set. But it also has a deleterious effect on cache since the chances of the two tasks using the same data is remote.
- Reduce lock contention and other cases of multiple processors going for the same piece of data.
- Reduce the number of IOs. IOs are really disruptive. As well as the amount of raw processing and large memory movements that can fill cache with data that is hardly ever reused, there is also contention for locks and inevitably a number of process switches.
- Reduce the number of network messages sent or received. Sending and receiving messages has all the same overheads of doing an IO plus the additional complexities of building network messages and handling the network protocol.
- Reduce the number of memory overlays. Memory thrashing is the worst of them all—practically everything is wrong.

These are all deeply techy things that your average application programmer would rather not think about. Furthermore, many points are outside of the programmer's control; they depend on the operating system or database software. This is why I call it the un-slippery slope, it's hard work going down it.

On the other hand, going up the slope is easy. Suppose you add an extra index to a database table. Not only do you incur the cost of the extra IO and processor to read and write the index, but you also increase the active memory footprint, take up database buffer space that could be used by other data, and stretch out the length of the transaction thereby increasing lock contention.

The kind of application dictates to some extent where you are on the slope. Tight loops doing numerical calculations are at the bottom of the slope and multiplying a 100,000,000 by 100,000,000 matrix is somewhere near the top. Industry benchmarks have small applications, they don't share the system with any other application, they are highly optimized to reduce IO and memory. In short, they are much further down the slippery slope than you can ever hope to achieve in a real application.

In the following sections I will look first at transaction servers and then business intelligence data access and investigate some of the performance characteristics and what can be done to optimize the application.

8.2   Transaction processing

Let us start by looking at an optimized transaction implementation. This is illustrated in Figure 8-3.

Summarizing what we see here, we have:

- One input and one output network message;
- A number of reads and writes to the data file, and
- A write to the log file, which could be on disk or tape.

In a typical configuration you find that the application logic takes in the order of 10 percent of the processor and the network and database systems take 30 percent each. The remaining 30 percent is idle and has to be because at higher than 70 percent utilization, queuing effects start deteriorating the response time so much that the system starts being unusable (see Queuing box). This is of course all a gross simplification but it gives the flavor of what is happening.

Where are the bottlenecks in this system? Let me do some "back-of-the-envelope" calculations. First the network (see Figure 8-4).

A 10 Mbit Ethernet LAN actually only delivers about 1Mbit/sec (unless it is switched). So we are talking about one or two 10Mbit LANs or one 100Mbit LAN. (On the other hand, if you used character-based telnet, which has a separate message for every byte, it would be a different story, and this is one of the reasons early Unix systems had such a problem with high transaction throughput applications.)

What about disk throughput? Another back-of-the-envelope calculation is presented in Figure 8-5.

What the calculation in Figure 8-5 shows is that there is no issue with disk throughput since a SCSI channel is rated at 40 Mbytes per second. The problem is

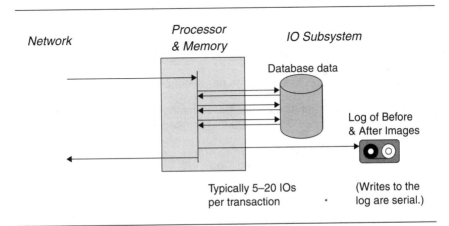

Figure 8-3   An ideal transaction implementation

Network Throughput Requirements

100 transactions per second

200 bytes in
+ 2,000 bytes out
= 2,200 bytes per transaction
= 220,000 bytes per second
add headers, etc., and convert to bits
= 2.2 MB per second approximately

Figure 8-4 Rough OLTP network calculations

that it implies 16 to 40 disk drives going flat out (see How Fast Is Disk? Box). Since IOs will not be evenly distributed over the drives, the system would need to have many more disks attached and the system must be optimized to ensure that there are not an excessive number of IOs to one disk. We end up with large disk farms, large numbers of IOs per second, but low data throughput rates. Disk caching will help greatly, but, even without it, there is not an insurmountable problem so long as the database software has the ability to spread data over many disks.

But note, taking a backup copy of disk to tape has the opposite profile. Properly configured (and using enterprise capable backup software) the limit on backups is usually the number of parallel runs, where each run cannot go faster than the

Disk Throughput Requirements

100 transactions per second

at 8 to 20 IOs per transaction
= 800 to 2,000 IOs per second

at 4,000 bytes per IO
= 3.2 to 8 MBs per second

if average 50 IOs per second per disk
= 16 to 40 disks

Figure 8-5 Rough OLTP disk calculations

Queuing

In a chapter about performance I am obliged by the IT Capacity Management and System Tuning Union to have a section on queuing:
I only remember one formula on queuing:

Total time = service time / (1 − utilization)

In other words, if the utilization is 50 percent, then the total time is twice the service time. If the utilization is 70 percent then the total time is a bit over three times the service time. This is for random arrivals and a single provider. Having multiple providers on a single input queue is much better.
The long and the short of it is that online utilization cannot be allowed to get much more than 70 percent, otherwise response times go through the roof. Of course, in batch you don't care and you can run the machine at 100 percent utilization.

minimum of the serial transfer rate of the tape device, the disk device, tape channel, or disk channel.

What about memory? Here, clearly, we could have a problem. The operating system, networking software, and database software are big hungry systems that need lots of memory for their tables and code. Spare memory is at a premium for the database buffer pool. If we were to have a crude implementation there could be a single copy of each application for each terminal. Since each application needs a database connection, it will be large, say 2 MBs. If there are 2,000 terminals this translates to 4 gigabytes just for applications, the addressing limit of many processors. The answer is to use a transaction monitor, and all mainframe systems have one (CICS on IBM MVS, TIP and COMS on Unisys ClearPath). What a transaction monitor does is allow programs and resources to be shared among all terminals. The number of parallel copies is then the number of active transactions rather than the number of terminals. The impact is dramatic. The active memory footprint is reduced and the memory can be used for more database buffers.

So what is the problem? In a well-balanced system with a highly capable IO subsystem, it is processing power, which brings us back to the un-slippery slope.

So let us look at some of the technologies I discussed in earlier chapters and how they change this profile.

8.2.1 Object interfaces

Object interfaces will normally have more network messages than a simple transaction message interface. I say "normally" because it is possible to have more or less the same number of messages by simply turning a transaction server into one large object. This is against the spirit of the object interface, so will tend not to be done. Instead, what would be one operation, for instance "credit an account," will

How Fast Is Disk?

The simple answer is that the best modern disk at the time I am writing does 10,000 rpm and has an average seek time of about 8 milliseconds.

This is incredibly fast—a single rotation takes 6 millisecs. In theory it could achieve 166 IOs per second if there is no head movement or 90 IOs per second if there is head movement (allowing for average seek time plus time for a half rotate).

The catch is that the processor has hardly any time to ask for a new IO. In the time between disk operations the system must:

* Get control of the channel
* Copy the data to the memory (probably with some buffering in between)
* Handle the IO finish code
* Wait until the processor is free
* Run application code until the next IO
* Process the next IO code
* Wait to get control of the disk (another IO on the disk may be in process)
* Wait to get control of the disk channel
* Write the data across the channel to the disk cache
* Move the disk head and do the IO

This all takes time and delays come in 6 millisecond chunks—the time for another rotation. Doing 30 or 40 random IOs per second and 60 or 80 serial IOs per second off one disk is doing well in a moderately busy system (rather than in a laboratory test).

Disk caching helps, of course, though clearly all the delays outlined above still apply. Reading data in a database buffer in main memory will always be quicker and incur less processing overhead than reading it from disk cache. However, disk caches are often very large and, by having battery backup to protect cached data over power failures, can save on writes as well as reads. But some activity does not benefit from caching at all. Large serial reads and writes (for instance while copying a database to backup) does not benefit from caching (unless there are effects due to reblocking—the cache subsystem reading larger blocks than the main system). Also random reads and writes on a large file (one much greater than the cache size) are not improved. An example may be the account detail records in a bank. Exactly the degree to which cache helps is extremely complex and hard to predict in advance, except by a comprehensive modeling exercise.

typically become two, "find the account" and "send a credit message to it," as was discussed in Chapter 3.

An object interface does not necessarily imply a doubling of the network messages. Many applications do something like—read an object, display it on the screen, and let the user update the record. This could translate to—find an object, get the data, display it on the screen, and update the object. Instead of two operations—read and write—there are three—find, get, and update.

But it could be a lot worse. Languages like Visual Basic positively encourage you to use attributes, not operations, which translates into a message to get every attribute value and a message to update every attribute value. The worst case could be something like—find the record, do ten messages to get ten attributes, display on the screen, and do two messages to update the object. Instead of the original two messages in the non-object case we now have thirteen messages. Since the overhead of message handling is so great (we assumed the network side, which includes the transaction monitor processing, took 30 percent of the processing power in the original case) we should expect this implementation to use much more processing power.

I have also ignored poor implementation decisions by object interface software vendors like poor management of connections (some CORBA vendors have one TCP/IP session for each object reference). But I don't see any point in dwelling on these since they will be fixed in the fullness of time (perhaps by the time you are reading this book).

The conclusion is that with object interfaces you have enough rope to hang yourself with plenty left over. However, hanging yourself is not compulsory, you can avoid the rope as long as you look out for it. This is true for all object interfaces—DCOM/MTS, EJB, or CORBA—and I strongly suspect the nuances of writing an efficient interface will exceed the performance differences between the technologies.

8.2.2   Transactional component containers

Transactional component containers have resource pooling similar to old-fashioned mainframe transaction monitors. Excepting the fact that they are modern pieces of software, which inevitably seems to mean they use much more memory to do the same thing, they should benefit in the same way.

Note, with vanilla CORBA you are on your own. It is up to your slick implementation to pool resources until the CORBA component model is available and mature. Writing a high-performance, transaction processing system in CORBA is masochism.

Assuming the object interfaces are used efficiently by the programmer as discussed above, I don't see why transactional component containers should not be capable of implementing large-scale applications.

8.2.3   Two-phase commit

The details of how the two-phase commit protocol works is described in the box (Two-Phase Commit) in Chapter 7. What you need to know is that when you update two or more databases on different systems there are additional network messages and disk writes. The message flow is illustrated in Figure 8-6.

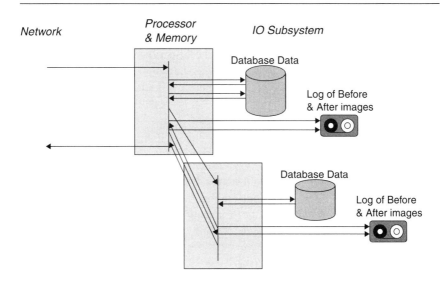

Network Processor & Memory IO Subsystem

Figure 8-6 Two-phase commit

What this shows is two databases being updated in one transaction on two different boxes. There is a network message from the master transaction to start the subtransaction in the other box. When the subtransaction has finished it sends a reply and, finally, there are two messages for the acknowledgment phase of the commit protocol. Both systems maintain their own log. Another source of delay is that the transaction takes longer, so database locks are held for longer and there is more lock contention.

In short, it is not good news. On performance grounds two-phase commits should be avoided whenever possible. Clearly, if a low percentage of transactions use two-phase commits, there is not a serious problem, but we want to avoid an architecture that incurs a two-phase commit on a large percentage of the transactions.

8.2.4 Message queuing

Message queues can be very efficient, since they allow a number of messages to be put into one block both for transmission over the network and for writing to disk. But there is a trade-off between reducing the overhead and elapse time in sending the message. For real-time messages, elapse time is paramount, so it is less likely there would be any message blocking over the network.

The wider issue with message queuing is that you must implement your own program scheduler. For instance, if you are using message queuing for real-time processing you may want to put all like messages into one queue. The easiest technique is to have one program emptying the queue but, on high-volume systems, this will not be fast enough. The alternative is to have several programs emptying the queue. But it is up to you to write the scheduler that decides how many programs run and starts additional copies of the program if the queue is too large (tasks that would normally be done by a transaction monitor).

8.2.5   Using remote database access for real-time transactions

Remote database access technology, on the other hand, is inherently inefficient for real-time transactions. It was this technology that is largely to blame for the poor performance of first generation client/server applications, also known as "thick clients" or, in Microsoft-speak, "rich clients." If you look back at Figure 8-3 it is easy to see why—every database call becomes a network message, or even several network messages, vastly increasing the network overhead. It is the database server that really suffers. If you need 20 transactions per second the transaction server might be handling 20 input and 20 output network messages but the remote database server is likely to be handling ten times that amount.

This situation can be greatly alleviated by using stored procedures. But note what has been done here, the database server has been turned into a transaction server. Compared to a transaction server, however, the database server has limited control over its ability to do multi-threading and connection pool management. This is because the number of parallel stored procedures being processed at any one time cannot be greater than the number of database connections.

Interestingly, stored procedures have been widely used in benchmark configurations. Some performance studies have used a configuration like Figure 8-7.

There are several points about this configuration that need to be understood.

- The purpose is to show scalability and the biggest bottleneck is the database. Therefore they need to take out as much processing as possible from the box running the database.
- The stateless sessions allow easy load balancing over the Web servers and the transaction servers.
- The purpose of the transaction server is to control the number of database connections, in other words, to avoid having one database connection for every end user.
- Such benchmarks are usually set up so that the data can be distributed over separate database servers, for example, by customer number range. The issues with this approach are discussed in the section below called "Is distribution an alternative?"
- By using stored procedures, there is one input and one output message per transaction to the database server. The total amount of hardware required

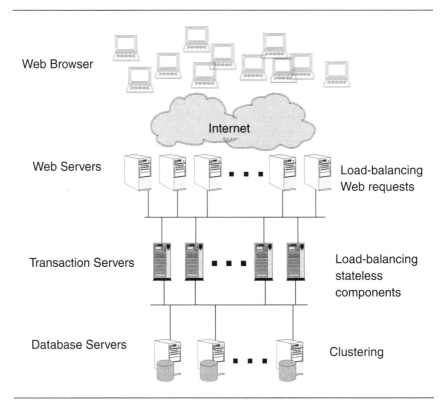

Web Browser

Internet

Web Servers — Load-balancing Web requests

Transaction Servers — Load-balancing stateless components

Database Servers — Clustering

Figure 8-7 Database server benchmark configuration

is greater than it would be if the transaction server was in the same machine as the database server because the number of network messages have been doubled.

- But the cost is not necessarily greater for two reasons. First, a large proportion of the cost is software, not hardware, and is priced by the number of end users, not by hardware capacity. Second, a large number of transaction servers can be used and each individual transaction server can be implemented on cheap commodity hardware.

In other words, the use of separate boxes for the database servers has a lot to do with benchmarking and precious little to do with real life. For instance, the advertised benefit of a separate database layer is to access several different databases within one transaction, for instance so that customer data can be shared across many applications. It would be much harder to optimize such a configuration. Any widely accessed database, like a customer database, could easily end up with a huge number of connections.

8.2.6   Conclusions on real time

The conclusion we can draw from all this discussion is that what is needed to build a high performance transaction engine was first understood and implemented in the 1970s and 1980s and hasn't changed much since. The industry has been rebuilding the same solution under different guises like database stored procedures and transactional component managers. The main difference has been the languages in which we implement the transaction logic. The other conclusion is that with the massive numbers of IOs and network messages there is no leeway. You must use software like transaction monitors that optimize the use of resources and you must be ready to review and optimize your disk IOs and your interface, especially if it is an object interface.

8.3   Batch

So far in this book there has been little mention of batch; the emphasis has been on new technologies and new applications where batch is less important than in the past. Batch may have a diminished role but it still has a vital role.

There are three basic reasons for batch. Two we have mentioned already—the need to support time-cyclical business processes (like payroll and bank interest accrual) and the need for housekeeping (like copying a database to backup). But there is a third reason—optimization. For example, suppose we have 100,000 new records to add, each with one index entry to insert. Each index entry insertion might require one or two reads and one or two writes, between 200,000 and 400,000 IOs, which typically translates to several hours of IO time. If we can sort the input in the same order as the index, the number of IOs is drastically reduced, perhaps to 10,000 reads and 10,000 writes. (If you want to be precise, the number would be close to the number of tables in the index, so it depends on the size of the tables and the population of existing records.)

The downside of using batch for optimization is that the updates are not done until the batch run, typically during the night. Many organizations would rather the database was up-to-date immediately, which besides giving a better service would simplify the code. Sometimes, however, the savings are so dramatic that removing them is out of the question.

Batch performance is becoming more and more of a problem. The reason is that with late night this and late night that, the online day has become longer and longer. The international nature of the Internet brings with it pressure for the online day to be 24 hours long. The time allowed for batch—the batch window—is shrinking.

I discuss the applications aspects of removing batch in more detail in Chapter 14.

From the performance perspective, the trick with batch is to have enough parallelism to keep all the processors busy (perhaps leaving enough for a residual online service). An enormous number of organizations haven't done this. It is usually not that difficult, as it is a matter of partitioning the input records over a number of programs. The biggest problem is programs that do a huge batch task in one transaction to simplify recovery code.

If you were designing from scratch you could and should eliminate these problems during initial design. In fact, you should write transactions so that they can be used for both online and batch, which means ensuring that they are short. Batch programs can then support parallelism from the start. On the other hand, retrofitting these changes to existing batch runs is almost certainly quicker, easier, and less risky than rewriting everything from scratch.

8.4   Is distribution an alternative?

With all these problems, wouldn't it be easier to distribute the application over several smaller systems? The answer is, regrettably, it depends.

The easiest distributed systems to implement are those where the application is inherently distributed. For instance, a warehouse control system spends most of its time processing information local to the warehouse. It needs connections to the central location to receive input data and queries, but the volumes should be low.

But how do you take a naturally centralized system like a bank database and distribute it over several machines? The first point is that to be truly effective you will want to distribute the data over a large number of machines. Distributing a 100-transactions-per-second application over three machines is likely to end up with machines that do 50, 30, and 20 transactions per second respectively. The problems of managing the 50-transactions-per-second machine aren't that different from managing a machine with 100 transactions per second. To make a real difference, distribution should be over, say, 10 or 20 machines.

The first step in implementing a distributed bank would be to ensure online transactions are routed to the right machine. We could do this by having the distributed systems each implement a range of account numbers. You don't want all the big business accounts on one machine and all the savings accounts for children on another, so you would have to look carefully into exactly how you are allocating account numbers.

Any task that isn't account number based, be it online update, batch report, or ad-hoc query, would have to be implemented by accessing all machines. For instance, suppose we wanted to find the list of accounts that are overdrawn, this now requires a search of all machines.

Many bank transactions not only do a debit or credit on one account, but also do an update somewhere else. For instance, the system might want to keep track of how much money is in the cashier's till. So where is this data kept? If it is on a different machine we have to implement two-phase commits. However, the machine that has the cashier's till records is going to have to process a large number of transactions, so it will have to be large—unless we distribute that as well. Alternatively, we could split the accounts by their owning branch but then account number–based operations would have to start by looking up the owning branch from the account number.

Having made the split, we now have to administer and manage many databases not one. Complex tasks, like handling new versions of the software and building disaster backup plans, take on an additional layer of complexity.

There are four points coming out of this discussion:

1. There is a great deal of extra coding—transactions, reports, and inquiries are all more complex.

2. Evenly spread dispersal of data is hard—the largest machine is likely to be supporting much more traffic than the smallest.

3. There is considerable additional overhead like two-phase commits.

4. It much more difficult operationally—put simply, instead of having one machine to manage, you have many.

The changes are so great that unless you have built the application from the ground up to be distributed, it is very hard to change later.

Many people promoting distribution are doing so to overcome a limitation in their preferred software technology. But the issues with scalability in software products are often not to do with the number of transactions per second, but the number of attached users. The distributed solution for banks using account number ranges totally fails on this score. If the bank has 10,000 users, each account-handling server must still each support 10,000 users.

The conclusion is that with the increased scalability of machines there doesn't seem much point distributing a single application only for performance.

8.5   Load balancing

In white papers and press articles, the message is that scalability equals load balancing. Let us look again at Figure 8-7. There are four tiers: browsers, Web servers, transaction servers, and database servers. Load balancing means having any number of Web servers, any number of transaction servers all working on the same application, and any number of database servers.

Load balancing of the Web server requires a special network router that fools the outside network into thinking that there is only one Web server (that is, only one IP address and only one name) whereas in fact there are a number of physical Web servers. As discussed before, such routers are available.

The other problem the Web servers must solve is ensuring that the data in all of them is the same. We have met this problem before—it is what I described before as the dual-active scenario, the only difference is that it could be many active and not only two. As we found in the resiliency discussions, the best solution is to put all the state in the backend database.

Scaling a single transaction service by load balancing over several physical servers is much harder. The dual-active issues apply here also if there is state (that is, if there are EJB stateful session beans). Therefore the number one rule is—no state. Even applying that rule, there is a further issue of balancing the work evenly across the servers. Let us imagine that we have some transactional component middleware with load balancing. At a minimum this means that every time a client requests that a new object is created, the objects may be located on one of several machines. This increases the overhead of object creation since the servers have to decide which server takes the object. This may or may not be significant depending on whether the application creates new objects often or only rarely. (But the downside of only creating objects rarely is that spreading the load evenly over many machines is much harder.)

The multiple transactions servers now have to update the same database, so how about load balancing the database server across several machines? The first task is to ensure that the database connections are assigned to the different machines in such a way as to disperse the load across the database servers. Assuming this can be done, then the multiple machines can share the same database by using clustering, as discussed in the last chapter in the section on the dual-active scenario. Whether we get good performance from the many clustered machines again depends on the application. If there are many reads and only a few writes, performance can be good. When there are many writes to the same physical blocks, performance will be poor. The killer is "hot spot" data; data that all the transactions want to change. Examples are control totals and statistics, the end of indexes (for example, the last block in a sequential index organized on date and time), and small volatile tables. Because of locking, you single thread through the hot spots (that means one program goes through the code at a time). Since the overhead of sharing buffers on a clustered machine is greater than on a single machine, single threading of hot-spot data on a clustered configuration can be even worse than on a single multi-processor system.

All this "it depends on the application" is the reason why vendors can show linear scalability for their products and why you can find so few examples in the real world. You have been warned.

The bottom line is that, if you want your application to respond well to load balancing or other forms of distribution, then you have to design it with that in mind. For instance, if you want to eliminate an index that is a hot spot you have to figure out which other applications need the index and find an alternative solution. This is another reason why modelers have to talk to techies.

My personal view is that the configuration illustrated in Figure 8-7 is balanced on a knife edge, and it will only work well on real-life applications after a major tuning exercise. Where possible, just have a single machine holding both the transaction server and the database server (possibly with a backup) and leave complex load-balancing techniques to the organizations that are pushing the boundaries of the performance and don't have a choice.

8.6   Business intelligence systems

I have used the words "business intelligence system" as a catchall for the whole range of machines from data access and decision support to data marts and data warehouses. But all these machines share two performance issues—processing ad-hoc queries and data replication.

8.6.1   Ad-hoc database queries

Large database queries are IO and processor intensive. The IO usage is obvious. The processor usage is from:

- Checking each record against the search criteria
- Moving data to the output message
- Sorting
- Parsing the query, including scanning the query text, building a processing plan, and optimization of the plan
- Managing temporary data
- Doing arithmetic calculations, checking for nulls

And much else besides.

Worse still, large queries will dominate the IO capacity. They also need large amounts of memory, for instance, to be used by the sort routines. They have a very disruptive impact on database buffers, filling them up with stuff no other program is at all interested in. In short, they squeeze out other work. It is hard to ensure database queries have no impact on production work even if they are running at low priorities. This is the reason why organizations have been so keen to move the database to another machine where the database queries can only get in the way of each other.

On the other hand, there are more and more pressures for having up-to-date data available at any time. This is partly a reaction to the Internet—for instance, customers or business partners checking the status of their orders. You can argue that this is no different from online inquiry transactions now, but I expect to see more of them, larger chunks of data in each query, and the provision of more flexible tailoring of the request. Of course, smaller queries aren't as disruptive as larger ones, but mixed query and transaction workloads will become an increasing challenge for database vendors.

8.6.2 Data replication

While data replication helps solves the ad-hoc query problem, it introduces a new set of problems of its own.

The technology for replication is basically straightforward; take a copy of the database and keep it up-to-date by applying the changes. It is neat to be able to take the changes from the database log file. When you review technology that does this, you should check that it does not apply changes from transactions that were subsequently aborted.

The network load for replication is large. The good thing is that it can be a few large messages rather than many small ones. You can get an idea of how much extra network throughput is required by looking at the amount of database log data created. For instance, if your system is doing 50 transactions per second and each transaction generates 4,000 bytes of database log then you need 200KBs per second. A dedicated Ethernet LAN connection should do the trick.

In my experience, the significant performance problem with data replication is loading the data on the target system. The reason this can get out of hand is that it is desirable for the query database to have more indexes than the production system. The IO overhead of a load may be not far short of the IO load on the production machine.

So what's the solution? Having huge quantities of memory to hold as much as possible of the indexes in memory is clearly an approach. Letting the target machine get behind and catching up during the night is also a possibility. Sorting the records before loading them would also save on some IOs.

As an aside, perhaps what is needed are some neat tricks from the database vendors. Perhaps they could have an adjunct index for today's data that could be merged into the main index as a background run. The index search would then have to look in both the main and the adjunct index. As I write this (in mid-2000), I am not aware of any vendor who has done something like this.

8.7 Backups and recovery

All of the above discussion leaves out arguably the single most important aspect of building a large system—the performance of backup and recovery.

There is a cruel logic about large systems:

- The more users there are, the more important it is not to have a failure.
- The larger the database, the more likely it is to experience a hardware failure because there is more hardware to fail.
- The larger the database, the longer the backup copy will take.
- The more transactions there are, the larger the log.

- The larger the log, the longer reconstruction of disk data will take since it has to reload the relevant data from last backup copy and reapply the changes in the log.
- Because applying the log takes so long, backup copies must be taken more frequently.

In other words, the larger the database, the longer the recovery, and the longer the database housekeeping.

Let us first get a yardstick on how big the problem really is. To do this we will take out our trusty back-of-the-envelope and do a few calculations; see Figure 8-8.

How long does it take to copy a database to backup? There are two questions: how many parallel streams can you run and how fast is each stream? Figure 8-8 illustrates that one stream copying at 4MBs per second takes a disastrous 70 hours to copy 1 terabyte. In practice, it is worse than that, because you might want a check phase and you can never reach maximum capacity. The conclusion is that for large databases you need both fast back devices and software that supports many parallel streams.

How much log is created? Say your system handles 2 million transactions per day (about the size of a medium bank). The amount of log data created for every transaction is very variable and depends on the details of the transaction, the database design, and database implementation itself. If we assume, as before, that there are 4,000 bytes per transaction then there are 8 gigabytes of log written each day. Within a few days, the disk will be full, so the log must be copied to tape and removed.

Say there is a disk crash. The data must be copied back from the backup and the log applied. If there is a weekly backup copy of the database that would mean on average, in our example, working through 28 gigabytes of log (three and a half

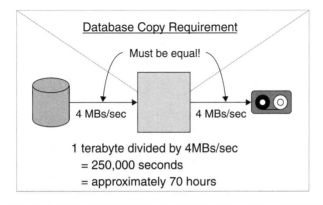

Figure 8-8 Database copy requirements

days' worth) and probably doing several million IOs to the disk unit. Hopefully, most of the data will be in disk cache or in the database buffers but, however we look at this, we are talking about many hours, maybe days. With the cheapness of today's disk units, the solution is to mirror the complete database. However, the organization still needs protection against catastrophe, in other words, software problems, or operations troubles, and needs the security of being able to do a complete rebuild of the database in an acceptable period of time, say less than a day. This requirement usually means taking a backup copy every day.

A final factor for performance is the time taken to reorganize the database when you change the schema. This is such a large subject and so dependent on the specific database product and the specific reorganization task required that I have no option but to leave it out.

8.8   Design for scalability and performance

While many of the issues I have been discussing are very technical, performance should be considered early in design, before the technology is even considered. There are three reasons:

1. The performance consequences of data distribution can be assessed.

2. The difference between deferrable transactions and real-time transactions should be noted. Using message queuing for deferrable transactions in preference to distributed transaction processing will be much faster (and more resilient, as I noted before).

3. The model gives us the data and transaction volumes.

Performance analysis is required at all levels of implementation design and during implementation. Until we get down into detailed analysis the primary technique is for the modelers and the techies to analyze the performance implications of the business process model. The techies need to see the flow of data and the data volumes, they need to know the scale of the task that faces them. Object models, class hierarchies, or entity-relationship diagrams do not give them this information.

The first step is to measure the scale of the problem. The simple expenses claim application discussed in the last chapter illustrates how this can be done. We know that we can reasonably expect the busiest times for submitting expense forms is likely to be early in the week and that the maximum number of people working simultaneously on the system cannot exceed the number of employees. By analyzing the business process we can compare the distributed and centralized solutions for the application and can estimate the load on each node and the data flow between loads. We should exploit the fact that the data sent between the expenses system and the payment system is deferrable, not real time.

At a more detailed level we can look at the actual expense report submission process. On one hand, we could collect all the expense report information on the workstations and send it in one message to a central server. On the other hand, we could have one transaction to the central server for each expense line item. The difference in performance will be significant but the volumes might not be high enough for us to care.

At the very detailed level, we can investigate the interfaces, code, and database usage profile to model the performance of the high-volume transactions.

Another issue in the implementation design to consider is performance monitoring. There is a problem here. In distributed systems technology there is very little instrumentation for measuring performance across the system rather than within a single node. The chief problem is different machines do not have exactly synchronized clocks, at least to the level of accuracy we need. It is very hard to say, for instance, that the ninth message that left box A at 2 seconds past 10:05 AM is the 24th message that entered box B at 5 seconds past 10:05 AM. So, if we find the reply to a message was slow, it is hard to track down exactly where the delay was. For this reason, for high performance distributed applications, it is likely that you will have to build some of your own instrumentation. I discuss this further in the next chapter.

8.9   Conclusions

I started this chapter by discussing the TpcC benchmark. Hopefully, you should now start to understand (if you didn't before) why these benchmarks are so remote from reality. All the code for resiliency (mirror disks, restart areas, and so forth) is out. All the code for system management (discussed in the next chapter) is out. There are no extra indexes for reports and no data movement to a data mart system. The price does not include the hardware for copying the database to backup. The applications are frequently written in tools not used by real application developers. The applications are optimized by experts. Sometimes the benchmarks use configurations that must be finely balanced where a better solution in real life would be more robust. The application is small and unchanging. The application has a small memory footprint, allowing cache and database buffer optimization. This does not mean that TpcC results are not useful, but just concentrate on comparisons and not absolute figures, and even then remember that if you change the development tools the results might change dramatically.

I expect many of my readers are still inclined to dismiss this chapter on the basis that hardware improvements will make it all irrelevant. The strange thing is that if I had been writing this ten years ago I would probably have agreed. But hardware advances seem to have been absorbed by transaction growth and inefficiencies in the software, and performance seems to be just as crucial today as it was then.

Even assuming we don't do anything stupid like abusing the object interface, hardware utilization will continue to rise. Some of the reasons are:

- Demands on the hardware will increase because of the requirement to reduce the batch window and pressure to do more database queries on the production system.
- Demand will also increase because of the use of object interfaces and two-phase commit.
- The Internet will lead to surges in demand at unexpected times; performance will fluctuate much more than it did previously.
- New applications are being developed all the time.
- Greater hardware resources lead to a greater tolerance of poorly performing systems.

Complacency on the performance front is misplaced. If you are designing a high-volume application today you must:

- Use a transaction monitor or transactional component manager.
- Ensure your object interfaces are used efficiently.
- Model the performance of the high-volume transaction.
- Ensure batch programs can be run in parallel and alongside online work.
- Keep transactions short (see Locking box).
- Avoid excessive use of two-phase commits.
- Control the number of indexes.
- Ensure your chosen database vendor can support multiple disk units for one table, that the disk configuration can be changed with minimum disruption and that logging can be mirrored and put on a different disk unit from the rest of your data.
- Ensure your chosen platform and database vendor can support the full range of backup and recovery features, including online backup copy, multiple streams for backup copy, online reorganization, automatic management of copying logs from disk to tape (or tape logging), support for many channels and disks, and high IO throughput rates.

Design for performance is important and something that must be started early in the design cycle and continued throughout implementation and delivery. Modelers must take some responsibility for performance and not leave it all to the techies. Even then, don't expect to get it right the first time. You will need to monitor the performance and make corrections. You will also need to benchmark the high-volume transactions early to assess the performance impact.

Locking

I have ignored the effects of locking in this chapter not because it isn't important but because by and large it can be solved.

There are two kinds of locks that will particularly impact performance—internal locks in the system software and database locks—and there is usually nothing you can do about the internal locks except use a different operating system and/or database vendor. Database locks can be record locks (also known as row locks), block locks (also known as page locks), or file locks. In most cases, you want to lock out the least amount of data and therefore record locking is to be preferred. The exceptions are when very large numbers of locks are being needed and the overhead of managing a large lock table becomes excessive.

In online database applications there are typically a number of "hot spots." These are small amounts of data that are hit with great rapidity. They are often data, such as accounting totals, statistics, restart data (described in Chapter 7), or even data for tracking activity that was originally put in to improve performance or management. The fact that they cause a problem only becomes apparent when the system is scaled up to production volumes. Block locks are disastrous for hot spots because there is a good chance that the records will be in the same block.

Sometimes hot spots can be eliminated. For instance, inserting many records into a table with an index on date and time will have a hot spot on the last table in the index, but putting the microsecond time as the first part of the index breaks it up. Of course the disadvantage is that the index no longer provides a time ordered view of the data, and there are additional IOs, so this change may be impractical.

There are several techniques for tackling locking problems. First and foremost, you must keep transactions short. Don't even think about a transaction that sends and receives a network message when locks are applied (two-phase commit excepted). Small transactions are important even for batch transactions or transactions that are emptying a message queue, otherwise you will never be able to run this work alongside the online day.

The second technique is to delay locking the hot spot records until later on in the transaction. It seems weird reordering your program logic for performance reasons, but that's life.

9

Security and
Systems Management

This is the third chapter in the sequence about distributed systems technology principles.

Security and systems management are enormously large subjects. To deal with the subjects comprehensively, we should at least consider: security, security administration, configuration management, problem escalation and management, performance tools, capacity management, cost control, and systems operation.

There are also many software products. There are software products for tape library management, disk management, batch scheduling, print management, performance monitoring, capacity management, database administration, and much else besides. Much of this software is platform specific. Like in the previous two chapters, I am going to assume you understand security and systems management on all the platforms in your organization. The issues I would like to discuss are concerned with security and systems management in a distributed environment. In particular, I want to take an application development perspective and ask the question: How do I develop distributed applications that are secure and can be managed well?

This chapter is like a sandwich. I discuss systems management technology first and the impact of systems management on application programs last. In the middle are two sections on security. The reason for this is that the application programming issues are closely related and it is easier to treat them together. Security is an enormously important subject, but ultimately it is an aspect of systems management.

9.1 Systems management technology

The vast majority of distributed systems management products, for instance CA Unicenter and Tivoli, follow the same basic conceptual pattern, which is illustrated in Figure 9-1.

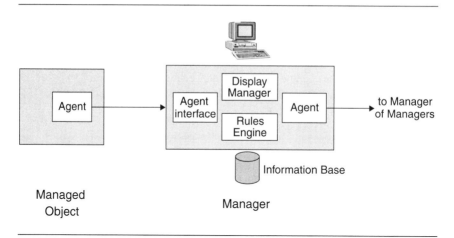

Figure 9-1 Distributed systems management

The model has a number of parts:

The **Managed Object**—the thing being managed. It may be a device from the size of a single card to a mainframe. It could be an application program, a database system, or even another manager. In fact, it could be more or less anything you care to manage.

The **Agent**—this resides in the managed object, gathering information, and shipping it to the manager. It may also do commands on the managed object, acting on the manager's behalf. The agent may be event driven (that is, waiting for something to happen), continuously monitoring the system, or both.

The **Protocol**—this is the protocol used between the agent and the manager. There are essentially three kinds of interaction between agent and manager: polling (the manager asks for information), alert (the agent tells the manager something has happened), and continual stream (the agent is sending regular updates). Protocols may support one or more of these modes of operation.

The **Message Format**—the messages hold the status of the managed object. The status is typically a list of attributes and data values. For instance a network router may have attributes to describe its network address, name, status, and traffic volume. Different sets of managed devices have different sets of attributes.

The **Manager**—the manager collects all the information from the agents, stores it, and displays it. The major elements in a manager are typically the agent interface, the rules engine, the information base, and the display manager.

The **Information Base**—this stores all the information collected from the agents. It can be as primitive as a few simple text files but it can be as complex as a full-grown object database.

The **Rules Engine**—this will be something like a scripting language for pre-processing the incoming data, filtering out what is irrelevant and highlighting what is very relevant. It may also consolidate many errors into one and send back commands to the agent for corrective action. Without the rules engine, system management is little more than remote operation. With the rules engine, tasks can be automated and information can be made more focused; this is where the real operational savings are made.

The **Display Manager**—shows the data textually, diagrammatically, or graphically, typically displaying information in traffic light colors to indicate areas of concern.

Actual products might have many other features like inventory control, software distribution modules, error reporting modules, and additional forms of communication with operators, for instance, links to pagers.

The best known standard in network management is the Simple Network Management Protocol (SNMP). Though it started out as a network management protocol, it is now widely used elsewhere. This is possible because it adheres to the structure described above; SNMP was designed to allow devices from one vendor to be managed by a manager from another vendor. SNMP is not limited to certain devices. Suppose you want an SNMP-enabled online coffee machine. You would need to define a new message format; it might have attributes like "Water status," "Brewing status," and "Amount of coffee left." Any SNMP manager would then be able to accept the messages. Most, of course, would do little more than display the raw text. A specialized manager might draw the coffee pot and show how full it was by means of a diagram.

The key to extending SNMP is defining the message formats. These message formats are called MIB formats. MIB stands for Management Information Base, which is the Information Base in an SNMP manager. As noted above, the Information Base is where the SNMP messages are stored. Each device will have its own MIB format defining the set of attributes it can report. Many of these MIB formats have been standardized, but it is very common for vendors to add their own extensions or create totally new MIB formats for additional managed services.

SNMP is effective at TCP/IP network management. It is less effective at managing system software elements and applications, mainly because the MIBs are not defined or defined to the level of detail needed to make them effective. (A full set of standard MIB formats is nearly impossible because of the variety of platforms and applications.)

Two important, more recent standards are WBEM and CIM, which are both under the control of DMTF (Distributed—was originally Desktop—Management Task Force). WBEM defines a standard for system management using HTTP as the protocol and XML as the data format. CIM stands for the Common Information Model and is equivalent to the MIB. In other words, a WBEM coffee maker might send a message that contains text like "<brewing>ON<\brewing>." There are ways of mapping SNMP MIBs to CIM classes so it is possible for one device to support both. A device that supports WBEM can typically be managed from a Web browser.

There are further alternatives. Unisys has a product called Single Point Operations (SPO) that simply picks up the console text streams that have been used to manage most computers for many years. It is likely that to manage a large environment remotely you will need several different technologies. Clearly, there is an issue with standardization, but many of those problems can be overcome by integrating managers. SPO, for instance, will raise alerts to CA Unicenter and SNMP agents can raise an alert to SPO. However, if the receiving system knows nothing about a certain attribute, all it will do is display the value as text.

Framework products like CA Unicenter and Tivoli try to manage everything. Most framework products have their own protocol and support SNMP as well. Then there are a variety of point products. Some people will tell you that choosing the best of the breed is the right decision, others will tell you to stick to framework products because of their greater integration. The jury is still out.

So how well does this model for systems management work? Our experience in this corner of Unisys is that it seems to work well if you start out slowly, start with one major problem and build out from there. You should tackle it slowly because configuring the environment is a significant effort and you must be ready to learn by experience. Installation of the software and the addition of the managed object into the management environment is only the start. You then have to consider what information you want to display on a regular basis and set up the diagrams and reports appropriately. You may need to readjust various parameters to change the frequency that devices are polled. You will almost certainly have to modify the rules. When you started out, you may have thought that you were primarily interested in a certain error message, now you realize you need to look for this error message only under certain conditions. You may find out that the problem you've been trying to solve isn't nearly as important as that problem over there. The evolutionary approach wins.

Managing a complex environment is inherently hard. Generic problems include:

- How do we distinguish between trivial problems and important problems?
- How do we prioritize problems?
- How do we assess the business impact of a problem?
- How do we stop ourselves from being overwhelmed by error messages when many of the agents are reporting the same problem again and again?
- How do we understand the dependencies on different elements, for instance the Web server application might depend on the network, the backend hardware, the database, the transaction server application, and so on?
- How do we detect if something is missing? For instance, suppose the payroll doesn't run because the changes weren't posted.
- How do we ensure the information base is kept in sync with the actual configuration?
- How do we handle the distribution of new software versions?

Clearly the distributed systems management model described above does not directly solve any of these problems though it does provide an environment that makes solving them easier.

There is an alternative to centralized management, which is local management cooperating loosely together. The fact that this can work is illustrated brilliantly by the Internet itself. There is some authority on the Internet that defines the basic network standards, for assigning IP address spaces and for giving out domain names, but much of it depends on ISPs managing their own local network and various country organizations managing their part of the backbone network.

This loose cooperation approach to distributed management makes demands on the technology. It's not so much a particular technology, it's more a set of design principles. The first of these is to value robustness above performance. The way to design a really fast network, for instance, is for every node to know exactly the fastest way to send a message to any other node. The robust way (used by TCP/IP) is to send the message roughly in the right direction and for the receiving node to send it on, until it finally reaches the other end.

The end goal of the loose cooperative approach is self-management. Under the general heading of self-management there are three components: self-recovery, self-configuration, and automatic version control.

Self-recovery is best done as near as possible to where the error is detected. This is what TCP/IP does. If the link fails to send a message, the message is resent. If the link is down, the layer above tries to find an alternative route. The general principle is to handle as much as possible before giving the problem to the layer above.

Self-configuration is simply looking around to find out what is there. A good example is PC "plug and play." JINI from SunSoft is a new technology in this area that holds promise. The interface to JINI is through the Java Virtual machine. The client uses JINI to search for a service (for instance, a color printer). The server then loads a small chunk of JAVA code in the client that provides the interface to the service (in our example, a device driver for the printer).

Automatic version control is, if you will, self-reconfiguration. It is about handling change to the configuration. A good example is Web documents. If a Web page has changed on the server, the browser will automatically load the new version. Using Web software instead of traditional workstation programs has led to a great reduction in management effort.

Self-management will become more and more important for two reasons:

1. Administrative costs are much less.

2. The configuration will change so rapidly in the future, it will need a computer to keep up with it.

The Web has encouraged a lot of thinking in this area and I believe we will see radical change in the direction of self-management in the next ten years.

At the moment the loose cooperative approach is far from replacing centralized management and probably never will entirely. However, as systems become more complex, it will become more and more important to handle as much as possible locally.

9.2 Security technology

Security is a hot topic, thanks to the Internet. Most of the press about security is either about hacking or about the government meddling in encryption standards. It is ironic that one half of the public discussion is about our inability to create secure systems—viruses and hacking—and the other half is about our ability to build such secure systems the government feels they can't snoop on us like they want to.

Security is largely about authentication, access control, and protection. Authentication is about identifying people and other users. Access control—commonly called authorization—is about giving users the authority to use a resource in a specified way. Resources can be big things—servers or databases for instance—or small things—transactions, database commands, or attributes in selected rows of selected tables in a specific database. Protection is about stopping unauthorized access to resources. Protection is my term; security experts split it into confidentiality (protection against disclosure), integrity (protection against tampering), and non-repudiation (protection against fraud). There is also protection against denial of service and physical protection to stop undesirables walking up to the computer, and so on. I have lumped these all together because this is meant to be a short book.

The technology discussions in this book are in the area of servers, middleware, and application development. I am going to assume that servers are in secure locations and are controlled securely. In other words, I assume that when we use the system software to give some people access rights and others none, the people (or viruses) can't circumvent the security by using holes in the operating system or utilities. This is a lot to sweep under the carpet and my excuse is that I've only given myself part of one chapter on this topic.

The traditional way of doing authentication is by usercode and password. Looking after your passwords is your responsibility. There are various ways of strengthening passwords protection, such as:

- Insisting the passwords are longer than eight characters.
- Insisting the password has a mix of characters and digits.
- Allowing no log-on attempts after three failures.
- Enforcing password changes every month.

The trouble with all these techniques is illustrated by me. At last count, I had ten passwords I am meant to remember. I have a standard format of characters and digits and increment the number by one every month. In spite of that, some systems need their passwords changed every month and some do not, so I've usually no idea where I have got to with the number. Many passwords have a different format so I can't use one format for all. Of course I write them all down. Some of the passwords are stored in Web cookies so you don't have to log on again. This is great for me, but if anyone steals my portable they would get these passwords. I suspect I am one of the more security conscious. There was a study of students choosing a password for their summer semester recently in which a huge proportion of the students chose the word "summer" for their password. Password security is going to deter the casual visitor but is unlikely to prevent a concerted attack.

A better form of authentication is to use special hardware assistance like smart cards or fingerprint readers. This is more user friendly, since the user does not have to remember a long list of passwords, and much more secure, since the passwords aren't written down. Furthermore, the passwords can now be long and random, and impossible to guess. The disadvantage is cost.

With the coming of the Internet another problem raised its ugly head. How do we identify the server? How do we know that *www.mylocalstore.com* is my local store rather than some impostor? The answer they have come up with is certificates. Certificates are most commonly seen when you start a Java Applet or possibly when you start an SSL session. (SSL is discussed below). The certificate has some text saying the server is what it says it is, and some information about both the server and the certificate issuer. There is also a button that if pressed will check the certificate with the certificate issuer. This can be done securely because the certificate contains a hash value that only the certificate issuer can check for validity. This of course hasn't actually solved the problem but only moved it. How do you trust the certificate issuer? The proposed answer is Public Key Infrastructure (PKI), a network of trust relationships where different certificate authorities approve of each other. As I write, this area is embroiled in controversy, which hopefully will be resolved in the near future. But within your organization you can still go ahead and build your own certificate system, for instance, by using the X.509 certificate standard, which is supported by many directory services packages.

All these authentication techniques are only good so long as the actual messages themselves are not being read. Someone sitting with a network monitor on the same LAN will see your password. If they are sufficiently expert they can spoof your dialog, sending messages as if they were from you. The solution to this problem is encryption.

Encryption is called weak or strong depending on how easy it is to break. What is strong today will be weak tomorrow as hardware gets more powerful. The strength of the encryption depends largely on the size of the key. However, even weak (for example, 40-bit encryption) takes a concerted effort to break unless you happen to have specialized encryption breaking hardware so you must really want to break the message to even bother trying. Weak encryption is enough to prevent causal snooping but not the professional spy.

There are two forms of encryption—asymmetrical (or public key) and symmetrical (or private key).

Asymmetric encryption uses a different key to encrypt than to decrypt. The great advantage of asymmetric encryption is that you can publish your key and anyone can send you secret messages. The disadvantage is that asymmetric algorithms are slow. The best known asymmetric algorithm is probably RSA.

Symmetric encryption uses the same key to encrypt and decrypt the message. Symmetric encryption is fast. The most widely used symmetric encryption algorithm is probably DES.

Cryptography is not only used for encryption. It can also be used for digital signatures. Digital signatures use asymmetric encryption, the private key to create the signature, and the public key to check it. The total message is hashed before the encryption is done, which ensures that the signature not only links the signature with a person but also ensures that the document contents are the same as when the signature was created. Clever, isn't it?

To illustrate how symmetric and asymmetric encryption can work, consider Secure Sockets Layer (SSL). SSL was originally designed by Netscape to allow any user to send secure messages over the Internet, for instance, to send credit card details. It is now being standardized by IETF (the Internet standardization body) who have developed the standard further under the name of TLS (Transport Layer Security). SSL allows you to send and receive messages over a TCP/IP session. You can tell a Web session is using SSL rather than normal sockets because the address will start by the letters "https:" rather than the normal "http:." Since the interface to SSL for the programmer is more or less the same as standard sockets, it is easy to implement on any product using TCP/IP sessions.

SSL uses asymmetric encryption when the session opens. The client asks the server for its public key. From this it generates a further key and sends this to the server, using the server's public key to encrypt the message. Both sides now generate an identical key that is used for symmetrical encryption for the rest of the session. Thus, while the start of the session is considerably longer than a simple TCP/IP session, the data flow thereafter is nearly the same.

Note that SSL does not have any password criteria. It does, however, optionally support certificates for both the server and for the client. In the credit card number transfer over the Web, the server may supply a certification but the client probably wouldn't. If you were using SSL as a secure connection to an existing application you may want to open an SSL session and then have a usercode/password dialogue to complete the log on.

A more comprehensive security scheme is Kerberos. In Kerberos, attached to every message is a ticket that identifies the user and gives them the authority to use the service. Acquiring the ticket is a two-step process:

1. Log on to the Key Distribution Center (KDC) using a usercode and password to get a Ticket Granting Ticket (TGT).

2. Use the TGT to get a ticket for a particular service.

This two-step process gives you a single sign-on facility because with one TGT you can get any number of service tickets. To avoid someone hanging on to a ticket indefinitely, all tickets expire and the user must log on again.

In Kerberos the KDC must be completely secure as it contains all the keys. The KDC is a potential bottleneck, especially over a WAN, though it can be duplicated.

As an aside, an interesting aspect of Kerberos is that it does not require a session. (It was designed for a Unix environment with a lot of UDP traffic; for instance, to NFS file servers.)

While Kerberos is more functional than SSL, it cannot support a secure dialogue with a completely new user, unknown to the KDC, and therefore cannot support a credit card payment over the Web from any person on the Web. Kerberos performance is excellent because it uses symmetrical encryption throughout. A downside is that for an application to use Kerberos, both the client and the server program must be programmatically modified (unless the Kerberos code is hidden by the middleware).

In the future, I expect many organizations will use both SSL and Kerberos. The likely scenario is SSL over the Web and Kerberos in-house.

Kerberos and SSL address the issue of authentication and network privacy but not of access control. In other words, neither answers the question of what to do within the server and within the applications.

Access control is about giving the users access to resources. There are three kinds of server security: access to the service, access to the operations, and access to the data. Kerberos provides security at the level of access to the service but it is up to the service to provide more fine-grained access control, in other words, access to the operations and data.

Managing security on an individual basis is too cumbersome for large systems: what you typically find is that there is a group of people to whom you want to give the same access rights. For instance, most clerical staff in a bank would need one set of privileges and the branch manager would need some additional privileges. Exactly how this is done ranges enormously between different server products. At one extreme, you can use tricks at the user interface. For instance, instead of defining the rights for every user one at a time, you might be allowed to define a security profile and, when putting in the security definition for a new user, you pick up an existing profile and then retype any fields that you want to change. This is great until you have to change something for a large number of users, in which case, you have to make all the changes to all affected users one by one. A better solution is role security. Every user is assigned a role and all users that have the same role have exactly the same privileges. Now if you need to change the security rights you just change the access right of the role. But what if you want individual users to have security like a particular role but with a few changes? Of course you could just define a different role, but other schemes are possible—for instance, allow users to have multiple roles. (This is often done informally by one person knowing two usercodes, and logging onto both.)

An alternative to role security is hierarchical security. Here a user may be given the right to pass on their security privileges to other dependent users. Also if you reduce the access rights of a user, you automatically reduce the access rights of any dependents in the same manner. This solves the user security management problem by devolving it. Unfortunately, there are some problems with hierarchical privilege control, in particular:

- If the master or lesser master leaves, the privilege structure must be unraveled and redone.
- A single user frequently needs several lesser masters to give them all the privileges they need to get the job done.

Role-based security is typical of transaction servers. Hierarchical security is typical of database security and is included in the SQL standard.

Transaction security checking is largely about figuring out whether the client is allowed to do an operation. Database security must consider not only the operation—retrieve, update, insert, delete, schema change, and security commands— but also the data. You may need to restrict access to selected fields in selected rows of selected tables. This is normally done by defining an SQL view, and allowing users access to the view but not to the underlying table.

In theory, database integrity is a function of the database system. In practice, a major part of the database integrity is actually enforced through the transaction logic. For instance, in a bank, the account total should be a summation of all debit and credit record amounts, but this major integrity constraint is not enforced by a database validity check (for example, by the SQL CHECK statement). It is "enforced" by the transaction programs being written correctly. It is usually unsafe to give update access to the database directly; you need to force people to use the transaction update logic. Thus users with access to the transaction server may not have direct access to the database. The two groups of people with direct database access right are typically:

- The database administrator, who has rights to control the database
- Those people who need ad-hoc query rights to the database

Likewise, someone with privileges to read or write the database system directly may have no explicit access rights on the file system that stores the database system files.

What we are seeing is that security is layered; the three layers in this case being the transaction server, the database, and the file system. The fact that a user may have access rights at a particular layer does not imply any rights to the layer beneath it. Also, to the layer beneath, the whole service looks like a single user— it does not see the service's users.

In highly secure systems there may be another dimension to data security, which is the computer equivalent of marking files confidential, secret, top secret, for your eyes only, or whatever. This is done by adding a security field on the data object (hopefully the data object is a reasonably large chunk of data, otherwise the system is impossible to manage). In theory you could replicate the whole paraphernalia of lists of roles and corresponding privileges for each data unit. In practice they would normally have a simple security rating (for example, 0, everyone can see it, to 9, only the boss can read it). A person's access rights on a table is then qualified by the maximum security rating associated with that operation. For instance, a person may have a read right of 3, which means that he or she can read any object with a security level of 3 or below. An interesting point is that in these secure systems, you are assigned a higher write security level than a read security level. It is logical (but it always makes me imagine the text disappearing as I write it).

For really secure systems there are specialized operating systems and specialized database systems. It is easy to get carried away thinking about more and more arcane security requirements, but the key point is to balance the requirements against the threats and the cost.

So how do we manage security when we have a distributed system where several frontend programs call several different backend services, each with their own discrete security management system? Today, you are largely on your own. While, for instance, Kerberos provide a uniform usercode management system it is up to the security administrator of each individual service to assign access rights to each user within the context of the service. Very few organizations could quickly tell you what privileges have been assigned to a particular user across the enterprise.

If a service detects a security error, obviously it should report it. In a seriously secure system it is important that any breach is not only reported but logged. Again today this is done on an individual service basis. For instance, it is hard to get a total enterprise view of whether some individual is probing the security of many systems.

In theory, there are no technological reasons why there should not be system-wide security control and logging. In practice, the vastly different security systems used by the different applications make centralized control of security hard. But if it were available, would many organizations use it? Security is ultimately in the hands of the department that owns the application. It is for them to define the roles and the people who fulfill those roles, not a centralized security organization. Any centralized security management function should be viewed as a service organization that implements the departmental and enterprise-wide security policies. It should win support through efficiency and cooperation, not through central dictate.

A final point: In practice hardly any of the major security violations are through using sophisticated techniques breaking the encryption code. Many IT systems are like a house with a locked front door but with a side window open. Above all, you need a conscientious security administrator.

9.3   Building application security

While today's organizations have many silo applications, I am promoting the notion of an integrated application architecture. This is illustrated (again) in Figure 9-2, this time extended to include other services as well as transaction services.

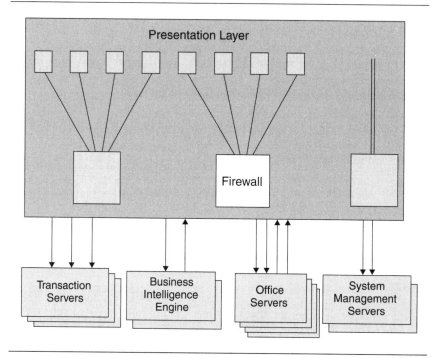

Figure 9-2 The presentation layer and servers

The basic model of security in this architecture is as follows.

As noted before, authentication must be done in the presentation layer because authenticating, say, a phone user is totally different from authenticating a Web user. The presentation layer is usually session-based: The user logs on, accesses one or more services, and logs off.

The presentation layer should offer to the users only those services that the user is allowed to use. After log on, the presentation layer associates a list of services with the user. In many circumstances, the presentation layer displays the list for the user to select which service they want to use.

Furthermore, each service should only use the transactions it needs and no more. For instance, a supervisor may be allowed to do more operations than a clerk. This can be implemented by role security; the clerk and the supervisor have different roles. If there is no system-provided role security, the role identifier can be included in a parameter in the service call and the access right checks done programmatically.

Finally, selective visibility to the backend data may be required. For instance, in a private bank only managers may be allowed to access certain accounts. This is much more likely to require programmatic support. The user identifier and the role identifier can be added to every message, and the program code selects data as appropriate.

There is a case for putting the user and role identifier in every message irrespective of whether the middleware supports all the security features you need. First, your needs might change. Security provided by the middleware usually assumes the user is directly connected to the middleware. But if the user is indirectly connected to the middleware, for instance, the users are attached through a Web server, it may be that it is only the Web server itself that the middleware recognizes as a single user.

(As an aside, this is another example of security layers. Many users might use a function in one layer, but to the layer beneath they all get merged together as if they were a single user. This is all very well when the function is a database system and the layer beneath is a file system, but not so good when the function is a presentation layer server and the layer beneath a transaction server. This is why you might need to propagate user information programmatically.)

The second reason for putting the user and role identifier in every message is to report errors accurately. When a security error is logged, the one item of information you will always want is the user identifier.

The good news in all of this is that since so much security is generic to different applications, there is ample scope for reusing components for security checking and for security error logging.

This is the basic model. To examine it in more detail let us consider three topics: circumventing security, handling internal violation, and integration with existing systems.

9.3.1   Circumventing security

The first obvious concern with this basic model is the question of whether security can be circumvented. There are a number of possible security weaknesses that should be examined, for instance:

- Using another program on the workstation or server that implements the presentation layer code.
- Breaking into the network between the presentation layer program and the backend server.
- Replacing the presentation layer program by a modified version.

I don't guarantee that this is a complete list, for we are now touching on the subject of network security and platform security, which is beyond the scope of this book. But a few general points can be made.

I think most people would agree with me that having a presentation layer program running on a workstation opens up many more vulnerabilities than having the presentation layer on a Web server. Figure 9-2 suggests that it is sufficient to have a firewall between workstations in the presentation layer and the backend network. Even with a firewall, a great deal of authentication must be handled by the backend server. The traditional solution would be to put all the authentication back into the back end. (Arguably all the presentation layer servers, like the Web server, should start their dialogue with the backend server by authenticating themselves. It would be possible in theory for the back end to check the access rights of the presentation layer on every operation as well as the access rights of the user.) An alternative approach would be to force all the workstation traffic through an intermediate server that, even if it does nothing else, handles security. This can provide application specific security control—an application firewall if you will.

A second point concerns the network. A typical network configuration in a large organization is illustrated in Figure 9-3.

Some explanatory comments on Figure 9-3:

- The data center could be reduced to one machine.
- Legacynet is a term for old networks.
- Other kinds of networks can be added at will.

The original point of this diagram was to show how to integrate multiple networks, but it provides an excellent backdrop for our security discussions.

The data center network is typically both high speed and secure. The number of nodes on this network is small. Malicious eavesdropping is difficult; first, because the network is mostly laid in the data center and, second, because it could

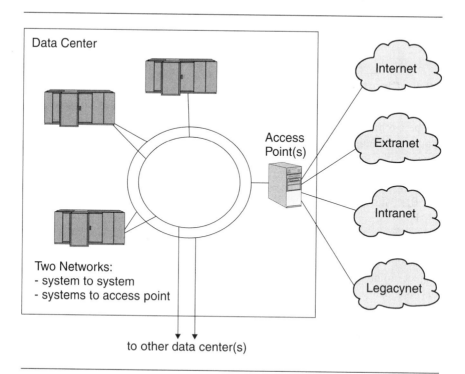

Figure 9-3 Network configuration

be a fiber network—ATM or FDDI. The link between the secure data center network and the insecure outer networks is through one or more access points.

The access point could be a firewall. This ensures messages coming into the data center are from a restricted list of machines and use a restricted list of protocols. If you are confident of the security of the presentation-layer server, you could put it directly on the data center network.

Can more be done to prevent circumventing presentation-layer security? One thought is to use Kerberos for all access to the transaction server.

9.3.2   Handling internal security violations

While circumvention is largely about stopping the outside enemy gaining access, what about the enemy within?

If you look at other examples of where organizations try to prevent internal corruption you will see three techniques used.

1. Have two or more people give permission for something to be done. For instance, have two people sign a large check.

2. Build fast detection systems for anything suspicious.

3. Assume violation is possible and build in recovery procedures.

You can do the same for very secure parts of your system. For instance, very secure operations can be logged and messages sent to the security administrator. Applications can be changed so security vital operations are done in two steps; one step to initiate the operation and another to "sign it off." Special care can be taken to recover sensitive data. Access to sensitive data can be monitored and reports sent to a supervisor.

Most of these techniques must be designed into the application. Security is a design issue, first in regard to identifying to the implementers which parts of the system have special security requirements and, second, to design the checks and balances described above.

9.3.3   Existing applications

Existing applications may not have this security infrastructure in place. For an existing online transaction processing system it is usually possible to "wrap" them with some code that can provide the security we want. This is described in more detail in Chapter 13.

There will be occasions when this will be hard, for instance, if the existing application has been bought from a vendor who won't let you touch the code. The worst case is probably when the security system is based on network addresses. You might be forced to build a gateway application that maps the security system described above to a bunch of sockets emulating terminals.

9.4 Application support for systems management and security

The reason why I put security and systems management together in a single chapter is that (besides making the book shorter—which I'm sure you agree is welcome) much of what is good for security is good for systems management.

One of the problems with much of existing systems management is that it manages the layers horizontally rather than vertically. This is illustrated in Figure 9-4.

Today, systems management is largely about monitoring changes in the state of the individual components. This is what I mean by horizontal management. But for some functions we must manage the flow in and out from user to database and back. Security is one example of this and the technique described earlier was to put the user identifier and the role identifier in each message.

Performance monitoring, which I discussed at the end of Chapter 8, has a similar vertical management requirement. To get a complete picture of performance, we need to know the performance of every step in the message flow. We could put all the message performance measurements actually into the message. Alternatively, we could put a unique message identifier (for example, user identifier plus a sequence number) in each message so that performance logs from different servers can be pulled together to trace the performance of individual messages.

A third example is fault detection. If there is an error detected somewhere, one of the problems today is knowing who was the end user and what was the input message when the error happened (and maybe was the cause). A good input logging system, together with the user identifier in the message tells you this information.

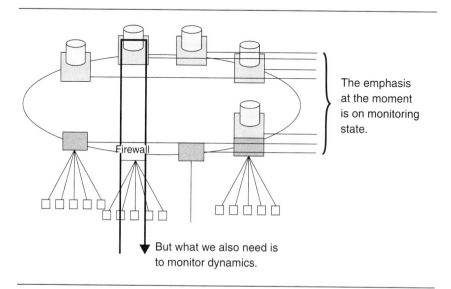

The emphasis at the moment is on monitoring state.

But what we also need is to monitor dynamics.

Figure 9-4   Vertical systems management

In short, logging is a general requirement. The log should always include

- User identifier
- Role identifier
- Message identifier
- Timestamp
- Error code

And often the input message data as well, unless that can be retrieved from a separate log using the message identifier.

Ideally, error information should be reported as soon as it is detected. You should also ensure that errors are reported only once to avoid flooding the system with error messages. A general point about logs is to keep them as small as possible.

Besides logs the other aspect of vertical management is monitoring the system, in other words, implementing continuous health checks on performance and functionality.

So how do we write vertical health check routines? The simplest way is to extend the end user application, for instance, if it is a Web application, create Web pages that return versions information or gather simple performance data like the elapse time of the last five transactions. Over time many of these quick probes will be developed. (I know one organization that, at the time of writing, employs some people to send transactions to the system every 15 minutes and time them with a stopwatch. I was told they found it very useful and were planning to employ more.)

I mentioned earlier the notion that system software was moving from centralized management to self-management, or more precisely, enhancing centralized management by self-management. The same is true of application programming. Most applications today are in the pre-centralized management phase, the "silo" management phase if you will, since every component has its own unique management interface. We would like to move from there to a consistent, distributed management system and all this discussion about logging as message formats is taking us in that direction by imposing an order and structure to aspects of systems management. But can we go a step further toward self-management?

As noted already, self-management is largely about self-recovery, self-configuration, and automatic version control. Self-recovery should always be an aim. The first rule is that programs should not stop unless they have to. For instance, if the database gets an IO error the database has a problem (maybe a localized, even a temporary problem) but the program is still running just fine so why should it stop? The program should report the error, reject that transaction and wait for the next transaction. It is up to the system administrator to panic (calmly, of course). More sophisticated self-recovery could be an automatic switch to the backup server.

Self-configuration is often already done to a limited extent by using the directory for configuration information. There is a progression from fast, hard-coded systems to slower, self-discovery systems that look like this:

- Configuration hard-coded in the program code.
- Configuration contained in a file read on program initialization.
- Configuration stored in a file or database but can be changed online (that is, any database changes and program internal table changes are made in sync).
- Configuration worked out at runtime by self-discovery.
- Reconfiguration initiated when configuration errors are detected.

As more and more systems become involved it becomes more and more important to move down this list. There are two reasons. First, the burden of managing many systems is greater than managing a few. Second, as systems become more integrated, the requirement to keep certain information in sync becomes stronger. Examples include user names, role identifiers, and server domain names, all of which may need to be known to many systems in the network. The ideal solution is for common configuration data to be managed centrally, perhaps by using directory services and for the application to retrieve the information at runtime. Most major middleware products can be integrated with directory services and this should be done. Even application shared data, like exchange rate tables, can be either held in a directory or held in a file that is found by looking up the file location in a directory.

But, if the application is meant to be running 365 days a year, 24 hours a day, there also needs to be a process to tell applications to refresh their local copies of the data and to do any appropriate reconfiguration. There are various ways of doing this. Giving applications an SNMP agent is one choice. Having a message queue for systems messages is another.

There needs to be a database, perhaps a repository, perhaps a configuration management tool, for holding the central configuration information. This would allow you to hold multiple versions of the configuration, to record the relationships between the different elements of the configuration, and (in theory) to control rolling forward and rolling back of configuration changes.

9.5   Conclusions

There are some important conclusions from the last three chapters on resiliency, performance, systems management, and security.

You have to be prepared to put code into your applications for handling multiple versions, security, error logging, performance monitoring, and error recovery, including switching to backup. This is a major reason why the notion that you can press a button on your design model and a fully working system will spring to life is premature.

A second important conclusion is that not only do technical design decisions impact these areas but so also do application design decisions. This is partly because the implementation designer needs to know in detail the precise performance, resiliency, and security requirements. There are trade-offs everywhere. For instance, as noted earlier in this chapter, for highly sensitive operations it is good to have a log of all operations on the object, but this would clearly be impractical on all operations.

A final conclusion is that there are real opportunities for code reuse especially in the areas of logging and error reporting.

These opportunities should be grasped. There often seems to be a rather cruel 80:20 rule that applies to programming that goes along the lines that 80 percent of the functionality is implemented in 20 percent of the time. A good part of the additional 80 percent of the time goes into implementing infrastructure code for performance monitoring, resiliency, systems management, and security.

The upside of implementing comprehensive infrastructure code is that, if you attack it early, it enormously aids testing and debugging new application development.

10

Implementation
Design and Components

This chapter is a linking chapter, linking the design discussions in the following chapters to the technology discussions in the previous chapters. The meeting point is the implementation design.

This chapter is about two subjects. The first is design in general, to provide a context for the discussion in the rest of the book. The second is implementation design in particular, since this is the part of design that most changes when looking at large integrated applications. The approach on implementation design is component-based. I am also assuming a green field application. How to handle existing applications is a subject for later chapters.

I am not going to discuss design in detail; I am going to make the assumption that you, or a person in your organization, understands design to the extent that you can build a successful "silo" application. The question I want to focus on is: What needs to change when you come to design a large integrated application rather than a small or medium sized standalone application?

10.1   Some general comments on design

In Chapter 1, I said that building an IT system can be broken down into business process change definition, applications functional design, implementation design, implementation, and deployment. A quick sketch of what is in these tasks is as follows:

- Business process change definition. This builds the business process model and indicates the desired change. The change could be nonfunctional requirements. (Nonfunctional requirements are requests for better performance, resilience, etc.)

- Application functional design. This builds the object model, designs the user interface and identifies the data storage requirements. Clearly the application functional design must be closely coordinated with the business process change. You could cut these two tasks a different way into high-level analysis and detailed analysis. High-level analysis is broadly the senior management demand for change, while the detailed functional specification is the proposed change as seen by the workers.

- Implementation design. This must include choosing the runtime and development technology, deciding on software tiers, defining components, and deciding which functionality is implemented by which components. Within this phase there needs to be a decision on whether to buy components from outside, to reuse existing components, or to build new components from scratch.

- Implementation. This breaks down into coding and testing.

- Deployment. This should include software installation, parallel running, data migration, and training.

To these tasks we should add two more:

- Understand the context. This is the first task. It includes understanding the business context, the existing relevant IT systems, the resources, and the skills.

- Project management.

Different design approaches split the tasks differently. Application functional design is often called analysis and design. Documentation could be split out into a separate task rather than assuming, as I have, that every task includes a documentation subtask. Data migration could also be moved into a separate task. Detailed program design (in contrast to the overall implementation design) could be moved into a separate task. Testing could be bundled in with coding. Implementation design could be split into software architecture design (dividing out the functionality among program elements) and technology architecture design (choice of technology, infrastructure design). In other words, there is not a hard and fast, commonly accepted classification. Furthermore, the word "task" is not used by everybody; the Rational Unified Process from Rational Software uses the word "workflow" and Unisys in its QuadCycle process for electronic business development, uses the word "discipline."

I personally think that, while the variation of names is confusing, the fact that different projects have a different task structure is good, not bad. In different projects the relative size of each task will vary enormously, hence a good task structure for one project is not necessarily a good one for another project. For instance, a project to change key business processes will have a very different task structure from a project to provide better management information. What every project manager needs is a checklist of candidate tasks and some sort of classification to help them find their way through the list.

These tasks can to some extent be done in parallel. Furthermore, working implementations can be produced long before the final version is available. Most authorities suggest that a big application should be built iteratively on a core implementation rather than do all the design at the beginning and all the testing at the end—the old fashioned "waterfall" model of application development. Most of the tasks listed above are done for each iteration.

To capture and enforce the notion of iterative development, modern design processes have taken to defining phases that are independent from tasks. QuadCycle has phases called Requirements, Architecture, Construction, and Deployment. The Rational Unified Process has phases called Inception, Elaboration, Construction, and Transition. Each of these phases can create implementations though the focus of the implementations change. In the first phase the purpose of the implementation is to confirm and elicit requirements. In the last phase the purpose is the final solution. This is illustrated in Figure 10-1.

Implementations from the early phases are essentially prototypes. There is no hard and fast rule on whether the prototype is going to be thrown away or whether it will evolve into an early implementation of the final system. If the project is a high performance transaction processing system, prototyping is probably best used only for eliciting requirements, to improve the user interface, or perhaps

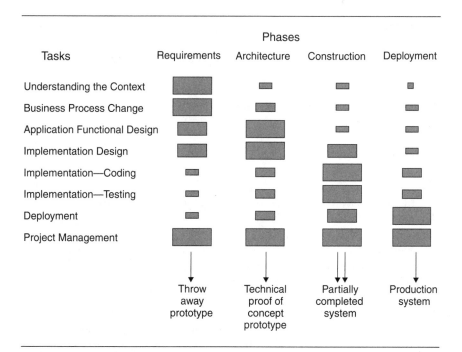

Figure 10-1   Tasks and phases

to prove a technology works. If the project is about displaying management information, then elements of the prototype might be in the final production system.

Designers, programmers, and project managers are all important in delivering a successful project. But just as important is a function called program management. Program management is about blending the IT development with the non-IT projects (for example, training, new business process design) needed to deliver successful business change. When IT application development was about automating existing clerical tasks, program management was not so important because everybody knew what needed to be done. But the more IT application development is about doing business in a different way, the more program management is key. For instance, a new Web-based ordering system will change the life for many people in the organization. It must meet the requirements of a new class of user, and must be properly integrated with backend systems, both IT systems and non-IT systems. The program manager's job is to ensure that all parts of the Web project come together. In any major project, there will not only be resistance to change but also justifiable criticism. Issues will be raised that must be fixed and fixed fast. The program manager's job is to identify early improvements and fixes. The program manager has ultimate authority on the project's priorities and business requirements definition.

All of the above applies to virtually any IT project. (The word "virtually" in the preceding sentence is in there because I can't think of any exceptions but I've been around long enough to know that that does not necessarily mean there aren't any.) Of course, if the project is to write a compiler, what constitutes an appropriate business strategy and functional specification is different from writing a banking application.

If you look at a selection of the design methods over the years, you will see that they have attacked the problem of design from one of three angles:

- User requirements
- Data structures
- Functions or processes

Methods that are strongly user-based start off by looking at the user interface. An example is Rapid Application Development (RAD), which is essentially about continual prototype refinement.

Methods that are strongly data structure oriented start off by analyzing the data content. An example is relational normalization, and years ago one way of starting the design was to take a paper form, turn it into an equivalent data structure, and normalize it. The origin of the modern approach to design was object-oriented analysis and design, which is a data structured approach.

Methods that are function-based or process-based start by asking what the business is doing (see Function vs. Process box for the difference between functions and processes).

Function vs. Process

The distinction between function and process is a subtle one but important for designers. Functions are about what happens—in other words, the end result. Processes are about how it works. There is a hierarchy; you can take a function and describe the process that implements the function. But the process description will be an interacting set of functions. You can then take each of these more detailed functions and describe the process that implements them. This is illustrated in Figure 10-2.

However, you can make a functional hierarchical decomposition that bears no resemblance to the process structure. In fact this is exactly what most organizations do—it's called an organizational chart.

Many design approaches in the past have taken a strongly functional view. Data flow diagrams are about functional composition not process decomposition (not many people know that) because they show only how information flows between the functions not the flow of work, that is, the order things are done to achieve an end result. People who like a functional view say "Tell me what needs to be done and I'll figure out how to do it." But the problems with straight functional decomposition are:

* It can be very hard to understand. You often can't understand why something is a sub-function unless you can see the process.

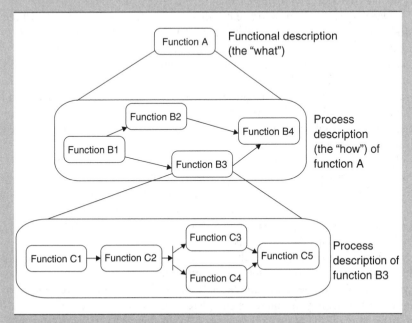

Figure 10-2   Functions and processes

(continued)

Function vs. Process   (*cont.*)

- Functional decomposition can easily lie. It is very easy to leave something out or add something extraneous.
- The functional decomposition can easily bear little relationship to what actually happens because there are so many alternative ways of doing something.

The conclusion is that you must see both function and process.

While in the past there have been methodologies that have taken one angle of attack to the exclusion of others, most experts these days would agree that you have to have a balance between all three.

The key characteristic of modern development processes for commercial applications is that they are model-based. Put simply this means, the business and implementation designs are represented by a series of diagrammatic views on a model. The model should not have any old diagrams. The diagrams must have precision—every element in the diagram must have precisely defined semantics. The purpose of the model is communication; the model should be used to convey information from designer to implementer, from designer to users and management, and from designer to designer.

One very welcome development is that there is strong support for the Unified Modeling Language (UML), which means that most people these days are drawing the same kind of diagrams. Thus in UML there are Use Case Diagrams, Class Diagrams, Sequence Diagrams, Activity Diagrams, Component Diagrams, and so on. The ideal is to be able to see the same model, switching between different diagrams, and zooming in from a high-level view to a more detailed view of the same diagram. The goal of modern design environments is not only to provide diagrammatic drawing tools, but also to keep the diagrams in sync—in other words, to ensure it really does show different aspects of the same model. Underpinning the tools is a repository. Put simply, a repository is a database for development tools that makes it possible for the tools to share data. The repository by necessity provides additional generic cross-tool facilities like version control, configuration management, object-level security, and so on. Most repositories are specific to the tool vendor but there are a few repositories in the marketplace, most notably UREP, that are general purpose repositories.

It is only possible for different diagrams to make sense of different views of the same reality if there are elements common to all of them. Imagine you have two photographs of the same valley seen from two different angles. It is much easier to reconstruct in your mind the complete valley if you see the same feature in both, for instance the same farm house or the same landmark. It is the same with a model; you will never be able to form a mental image of the model from multiple diagrams unless you can see that thing A in one diagram is the same as thing A in another diagram, in spite of being drawn in a completely different way.

The "things" that are in common in most diagrams are objects. These are "business objects" and not to be confused with implementation objects like program objects or workstation GUI objects. Business objects may be solid things—machinery or people—or they may be things that, in years gone by, were represented by pieces of paper and now are represented by records in a computer—for instance, accounts or orders. In all cases, they are things meaningful to the business.

So: how good are modern design processes? And how well do they work for large integrated applications?

These are hard questions to answer. In fact, I think it is fair to say that nobody really knows. One reason for this uncertainty is that there are a number of factors that are so important for a successful project that everything else is put in the shade; in particular:

- There must be strong project management.
- There must be strong business leadership. Business does not necessarily speak with a single voice and factions may set out deliberately to undermine the project—especially if jobs are on the line. Furthermore business conditions will change.
- There must be a good implementation design. Besides delivering good technical characteristics (fast, secure, etc.), a good implementation design makes it easier to change functionality, so design errors can be more easily rectified.

The main alternatives to a modeling approach are:

- Write the requirements and functional specification in English, not in diagrams.
- Use a rapid application development method, showing early versions of the application to the end users and changing it according to new requirements.

Both these approaches work for small applications. Sometimes they work for big applications, and sometimes a modeling approach fails for big applications. But large functional specifications written in English are usually unintelligible. People think in pictures and they do modeling in their heads—visualizing what the system looks like—even if they don't communicate their models well to other people. Some diagrams are essential, and using diagrammatic techniques that everyone understands is far preferable to inventing your own. Rapid Application development, on the other hand, is good for designing screen layouts but useless at anything else. For example, if the application is about changing a complex business process, trying to unravel the essence of the proposed new process from a bunch of screen layouts is almost impossible. Much of what has gone wrong with Web projects has been the integration with the backend systems, and Rapid Application development provides little to help you address this issue. A modeling approach to design is here to stay.

10.2   Implementation design

Moving from application functional design to implementation needs an intermediate step—implementation design. Implementation design consists of at least the
following:

- Deciding on the development and runtime technology to use.
- Designing the layered structure—that is, deciding how to spread the func-
  tionality over the layers.
- Identifying the major runtime objects in the implementation.
- Deciding how to group objects into components.
- Defining the component interfaces.
- Designing the common system management and security components and/or
  routines.
- Identifying reuse opportunities.

Going from detailed functional design to implementation design is not a
one way street. It is only during the implementation design stage that you can really
understand the performance and systems resiliency aspects of the system (or put
another way, the possible cost of the implementation). Also reusing components
may make you reconsider aspects of the functional design. This is a small-scale
version of the phenomenon you see when implementing an application package in
which the organization is forced to change its business processes to fit the package.

We have discussed technology a good deal in the previous chapters and the
primary conclusion is that there is no right answer for everyone. Besides which,
technology is changing rapidly; any right answer now may be the wrong answer in
the near future. Thus, where possible we should try and keep our technology
options open. For the rest of this chapter, however, we will assume that we will be
designing applications that are based on components and using object interfaces.
In concrete terms, this discussion will be relevant for designs based on COM or
Java or a combination of the two. In practice, of course, there will be existing
applications, which are discussed in later chapters.

Let us start with the layers. In Chapter 6 I discussed a two-layer architecture—a presentation layer and backend transaction or data intelligence engines
(see Figure 6-5). In this chapter I take this down a level of detail and discuss layering of components. I will start with the user interface.

10.2.1   The presentation layer

User interface components must be organized around the user interface structure,
one component per Web page for instance. There is a dilemma here. On the one
hand, if you use a facility like Java Servlets, which is essentially a programming

tool, you can easily build some code that is well structured for the business task in hand but that provides no support for building the screen formats. Building or modifying anything more than trivial Web pages is hard. On the other hand, if you use a tool such as Microsoft Active Server Pages or Java Server Pages, you can use a Web page editor to build your HTML. That is great for HTML, but reading anything more than trivial business logic in these tools is painful. It is the simple things that destroy readability, like indentation. People writing HTML indent it to show how visual bits are grouped into bigger bits. People writing programs indent it to show the program structure like loops and conditional statements. Now we have to put HTML and logic in one text file; indent according to the HTML and you can't read the program logic, indent according to the program logic and you can't read the HTML. Until this problem is solved it is best to split them. You should aim, if you can, to use a visual tool for building the visual interface and have one or a very few calls to the business logic component to collect the data. The implication is that for each screen there is one component for formatting (or ASP/JSP page or equivalent) and one for the business logic. Similar arguments apply for other interfaces like the script for an IVR (Interactive Voice Recognition) software package.

The next question is: What does that business logic component do? To answer that question we have to first address three crucial subjects: mapping business model objects to implementation objects, grouping objects into components, and reuse.

10.2.2   Mapping business objects to implementation objects

This is an area where the proponents of modern design methods do themselves no favors. In the literature you will see designs that describe traffic-light control systems alongside banking systems, and classes that implement an operation that displays "Hello World" alongside a class that implements an invoice or an order. I suspect the reason people mix up objects from so many different contexts is to emphasize their belief in the statement "Everything is an object." Well, yes, but once you decide that everything is an object, calling things objects no longer becomes interesting. What gets lost is the fundamental difference between different sorts of objects, and the most fundamental difference is the difference between objects in a business model and objects in an implementation.

While objects in a business model are things like "account," "customer," "invoice," "order," and "product," objects in an implementation model are:

- Program objects—chunks of memory (state) with associated processing routines (operations and methods).
- Database objects—chunks of data on disk, and maybe some processing routines.
- Interface objects—virtual objects implied by a middleware directory (I will explain this more below).

- Hardware objects—a lump of metal, plastic, and/or silicon.
- Display objects—things you can see on a screen or objects (like ActiveX controls) whose primary function is to create displayable output.

An object in a business model is likely to be represented by one or more database objects, one or more program objects, which may or may not be at the receiving end of an interface object, and maybe a display object.

Ah, do I hear someone say, but the whole point about object-orientation is that objects are natural and that they make this mapping easy? They do, up to a point. There are always some crucial differences, such as:

- Not all business objects are implemented. Parts of the business process may simply not be tracked in the application.
- Many implementation objects don't correspond directly to any business objects. The output from a database retrieval, objects for system management, and objects controlling a button on a screen are examples.
- Implementation objects frequently have a different lifetime. A program object dies when the program dies. A database may hold a record for a customer who no longer exists. Middleware such as CORBA provides a mechanism for storing long-lived object references using the Implementation Repository so you can have long-lived object references and actual implementation objects flicking into life and out again. (By way of a reminder, the Implementation Repository allows for object references to be converted into strings and converted back to object references for the lifetime of the object.)
- The class hierarchy for business objects and implementation objects may differ. An implementation object may belong to a class of debug-traceable objects which has some special code that writes to a log when the object is created or deleted. On the other side, super classes that have meaning in the business world may have no meaning in the implementation. For instance, in the business model, customers may be refined into business, people, and non-business organizations. The implementation may choose to ignore these subtleties; what is left of this analysis may be no more than a single field indicating the kind of customer.
- A class of business objects may be physically dispersed across multiple systems.
- A single business object may be replicated across many databases, possibly with a different format in each. Product data in an ordering processing system may be very different from product data in a manufacturing system.
- A business object may move from application system to application system. An object representing an insurance claim may be created in a local application and lose many of its fields when stored in the main database.

It is best to think of implementation objects as temporary proxies for business objects rather than business object implementations. In most cases, the state of the business object will be stored in a database, possibly dispersed among many tables. The proxies come into existence to provide a temporary business object look and feel to the data.

Put another way, the business objects disappear under the surface of the implementation and are hard to see. What you are left with, if you design the implementation carefully, are the interfaces to the business objects.

It is extremely important to understand the relationship between business objects and implementation objects and you should not always expect it to be a one-to-one relationship. It is only by understanding the relationship that is it possible to know what to change in the implementation when the business changes.

10.2.3   Grouping objects into components

One of the problems with using object-oriented class libraries for reuse is that you often find that a number of different objects go together. For instance, you find that the definition of a bank account class is hard to separate from the definition of a credit record class and debit record class. This means one class definition by itself is often not a self-contained unit suitable for reuse. One of the advantages that many authorities have seen in the component reuse model is that components can contain multiple objects, so objects that belong together can be implemented together.

(As an aside, if you read about transactional component middleware— COM+ and EJB—you will see that there is often an underlying assumption that one component equals one object. It does not have to be so, but programming is simpler if only one object is exposed to the client and all other objects are hidden within the implementation.)

But first, what is a component?

I am going to go with the following definition: A **component** is a program element (either compiled or interpreted) that can be "called," that is, it provides an interface. An **interface** is the definition of the operations that a client can invoke on the component. **Program elements** are executable files (possibly interpreted) that can be lifted from one context and run in another. Some points about these definitions should be made:

- Traditional programs aren't components because they can't be called. But programs can be lifted from one environment and used in another— programs are reusable. (Programs by my definition are program elements.)
- I have said nothing about threads, processes, and address spaces—in other words, nothing about how it actually runs in a computer.
- I have said nothing about whether the interface is object-oriented or not. Components without an object-oriented interface include Windows DLLs, RPC servers, and Cobol online transaction programs (which are called by the transaction monitor). The fact that components can be lifted from one context and used in another is much more important than the fact that the interface is an object interface.

My fundamental rationale for these definitions is that it makes a distinction between three kinds of things: the management and assembly of reusable things, specific concepts like object-orientation, and specific environments (like transaction component middleware). The definitions are not formal or rigorous but they will suffice. As I said before, no one controls computer definitions, so you are free to disagree.

I noted in the previous section that business objects were likely to end up as little more than interfaces. My definition of component, therefore, hints that they are implemented as components. As a general guideline that is a good, but there is more to it than that. There are several factors to take into account:

- Horizontal objects—ones that handle cross-application functions such as security and error reporting—should not be mixed with vertical objects— objects that implement business logic and are application specific.
- There should not be a large number of small components, otherwise application maintenance will be unmanageable.
- Components, where possible, should be split along business process boundaries.
- Business objects that are tightly coupled need to be in one component.
- Reusable routines should be put into components. It may be appropriate to group similar routines together into one or a few components rather than have one component per routine.

As you can see, there are no hard and fast rules; we rely on the designer's good judgment. But the fundamental point to keep in mind is change; the component is the lowest unit of change. Parts of the application that change often should be in their own component. Put another way, the faster the change the smaller the components.

I discuss in the next chapter the notion that the particular kind of business object best suited to be a separate component should be a business process tracking object. This aligns the object model with the business process model.

Finally, reuse should be considered. If a component already exists, take it.

10.2.4 Making reuse work

The computer industry has high expectations for components. The reason is that many people believe that we are on the verge of a revolution where component reuse will revolutionize software development.

The key idea in this thinking is that, setting design and project management aside, there are three basic roles in implementing a system.

1. The programmer who writes reusable components

2. The assembler who writes scripts that call the components

3. The administrator who writes the deployment descriptors and configures the production system

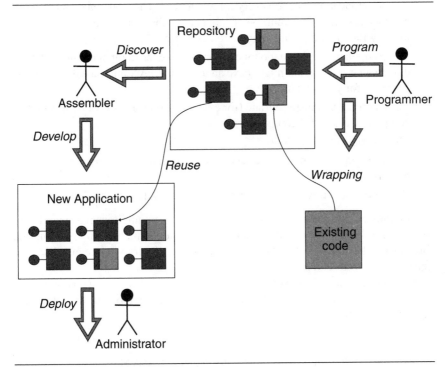

Figure 10-3   Serendipitous reuse

The model is illustrated in Figure 10-3.

The assembler creates the applications. The programmer writes the components and places them in the repository where the assembler can find them. The administrator sets up the new application in its runtime environment.

The difference between this thinking and earlier approaches is the split between component programmer and assembler, where previously they were combined into the single function of programmer. The logic behind the split is twofold:

- Ideally, the system can respond quickly to business change by changing the script or by modifying the deployment parameters.
- Components can be reused. Reusable components should be more battle-hardened (better tested, with better performance) than components used only once. Hopefully a market will develop for buying reusable components.

The fundamental question is: Is this model realistic? If so, is it always realistic or is it only realistic within a certain set of conditions?

Component reuse is often presented as identifying a functional gap and finding a component that implements the required functionality. I call this **serendipitous reuse**. But there are many reasons why the component may be unsuitable, for instance:

- The component may not do everything you need. The question then becomes whether you can live with the shortfall, change the component, or fill in the missing functionality with another component.
- The component might do too much. For instance the component might be doing some printing but might have an unwanted FAX interface that is inappropriate for your end users.
- The technology is inappropriate (for example, you want a Java Bean and the component is a COM component).
- The component is too slow.
- The component might not interface with your security or system management routines.
- The component might use a different database vendor's technology.

Finding an exact fit is hard. Therefore to make serendipitous reuse work you need a large library of well-documented components, many implementing the same or similar functionality. Given the size of the library you are also likely to need a specialized search tool.

In a large project it is even harder. In Figure 10-4 there are two applications illustrated. One is a simple application of script and component. The other is a more realistic complex application.

Simple configuration—serendipitous reuse is practical

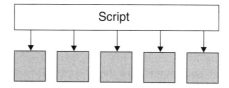

Larger, more realistic, configuration

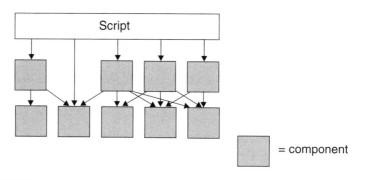

= component

Figure 10-4　Component dependencies

Whereas serendipitous reuse may be good for the simple application, it is unlikely to be effective for the complex application because components use other components. Components supporting business objects are likely to need to call other components that control access to common data (the customer and product data), common infrastructure (security, system management, printing, e-mail interfaces, etc.), and standard routines (interest rate calculations, date manipulation, etc.). Find two components over the Web, for instance, and it is unlikely that they will call the same system management error reporting interface or the same customer information retrieval interface. Businesses have problems agreeing on standards for business-to-business communication, and software vendors are not famous for their cooperative approach to standards development, hence I suspect component vendors are unlikely to agree on consistent interfaces. There is a domino effect; choose one component and you find yourself being forced to use others.

The alternative approach to serendipitous reuse is **architectural reuse**. You can think of serendipitous reuse as bottom-up reuse. It is analogous to building a house by looking around for suitable building material. If you find something you like you change the design to fit it in. Architectural reuse is top-down reuse in the sense that the architecture is paramount, you work on reuse opportunities while defining the architecture. Reuse happens because you design it in; it is analogous to designing a house from standard components—standard bricks, standard door sizes, and standard window frames. The key practical difference is that with architectural reuse you start by defining the interfaces and then look for components that implement the interfaces, rather than looking at the component and living with whatever interface comes with it. Components that are most likely to be used by architectural reuse are:

- Horizontal components: For instance, there are many advantages in enforcing one or a few security components, one or a few error-reporting components, a common printing implementation to be used consistently across many applications.
- Interface to common data: For instance, customer and product data is likely to be used by many applications. This is discussed further in Chapter 12.
- Interface to common routines. Examples are routines for interest calculation, date manipulation, string manipulation, and so on.

Architectural reuse enforces the architecture.

Many might feel that architectural reuse looks like a feeble vision compared to the grand vision of serendipitous reuse. But I don't think the grand vision will ever be achieved; I don't believe that the serendipitous reuse market will ever be enormously important. It has a role for components at the edge of the architecture, for instance, components that deliver parts of screen displays (grids, tables, moving pictures, and so on) or that do standalone functions like statistical analysis. But for the core applications, you will find that the domino effect ensures that when you start buying components you end up buying an architecture. This is not necessarily a bad thing so long as it is done consciously. But it is a different approach; you are not buying a component to fill a gap. Instead you will be taking a working blueprint and replacing the parts you don't like.

In this section I have concentrated on component reuse but this is not the whole story. The range of reuse opportunities is illustrated in Figure 10-5.

Reuse has been used for screen layouts, screen format parts, design patterns, documentation, testing routines, symbolic code (program source), practically everywhere in fact. When you copy an example from a text book, this is reuse. Encouraging reuse is important in every IT department. Programming groups should build a "pattern book" of code that works. Reuse of the screen formats is particularly important as it can be used to enforce a common look-and-feel over many screens and to ensure that, when the same kind of data (for example, an address) is displayed, it is always displayed in the same way.

There may be opportunities for reuse either when two classes of business objects have the same superclass or when there are business processes that are very similar. (For example, checking accounts and savings accounts are likely to belong to a generic "accounts" superclass and also to have many similar business processes.) This is probably best handled by the reuse at the symbolic code level rather than with components, if only because what is the same today may not be the same tomorrow—similar processes may later diverge.

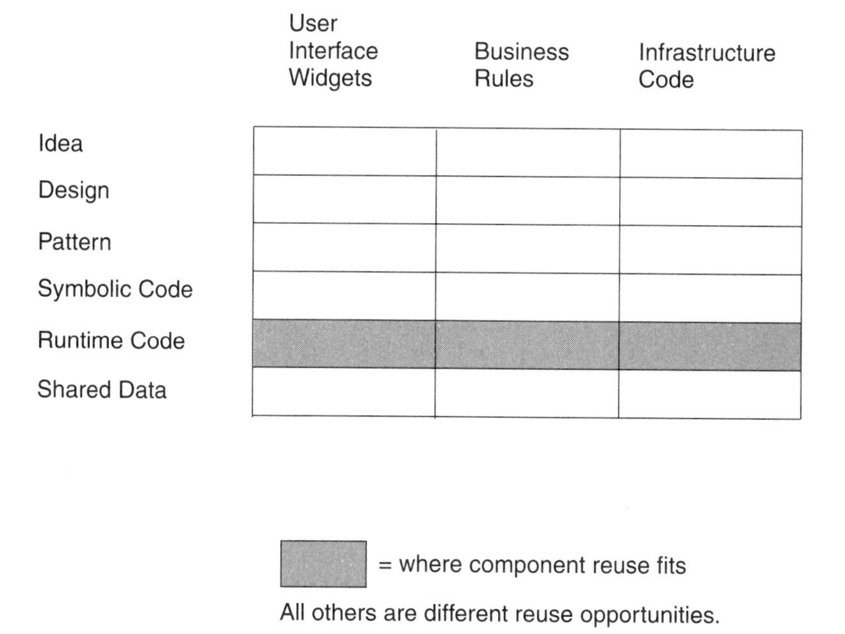

	User Interface Widgets	Business Rules	Infrastructure Code
Idea			
Design			
Pattern			
Symbolic Code			
Runtime Code			
Shared Data			

▩ = where component reuse fits

All others are different reuse opportunities.

Figure 10-5 The range of reuse possibilities

There have actually been many successful examples of organizations using reuse, but in my experience it is enforced reuse from the top that works, not bottom-up reuse from broad-minded, cooperative programmers. In short, we already know architectural reuse works.

10.2.5   Completing the implementation design

I haven't finished describing all the steps in the implementation design, in fact I have only gotten as far as the user interface, which I described as requiring two components for each kind of user command, one for formatting and one for business logic. I will call these components the **formatting component** and the **presentation logic component**. In general, it is unlikely (though not impossible) that presentation logic components will be reused across different presentation-layer servers.

Earlier in the chapter I discussed business objects and noted that their behavior maps to interfaces. The interfaces are implemented by **business object components**. We want as much of the actual business logic processing as possible to go into the business object components for two reasons:

1. It is more efficient for data intensive processing to be near the data.

2. There are possibilities for reuse over multiple interface channels.

Presentation logic components call one or more business object components and business object components communicate with other business object components. All communication can be through real-time or deferrable messages. The logical picture is illustrated in Figure 10-6.

But physically we want to hide the details of the middleware technology from the business object components. You can do this by introducing **mediator components**. The mediator components are like the oil in the engine that allows it to run smoothly. Mediator components do more than just hide the middleware. They provide a home for many of the calls on infrastructure code—monitoring performance or switching to backup servers. They also allow the presentation logic component to send the mediator a big message and have the mediator break it down into many calls on the business objects. There are several advantages to using mediators:

- It is fast—if more than one business object operation gets called by one user command there is only one message over the middleware.
- The business object component interface can be written for reuse without worrying about network performance issues.
- The mediator components handle all technology issues associated with the middleware. It would be possible, for instance, to write them in Java while the business object components are written in C++.
- The mediator components provide a home for special system functions, like code for switching to a backup server or tracing user activity for debugging purposes.

Presentation Layer

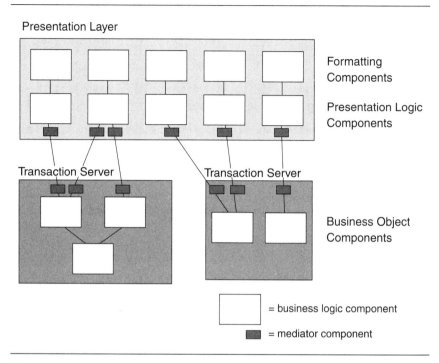

Figure 10-6 Component layers

Business object components may also call other business object components. If the call is across some middleware, mediators should be introduced there as well to protect the business objects from the technology.

This is just a starting point of a layered design. Additional factors to consider are:

1. Distribution of local and enterprise wide data

2. Batch processing

3. Business intelligence

4. Integration with e-mail and other groupware/office products

The first three of these will be discussed over the course of the rest of this book.

10.3 Conclusions

This chapter has proposed a generic component structure for green-field applications and discussed the task of implementation design. It introduced a basic outline of development and discussed the modern modeling approach to design. The distinctive features of the modern approach to design are iterative development and the use of models.

The main body of the chapter was devoted to implementation design, in particular how to break the design into components. Three types of components were defined that make up the application functional structure: formatting components, presentation logic components, and business object components. To these were added mediator components whose function is to hide the application functionality from the physical concerns of writing efficient, scalable, resilient, secure, and manageable distributed systems.

Reuse was discussed. The key point is to have reuse enforce the architecture. The danger is that reuse can undermine the architecture. The technique is to manage the interfaces during architectural design.

The next two chapters look at two aspects of this large picture—business processes and information. The chapter after these two goes back to the concerns of this chapter and tries to pull it all together, specifically looking at the issues of existing systems and managing change.

11

Implementing
Business Processes

Understanding business processes is key to implementation design. The purpose of this chapter is to explain why.

So far in this book I have been pretty sloppy in my use of the words "business processes." In the first chapter I talked casually about the need to support business process change and the increased emphasis on business processes that span departmental boundaries. And in the previous chapter I talked about the importance of business-process modeling for identifying components. Mea culpa, but then so is most of the rest of the computer industry.

Business-process modeling is not quite in the mainstream of IT application design. The activity model—the UML model for business processes—was one of its more recent additions. Go back to the mid-1990s and earlier, and hardly any design methods paid more than lip service to business-process modeling. It was only when Hammer and Champy wrote their book *Re-engineering the Corporation* (New York: Harper Business) in 1993, which made business-process reengineering fashionable, that the IT industry sat up and took notice of business processes at all.

Furthermore, the phrase "business processes" is often used interchangeably with the words "business logic" and "business rules." I always cringe when I see the words business logic or business rules. On one hand it makes business sound like the work of logical automatons, which is not my experience. On the other hand I never know what the speaker means, because business logic (or rules if you prefer) is scattered about everywhere. There are data verification rules, workflow rules, database integrity rules, formula rules, legal rules—what are they talking about? Mind you, I do it myself and everyone nods sagely.

So why not leave it that way; why worry about business processes? What I hope to show you in this chapter is the degree to which technical decisions are made on the basis of business process understanding. Also, though not explored further in this book, technology creates business opportunities and the way to take these opportunities forward is for the technologists to sit down with the business planners and discuss business processes.

Consider this simple point: It is only because business processes are integrated, that IT applications must be integrated. If business processes were stand-alone things that only had an impact on one small section of a company there would be little need for IT to be integrated (and life would be much easier).

Business processes are integrated in several ways, for instance:

- Some business processes are sub-processes of other larger business processes.
- Business processes can initiate other business processes.
- Business processes share information.

Consider a car rental process. There are many business processes: handling new rentals, handling returns, checking and cleaning cars, moving cars between offices, handling accident reports, and so on. They are all interconnected. Traditionally, we have implemented systems like this without really thinking about business processes at all. We have taken them as a series of discrete transactions against a car rental database and maybe hold a separate database for keeping an inventory of the cars. The application designer would have seen what the agents needed to do and turned it into a sequence of screen formats, the database designer would have identified the major tables. The programmer would take it from there and probably discover errors in the design and work his or her way around them.

Now what happens to this system when a gold/silver/platinum/blue/premium/etc. card is introduced? The new rental part of the IT system is irrelevant to these people because all they need do is make a phone call and the car is waiting for them. What happens to the system? There will probably be a new application written. The last bit will be a messy integration with the original rental system—perhaps the card system pretends to be a terminal on the new rental system. (Perhaps it prints the information and someone retypes it into the original system.)

If we take a business-process perspective we see that there is one long process—the car rental process of which new rental is only a part. The original new rental process and the card member rental process are alternative sub-processes of this central car rental process. If the original system was written with a clean break between sub-processes, the new sub-process could be slotted in with a minimum of disruption and the result would be a much cleaner design, easier to change, easier to maintain, and probably faster and more resilient as well.

By analyzing the business processes we understand so much more about the possible implementation, in particular:

- It gives us the fault lines for change.
- It gives us the constraints for data distribution.
- It gives us the requirements for performance.
- It gives us the requirements for data resiliency.

The fault lines for change between business processes or between a master business process and its subordinates was illustrated by our above example. Put simply, the unit of change in the business is the business process or sub-process. By aligning the implementation components along business-process lines we reduce the number of components that need to be changed.

On the data distribution front clearly all the data could be centralized. But if it isn't, we need to locate the data near the business processes and again split it along business process boundaries. Not only should this be more efficient and responsive to change, it is potentially more resilient as well. What if the network to the central system breaks down? Using the business-process analysis we can figure out what objects are required to carry on processing locally. A solution to maximize resiliency would be to keep local and global copies of various pieces of data. The business-process analysis tells us when we can make the copy and when it must be synchronized. For instance, a copy of the new rental information needs to be available to other rental offices in the time it takes to drive to a new return location.

Understanding business processes is of crucial importance for technologists as well as modelers. This chapter is about understanding business processes and understanding how they relate to information and to implementation issues.

11.1   What is a process?

Some of my readers will at this point be wondering where I draw the line between business processes and all the other things an organizations does. I take the view that almost everything a business does can be described as a business process, it is just that some processes are better defined than others. Business-process analysis has its roots in improving manufacturing, which is obviously regimented and repetitive. One of the insights from the business processing reengineering revolution was that the notion of processes is much wider than that and some of the same thinking can be applied outside the factory.

A process is a series of activities that delivers something, be it concrete or abstract, a solid thing or information. Examples of processes are cooking a meal, opening a bank account, ordering and delivering a pizza, buying a car. Some processes can be well-defined, meaning that they can be repeated consistently time and time again. Some processes are by their very nature not well-defined at all. Design and research are examples of processes that are impossible to define, at least in detail. Closer to home, so to speak, look at IT development itself. For many years IT development was considered an area where processes had little place but the work on quality management put a stop to that. Even IT management should be about managing processes and process improvement. Process improvement itself is a process.

We will explore the notion of processes by looking at an example outside of IT—building a house.

A well-defined process breaks down into an ordered sequence of activities; in our example building foundations, building walls, and building the roof. Some activities can run in parallel—wiring and plumbing, perhaps—and some are repeated. In most cases there is a wait between one activity ending and the next starting, for instance, while waiting for the plumber to arrive. A good deal of process improvement comes from analyzing the waiting period. For instance, a building contractor will try to ensure the builders are busy and not waiting for bricks or concrete to turn up.

An activity can itself be a process; wiring a house is a process in its own right. It's a question of what level of detail you want to analyze the process. The lowest level of detail—the activity that is not subdivided further—we will call a task. A task is usually done by one person in one place at one time and requires the application of some skill or resource. Tasks are discrete; they are taken to completion or undone completely. In our example, laying a single brick might be a task.

These processes are shown diagrammatically in Figure 11-1.

Not every process flow is a simple set of sequential or parallel activities. In most real-world processes there are alternative routes. For instance, building a

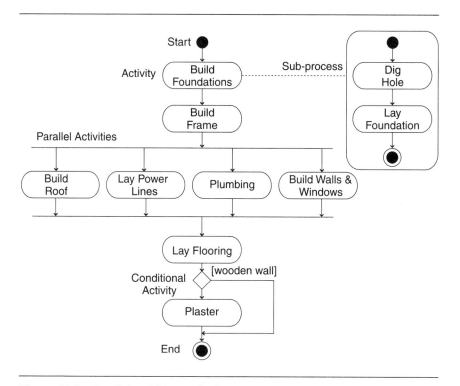

Figure 11-1   Parallel activities and sub-processes

house in concrete is somewhat different from building it in bricks. The more you look at the details of a process, the more alternatives you find. In many real-world processes there are loops; laying a wall with bricks is clearly a repetitive process. Sometimes it is the whole process that loops back on itself; put another way, the process is ongoing. The process of checking whether a nuclear reactor is at a safe temperature is, one hopes, ongoing. (What is delivered from a looping process? In this case, a safe reactor.)

We have seen that processes can be sub-processes of other larger processes, but this is not the only relationship between processes. Many processes trigger off another process—what we can call "send and forget." While building a house for instance, bills are incurred and payment processes are started. If the company is lax about paying its bills it does not immediately stop the house being built, so from the point of view of the house building team the payment process is not their responsibility. In no way could one say that the payment process is a sub-process of the house building process even though the house building process made the order that triggered the payment.

What I have described so far is a very prescriptive way of viewing processes; the process is a rigid series of activities. I like to think of this as the military approach because of the propensity of the military to drum process steps into raw recruits by insisting they "do it by numbers"—shouting out numbers for every step of the way. The opposite extreme is not specifying any order or alternative routes or perhaps even specifying some of the activities, but laying down some rules.

Prescriptive processes can be shown diagrammatically as noted earlier or documented by a series of numbered steps. You can even use a computer-like structured English.

Rule-based processes are typically documented in normal English (for example, the rule book in board games, the policies and procedures manual in business), but it could be documented in a formal rules language.

Contrary to popular belief, the military isn't always stupid. The reason they "do it by numbers" is efficiency. A prescriptive approach is fast and repeatable and the process can be followed without thinking. For some processes, like sales, for instance, it is hard to be prescriptive, although I've certainly been visited by salesmen at home who have clearly been following rigid rules. Sometimes prescriptive processes often turn out to be less prescriptive on closer inspection. At least that seems to be the case when I have tried to assemble some flat pack furniture.

There is another alternative and that is following a plan. Builders cannot be prescriptive about all of the detailed steps in building any house. They are following a plan. What you then need is a process for converting the plan into a one-off process definition.

Organizations need to analyze processes to improve their efficiency. Having a process diagram, like Figure 11-1, is a useful first step. Analysis may be on error rates, costs, or resource utilization. For the latter the focus of the analysis is not so much on the activities as the lines between them, because the lines usually represent delays or queues for resources. For instance, when looking at the "building a house" process, the analyst might be interested in ensuring there is no delay waiting for bricks, and they might also be looking for a way to ensure the bricks are not delivered before they are needed. Alternatively, the analysis might highlight resource constraints. Suppose there are a limited number of electricians whose task is to wire a number of houses being built at around the same time. The process analysis might try to optimize their usage.

On the other hand, the end result of process analysis may not be small incremental change but massive change. In our house building example, this could be moving to on-site assembly of walls and roofs that were previously built in a factory.

Let us summarize these points:

- A process delivers something, usually some goods or a service.
- A process follows a plan that defines the order of the activities.
- Activities can sometimes be processed in parallel.
- Activities can be conditional—put another way, process plans can have path choices.
- An activity can be a process in its own right or it can be a task. A task is an activity that cannot be subdivided and cannot be half done (that is, if there is a problem, it must be undone). A task is typically done by one person, in one place, at one time.
- A process can start another process (send and forget).
- A process may be ongoing, meaning that it loops back on itself.
- There are two extremes of plans; at one extreme the plan is very prescriptive and defines the steps in detail (the military approach). The other extreme is a plan that defines the rules that must be obeyed (for example, build the walls before the roof) but gives maximum flexibility within the rules.
- In practice, process execution may deviate from the plan especially if something goes wrong.
- An organization will have many processes going on at any one time. The processes are likely to be competing for resources.

11.2 Business processes

Since a business exists to deliver something—be it goods or services—processes are the essence of business. The fundamental activities of every business can be described as processes. All a business does is operate processes, manage processes, sell and market process deliverables, and plan how to change processes in the future.

Almost every part of a business can be described in process terms. An example of a high-level planning process is an annual budgeting process. The deliverable is the budget plan.

Typical processes in a manufacturing business include

- Buying supplies
- Controlling goods into and out of warehouses
- Manufacturing
- Delivery
- Order processing
- Billing

Typical processes for a bank include

- Opening an account
- Closing an account
- Processing debits and credits
- Handling overdrawn accounts
- Processing requests for information (for example, in support of a mortgage request)
- Paying interest
- Clearing checks

Typical processes in every business include

- Payroll
- Processing expense claims
- Taking on a new employee
- Paying taxes
- Generating annual accounts

Non-business organizations, like government departments, can also be described in process terms. Processes might deliver health care, a trained army, or a successful election.

11.3   The alternative view—functional analysis

Viewing businesses as processes is not in the life blood of the IT industry. The alternative is functional analysis (see Function vs. Process box in Chapter 10). All classical forms of systems analysis and some modern techniques like use case analysis are forms of functional analysis.

Clearly the functional approach often works. Many business processes are straightforward and so well understood by everybody that explicitly highlighting the process flow does not tell anyone anything they didn't know already. A functional approach is also good at automating what people are doing already, like turning paper-based processes into equivalent computer-based processes. Again the reason is that the processes are clearly understood.

The difficulty comes when the business processes are not clearly understood. There are three kinds of IT projects (this follows the ideas of a book called *The Information Paradox* [New York: McGraw-Hill, 1999] by consultants from the DMR group). Automating existing processes is only one of them. The other two are:

- Improving information quality and flow
- Support for business-process change

The functional approach is inadequate for both of the above. It is not categorically wrong, but it is incomplete and, used by itself, there are two dangers.

The first danger is that the functional approach is departmentally driven. To be fair, it is very difficult to break out of the departmental straightjacket. Departments make the business case, pay for the development, and judge the results. (Furthermore departments are social groups and have been known to put their own prosperity above that of the organization.) Many business processes cross departmental boundaries; order processing, customer relationship management (CRM), billing, to name but a few. Data quality in particular is a cross-departmental concern. For instance, a sales person submits an order form on which the first line has the total price and all the other lines have zero price. The sales department doesn't care. Their only concern is reducing the hassle of filling out order forms. But the marketing department is analyzing which products are doing well and which are doing badly by using false data.

Second, functional analysis is not a good tool for analyzing how to change the business. This does not mean that it is useless. Functional analysis does deliver a good insight into how systems work now; people can mull over the model and think of other solutions. However, the focus on any process improvement should be on the output of the process and this is lost in the functional model. A particular case in point is that functional analysis does not tell you whether the traditional order in which activities are done is a trivial historical accident or fundamental to the process. For instance, it is fundamental that you build the house frame before the roof, but not fundamental whether the plumbing or the wiring is done first. Flexible IT applications should not force an arbitrary order to a series of actions where none is necessary because, when you come to put a new interface on the old system, the old order will only get in the way.

I would be prepared to bet that many, perhaps the majority, of order-processing systems are merely computerized form filling and the database is little more than a store for electronic order forms. Computers can do much more. For instance, the proposal system could be linked to the order entry system. The order entry can be integrated with the catalogue or the configurator. The discount approval system can be linked in. The order system can be linked to manufacturing and delivering systems, and the whole thing integrated to answer the simple question that is often so difficult to answer—what happened to my order? If there is some problem in manufacturing and the thing can't be built, the manufacturing system might look at the order system and e-mail the sales person. The only way to reach these conclusions is by looking at proposal, ordering, manufacturing, and delivery processes as stages in one big process, not a series of isolated "silo" applications.

There is a problem, of course—a dark lining to a silver cloud. As I described above, the functional approach is convenient for management. It's hard to say to one department that their application is delayed while we try and include the requirements of another department. I will discuss this issue more in the last chapter. Suffice it to say now that one of the main reasons why IT applications are a barrier to change, rather than an enabler of change, is because they have been built along functional lines.

11.4   Information and processes

Information in business has little meaning outside of the context of processes. The vast majority of data is either part of the process (for example, an electronic copy of an order), supports the process (for example, customer information) or is telling management how processes are going on. Without understanding how the data relates to the processes it supports, the data is meaningless.

Most information used in business computer systems falls into one of four categories:

1. Plan objects: Information about the process plans—for instance, an airline timetable or a work schedule.

2. Tracking objects: Information about where an individual process has gotten in its execution (for example, where an order is in the manufacturing/delivery cycle).

3. Resource objects: Information needed by the process, usually information about resources or information external to the business (such as customer data, product details).

4. Result objects: Information that is itself a process deliverable.

For example, if the process is about delivery, then the tracking objects keep tabs on where the delivery is, the plan objects define the delivery schedule, the resource objects hold the customer information and the vehicle information. The result object is a delivery note signed by the customer, which may not be part of the IT system.

The relationship between processes and information is illustrated diagrammatically in Figure 11-2.

For every active business process (for example, for every order being processed) we normally have one tracking object. For order processing this object is the record of the order. For manufacturing this object keeps a record of where, in the manufacturing process, is the thing being built. Note it is an object not a row in a relational table; it could be complex. If you are building an aircraft, the manufacturing object would be extremely complex and probably distributed over many systems.

The result of one process might be a resource for another. For instance, a process for introducing a new product creates the product information used by

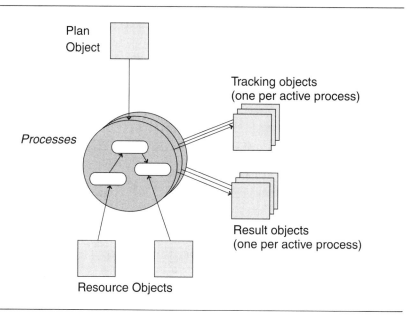

Figure 11-2 Processes and data

many other processes. One would anticipate that all resource objects have associated business processes that create, maintain, and delete them. This is illustrated in Figure 11-3.

Typically in implementation terms it is very common to merge the result object with the tracking object, like for instance order processing—the half-

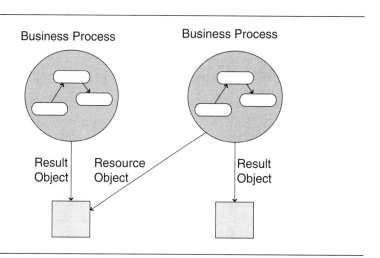

Figure 11-3 Business processes for resource objects

finished order tracks how the order processing has progressed; the completed order is the result.

Subprocesses may or may not use the same tracking object as their master process. The two alternatives are illustrated in Figure 11-4. I have called the alternatives: **shared tracking objects** and **copied tracking objects**.

Sub-processes that use shared tracking objects use the same tracking object as its master. The advantage of this approach is simplicity. The disadvantage is that some information from the sub-process may be of no interest when the sub-process has finished, so the object gets cluttered with uninteresting data.

Sub-processes that use copied tracking objects make a new tracking object. Information can be read from the master tracking object if necessary at the beginning of the sub-process and information passed back to the master tracking object at the end. The advantage of this approach is that it is easier to distribute the processing. The sub-process object can be in the local system. If there is a failure the sub-processing tracking object can simply be thrown away and the sub-process restarted. If we think back to the original example in the chapter—the car rental process—we can see the sub-process of gathering new rental information can be done on a local workstation and the completed data copied to the central system.

An example of copied tracking objects in IT development process is objects checked-out from repositories or configuration management products.

Tracking objects typically exist for the duration of the process and, in many instances, for a long time afterward for trend analysis. In a data warehouse system the large bulk of data is typically held in a central "facts" file, which is nothing less than a historical collection of the tracking objects for key processes like orders and payments.

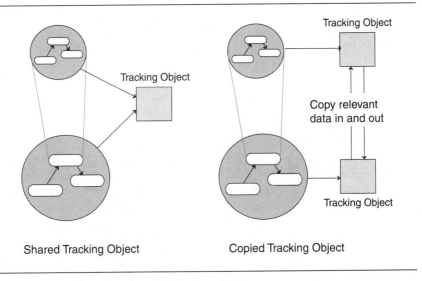

Figure 11-4   Shared and copied tracking objects

11.5 Processes and computer applications

In this section I will look at the relationship between business processes and IT applications.

First a preliminary comment; many computer applications are just passive receptacles of information (especially if they are simply replacing paper-based systems) and the actual flow of the business process is not enforced by the computer system. An example was the car rental process—the driver (normally) controls where and when the return process is done. The notable exception to this generality are workflow systems.

11.5.1 Business rules

There is a lot of talk these days about business rules and questions are posed about where they should reside. I have a simple answer—they should reside in the same location as the tracking object. Does that mean the transaction server? Normally. A counterexample is copied tracking objects, illustrated in Figure 11-4; for instance, the new car rental object that resided in a workstation and is loaded to the central system when it is complete.

For me the term "business rules" always summons up an image of a rule-based system controlling the process flow (for example, a rule such as: you don't give away the rental car keys until you have gotten a signature on the form and a credit card image). But in reality the vast majority of business rules are data integrity rules or data processing rules. Put another way, they are part of the transaction processing rather than controlling the flow between transactions. Rules that do control the process flow are usually simple, almost trivial checks, and there is little benefit from having them off elsewhere. Much of the talk on business-rule layers is inspired by the smother architecture described in Chapter 1, which assumes many complex systems can be held together by a rules engine.

Commercial application systems are complex, but it is a certain type of complexity. They are not algorithmically complex like a database query optimization algorithm, they are complex because there is so much of it. A non-business example is a tax form. None of the questions are particularly difficult (so long as you can understand them at all) but there are so damned many of them. The complexity is through having a large number of simple things. The challenge for the developer is not so much understanding the rules, it is finding them—at least finding them all. The best technique is to group related rules together. As I said, the vast majority of the rules are data integrity rules and, by necessity, belong with the tracking object. A simple solution is therefore to put all the rules with the tracking object. In implementation terms this suggests: have one component per tracking object data with the object itself residing in a database.

11.5.2   Real time vs. deferrable

Business processes occur in bursts of activity when somebody is doing something followed by long periods of waiting—the expense claims process being a typical example. During the burst the tracking object must be updated in real time. For instance, when the car rental company gives a customer some keys, the record of the transaction must be on the system. On the other hand, as discussed before, there can be a delay moving the rental record to the central system.

This pattern is very typical. When a task is updating a tracking record it must be done in real time. When a sub-process needs to return information to its master or when one process initiates another, deferrable, secure messages are usually ideal.

Note, it is only from a consideration of the business processes that we can work out the business impact of the computers or network going down. For a car rental company, it is not being able to reconcile car rentals with car returns immediately. The business must decide whether this matters, because all the information is on the car rental form handed in on return—unless the form is lost, of course.

What about changing the resource objects, such as updating customer details? The first point is that the tracking objects should not duplicate resource information. For instance, an order form should not copy the name and address of the customer; it should point to the customer record. The reason is that if the customer's details are changed you don't want the order to go wrong. (A comment for data analysts of long standing, this is like ensuring the relational data is in third normal form.) What if the customer object is deleted? In an ideal world, not only would the order tracking object have a reference to the customer object but the customer object would have a reference to the order tracking object or at least a way of finding the outstanding orders so it could cancel them. Such levels of data integrity are rare but enormously valuable. This is what computers should be doing—telling you when things have happened rather than absorbing information and never giving it back. Again the cancel messages to the order tracking objects will in most cases not need to be in real time.

11.5.3   Data distribution

In the main, tracking objects don't have any connection with other tracking objects. A set of tracking objects can therefore usually be distributed with ease. The issues, as always with distribution, are

- Controlling and securing the data.
- Searching for particular tracking objects.
- Doing anything (for example, batch update) that needs to see all tracking objects for one business process.

The car rental system illustrates these advantages and disadvantages well. In most cases, storing the car rental record in the local office is optimal because most people return the car to the same office they rented it from. However, is it a good idea to trust the safety of the data and the security of the system to personnel in a local car rental office? Another disadvantage of distribution is that, if the central office wants to find out information about the current rental contracts, they cannot without searching all the local offices and consolidating the results.

The car rental process example has already illustrated that sub-processes can be physically distributed from their master process. The advantage in doing this is efficiency; the task is processed locally and the number of data movements over the network is minimized. Furthermore, the sub-process can easily be aborted and restarted again. The downside is that there needs to be a tracking process in the master to know who is responsible for the sub-process, in case questions need to be asked about what happened to it.

Resource objects pose a different set of problems. Sometimes they can be distributed easily. For the car rental system the resource objects are records of the cars, and I expect most cars spend most of their time at one office going through a cycle of being rented, washed, and rented again. Therefore it may be optimal to keep the car object in the local office system. The problems are similar to the car rental tracking objects. Suppose for instance, the police see a rental car breaking the law and ask the car rental company who is the driver. Distribution in this case makes the query more difficult.

We noted before that tracking objects should not duplicate resource object data, but what about resource objects being duplicated in different databases, perhaps with a different layout? Sometimes, there are good reasons for doing this, such as:

- Performance—access need not be over a network.
- Resiliency—when the centralized information is unavailable, applications can continue to run.

Since information like customer details and product details is extremely pervasive, the issue of data duplication is often faced. This is discussed in the next chapter.

11.5.4   Long transactions

When a user is doing a task in a business process they are typically doing a series of operations against one tracking object. They don't want to have to identify the object every time they do something. For instance, if the business process is about processing an insurance claim and the tracking object represents the claim, they don't want to write in the claim number every time they transmit. When they have finished one claim they start work on another, in other words, switch to another business process and work on that. They do all of this in the context of a single security log-on to the system. This is illustrated in Figure 11-6.

Transaction systems have traditionally had difficulties with long task sessions. The root of the problem is that for performance reasons you want short transactions while task sessions look very much like long conversational

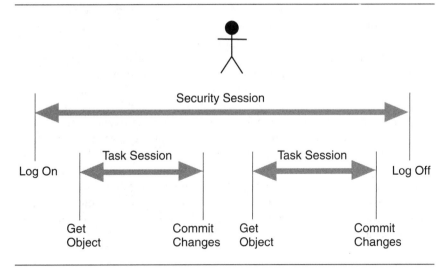

Figure 11-5   Long transactions

transactions. The task system may have many interactions with the system, all being done by one person and most targeted at one object, the tracking object. You don't want anyone else messing around with the same data at the same time, and at any point in the dialogue the whole task may need to be aborted. Insurance claim processing and new car rentals are typical examples.

There are several ways to solve these problems. If the task has one or more reads, but only one update, then a simple detection scheme is probably appropriate. The object contains a counter or a timestamp that indicates when it was last updated. If the counter or timestamp hasn't changed between the time of the first retrieval and the update, then no one else has been working on the object. If the counter or timestamp has changed, someone has been working on the same object at the same time, and the update must be aborted.

For longer tasks, or ones with multiple updates, a "pseudo lock" (a lock enforced by application code) may be appropriate. A pseudo lock is implemented by adding an attribute to the record that identifies the user that is updating the record. Every screen (pseudo locks were invented a long time ago) becomes a single transaction but, if another user tries to update the record while the pseudo lock is on, they fail. The biggest difficulty with pseudo locks is that abort logic must be hard coded.

An alternative is to copy the data locally, work on it locally, and copy it back when finished. These are often called check-out/check-in protocols. Aborting the task is much simpler with check-out/check-in—the checked-out copy can be thrown away. However, we still have the possibility that someone else could have checked out the same object at the same time. When they check it in, they overwrite the earlier update! Both of the techniques discussed earlier can be applied. If a counter or timestamp is used, the second check-in fails. If a pseudo lock is used, then the second person is not allowed to check the object out in the first place.

Note that, coming from the technical end, we have rediscovered the notion of the copied tracking object scenario, illustrated in Figure 11-4. Check-out/check-in creates a copied tracking object on the workstation.

The way to think about these long tasks is to distinguish between object ownership and atomicity. Often what you find is that atomicity is supported well by short transactions but there is a requirement for one person to own the object for a longer period of time. Processing an insurance claim is an example. There are a number of actions against the claim, which correspond to short transactions, but there is a longer period during which one person has ownership of managing the claim. You can implement the same with check-out/check-in. Someone can own an object and keep a local copy and every now and then check in their latest updates. The interesting business point about ownership is that ownership can be moved. It is possible, for instance, to check out data to one user, move the checked-out data to another user, and for the second user to check in the changed data.

11.5.5   Generic business processes

An interesting twist on the whole area of business processes is seen in departments like call centers. Here staff are receiving and making calls all day for a variety of different business processes—taking orders and handling questions for instance. But there may be a generic business process for handling calls. For instance, the call-center staff might be instructed to look at the customer records and ask whether they want to receive information about a new product. From our analysis there is one task but two tracking records; one for the call-center process and another for the business process (for instance, the order) being handled.

11.5.6   Batch

In an earlier chapter I stated that there was a need for batch for business tasks such as payroll or interest accrual.

From a business-process perspective, batch is required when a time event triggers the next stage in the process. The time event does not have to be anything so exact as 21:00 on the 2nd of August. If could be simply "every evening" or "on the last day of the month." The implementer wants the business to define the period as imprecisely as they dare to give him or her maximum freedom.

11.6   Business process flexibility

The primary reasons for taking a business-process view on IT is to handle change. How can we design to anticipate change?

Business-process change is often associated with a new frontend technology like the Web, or voice, or self-service terminal. In our business-process model these typically require changing a sub-process. This might only be the low-level sub-process associated with the task session or there might be additional processes involved. Typically a new interface comes with a new sub-process, as we saw with using the Premium/Gold/Whatever card for car rental. Using any new input device introduces a new set of security and management concerns. However, by analyzing these situations as processes and sub-processes we can isolate the parts that are changed and the parts that are the same. I would recommend, therefore, separating processes and sub-processes into different components. This subject is discussed in Chapter 13.

The second form of change is more difficult to handle because it does not fit easily with the component model. Think again of a bank but this time wanting to introduce a new type of bank account. They will probably decide that they want to have a bank account that is like an existing bank account but with a few changes. The IT community has invented two good techniques for handling this kind of change:

1. **Parameterized routines.** The bank account processing could be generic and, for every place where there is variation, the routine takes the account type and looks it up in a table to tell it how to handle this for this particular account.

2. **Subclassing.** With object-orientation we could have common class for the common bits and subclasses for all the variations. The advantage of this approach over parameterized routines is that the subclass can have new attributes as well as new logic.

Both of these have their role. This subject is discussed in more detail in Chapter 14.

11.7   Conclusions

What I hope I have done in this chapter is to explain what business processes are and why they are so important for IT implementations. In particular a business-process perspective helps in several important ways:

- It provides a tool for improving the quality of data by letting you understand where the data comes from, how it is used, and its impact on the business.
- It provides the fault lines where the system will change, which has a direct bearing on deciding how to split an application into components.

- It defines which message flows between processes are deferrable and which must be in real time. This is essential information for building a good middleware implementation.
- It provides the rationale for resiliency requirements.
- It provides the rationale for performance criteria.
- It provides the underlying basis for the discussion on security requirements, especially if we are seeking to protect against internal threats.
- It provides the underlying basis for the discussion on data distribution.

The reasons why techies as well as modelers must understand business processes are, first, because building the architecture is a cooperative effort between techies and modelers, and second, because it gives the real constraints that the IT infrastructure must handle.

Most IT systems today not only don't implement some aspect of some business processes well, they also over-engineer other aspects. The reason is that business constraints are not being accurately converted into IT technical requirements. You will find probably the worst examples of this tendency in large RFP (Request For Proposals) from governments and other large organizations (including businesses), which typically express technical requirements in large sweeping commands (like—all recovery must take less than 5 minutes). The demand to over-engineer is a major reason for delay, expense, and subsequent project failure.

Process Implementation Diagrams

We need a way to show how processes are implemented and, as I write, there are no standard diagrams in UML that quite capture all the elements I want. What I want to show is the following:

- Processes
- Business objects used by the processes
- Computer systems—because I want to show distribution
- Presentation layer elements
- Message flows between the elements

So I have come up with the following, using the car rental as an example (see Figure 11-5).

The purpose of this diagram is to help the implementation designer visualize the major features of the business-process implementation. In particular, it is to help discuss issues about data distribution and middleware requirements, especially performance and resiliency.

I am not particular about the exact diagrammatic conventions and would welcome alternative ideas. But what we do need is a diagram that can serve as the topic for discussion between techies and modelers.

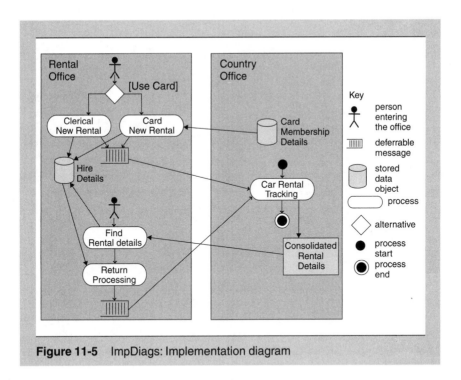

Figure 11-5   ImpDiags: Implementation diagram

12

Information Access
and Information Accuracy

This chapter and the next are largely about the need for integration rather than the technology for implementing integration. Taking a three-tier slant on the world, this chapter is about the data tier while the next is about the presentation and logic tiers.

As the title implies, the two main subjects for this chapter are information access and information accuracy. At the end of the chapter, there is a section on information administration.

12.1   Information access

The requirements for information access differ according to the user. I already touched on this subject in Chapter 6 and for your convenience I have duplicated Figure 6-2 in Figure 12-1. In Chapter 6 the focus was on the types of middleware. In this section, I want to focus on the design questions of who uses the data and whether they should use a data mart or data warehouse.

When we move to the top right hand corner of this diagram we are moving into the territory of data marts and data warehouses. This technology is predicated on copying the data from the production system to the data mart/warehouse system. Before the data is loaded in the target system it can be processed in several ways:

- It can be reformatted. Internal codes can be changed to meaningful text.
- It can be filtered. Unwanted rows can be thrown out.
- Unwanted attributes can be thrown out.
- Data from several databases can be merged.
- Data from two or more tables can be merged ("joined" in database parlance).
- Summary data can be calculated and the detailed information removed.

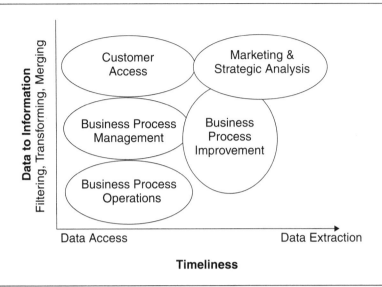

Figure 12-1   Data access users

The notion of copying and merging from several databases is illustrated in Figure 12-2, another diagram previously shown in Chapter 6.

Most of these reformatting operations can be done on production data. There are two fundamental reasons why people want to use a separate database: performance and historical data.

The overhead of doing queries on the production data can seriously impact production performance as discussed in Chapter 8. But the impact on other users is not the only performance concern. Using another database allows the data to be reformatted more efficiently for access. There is a great deal made in the literature about "denormalization" of data warehouse data. This is largely about turning internal codes into text by joining lookup tables with data tables (for example, turning a code like "LHR" into "London Heathrow"). This is a typical way the data can be reformatted for faster queries but there is no theoretical reason why a similar operation cannot be done directly on the production database.

A further reason for copying the data is that the query database might hold records for a longer period than the production data. Actually, arguably there should be an independent archive database. (As an aside, there is an opportunity for the database vendors to attack the problems of archive data directly. Why not have data like bank credit and debit records stored once in a special archive database that is visible from both the production database and the data warehouse database?) Note, however, that there are some complex technical issues in searching the archive (see Historical Data and Format Changes box).

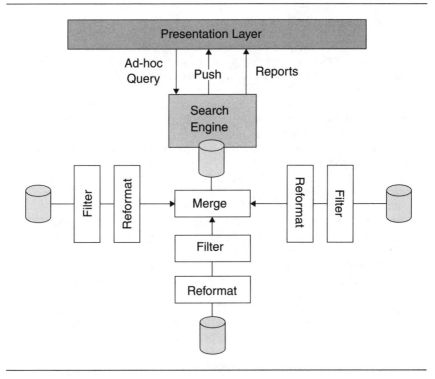

Figure 12-2   Business intelligence server

I have so far used *data mart* and *data warehouse* synonymously. Many would take violent disagreement to that stance. The thinking behind the concept of a data mart was to have a cheap and cheerful search facility without the enormous effort of creating an enterprise data warehouse. The counter view is that if you create a number of data marts then in the future it will be hard to merge them into a larger data warehouse to create a better enterprise view of the information. Unfortunately both views are right—their criticism of their opponents is on target. My bias is toward data marts, but that is largely because I am not at all sure the benefits of data mining on large data warehouses are as significant as advertised. I also feel that organizations should take the notion of a searchable archive database more seriously and use this as the staging post for extraction to local search databases.

I also have not mentioned data replication technology. When people discuss data replication they are usually not thinking of classic data mart or data warehouse applications. Instead they are thinking about the issues of replicating comparatively small amounts of data to large numbers of users, in particular for mobile users who will not always have access to the production data. Examples would be copying product information to a mobile sales force. This problem has

Historical Data and Format Changes

Over a period of time, the data structure of an object changes—new attributes will be added, changed, and deleted. Since we want to archive data or put it online in a data warehouse, what do we do with copies of the data that use the old structure?

There are two alternatives: live with multiple versions or try to convert all the old data to a new format. At an operational level, the second option has two problems. First, you may have to invent new data values for any new data fields. Second, the reorganization of large historical collections of data may take a long time, especially if a field being changed is used in an index. But even if these are easily overcome, there may be a more fundamental reason why not to attempt a reorganization. If, for instance, you make radical changes to the order processing system it could be that an order from before the change and an order from after the change are so different there is no direct correspondence between many of the attributes.

This is not only an issue with changing the database schema, it could be an issue with the data itself. Suppose you have a product table and each product has a style number, and then you decide to repackage the product so components that were part of one style are moved to another style. At the same time you create a bunch of new styles. A historical search to find out how much of something you sold becomes a difficult query that can only be solved by someone with a intimate knowledge of the product history.

So what's the solution? You have to take a pragmatic compromise. If the changes are slight and reorganizing the data is feasible, go for it. If the changes are severe, then start a new version of the historic data and have users merge the data from both databases if they want to see the complete picture. It's not a clean solution, but there is no elegant answer. You might want to consider adding a version number to each table in the archive or warehouse in anticipation of change.

unique challenges of its own and to do it justice requires more room than I am prepared to give it, because it is tangential to the main thrust of this book.

One way to find our way through this morass of different technologies all vying for our attention is to build a clearer picture of who are the users and what are their requirements. This I now attempt to do.

12.1.1 Basic process information

Everyone in business operations will need access to some basic information, and every one of our object types—tracking objects, resource objects, and plan objects—need some basic online inquiry facilities. This is to satisfy questions like: Is this product still available? How much does it cost? What styles do I need? Is this bank account overdrawn?

Some 4GL generator products, such as Unisys LINC, save large amounts of programming effort simply by generating all these inquiry screens for you.

Currently this kind of information is usually separated from HTML documents made available over the Web. In the future there will be more integration. For instance, a button on the product information screen could retrieve the product overview manual or the brochure. Or, when products are deleted, the product brochure could be automatically updated with "no longer available" on the front cover.

12.1.2   Process management

This is the basic management information; in the past it was (okay, still is) provided by overnight reports that were (are) printed and distributed in the morning. The kinds of information provided include:

- Status reports—for example, telling a sales manager the orders taken in the last week, month, or year.
- Errors—for example, what orders have errors in them? What invoices haven't been paid? What accounts could not be processed last night?
- Statistics—for example, stock levels, sales figures, how many of each product line have been sold, where, when, and by whom.
- Trend analysis of key items, which is required for demand forecasting.

What all these reports have in common is that they are reports about what is happening in the business processes. It is information for people monitoring the business processes in contrast to the category above, which is for people who are part of the business process.

Increasingly this information is becoming more online. For instance, the daily report might still be a useful notion but it can come in the form of a spreadsheet sent by e-mail or put into a Web page.

Programming reports is a great deal of work. Furthermore, it is never-ending; management always wants something different. There are many products available for report generation, typically built around SQL queries processed directly on the database. Given that networking and disk costs are declining, it is becoming more economical to ship large quantities of data on a daily basis to local servers, even to workstations.

One consideration is to use data mart technology. This is not complex data mining—that comes later. Data marts, per se, do not solve all the problems of process management information access; you might still generate and distribute reports, but you would hope that most reports are replaced by users accessing the data mart directly. They won't do this unless there is a good user interface; these users are not power database query users. But there is not a strong requirement to do extensive reformatting of the data since, for process management, you typically want to see the data as it is seen by the process workers. If they use codes, the process administrator is likely to want to see the same code—after all they might be responsible for assigning the codes. The advantages of using data marts increase when the raw data is in multiple production databases.

12.1.3   Process improvement

Process improvement starts by analyzing the dynamics of the business process. Questions that need to be answered are where are the delays, where is the cost, and where are the errors coming from? The IT system cannot answer all of these questions, but in theory it could answer them a good deal better than it usually does in practice. For instance, the time taken for the order to be submitted, fulfilled, and distributed could be captured simply by storing a few date and time attributes in the order record. The error rate from orders could be captured. Perhaps this information is being collected and analyzed more than I think, but I suspect people rarely think of gathering basic process improvement data when they are designing a system.

One generic issue is that the business-process flow from order, manufacture, and distribution is frequently implemented by sending the data from machine to machine so there is no total picture of the complete process. While this isn't implemented in many systems now, in the future it probably will be, not for process improvement reasons but because electronic business is exposing the business processes to the outside world. In this case, people want to know what's happened to their orders. Which brings us to the customer view.

12.1.4   Customer view

With the Web, customers will increasingly want information about products, prices, account status, and the status of their orders. These, in the main, are the same information requests we saw in basic process information.

It is likely, for security reasons, that you will want to treat customers as a separate presentation channel from internal users. I described in Chapter 10 that there is a layer of business object components. These should provide the basic inquiry information used by all the different presentation channels. Above this layer you will need to provide unique customer-oriented presentation, and probably some business-process logic and additional security checking.

Note that data marts are inappropriate for typical customer access. Customers want to see the most up-to-date data. If they submit an order and then immediately look to see what orders they have in the system, they will be very confused if the order they just submitted is not there.

12.1.5   Marketing and strategic business analysis

Marketing needs access to the data to help them design new marketing programs and for tracking the program's progress. The facility required for tracking campaign progress is to put another process management report, as discussed above.

An effective marketing campaign must have a well thought out target—that is, a list of customers to try to sell to. Targets are usually defined by factors such as age, wealth, and particularly, by what the customer has bought in the past. This relies on having good sales records and good customer data.

Strategic business analysis—in other words, deciding the business direction—has much in common with marketing from an information access point of view. Both have a requirement to look at long-term sales trends and analyze it by customer type, by geographic region, by product type, and so on. This is the classic data warehouse type application. The sales data is the central "facts" file and the other data provides the dimensions along which the facts are analyzed. I am sure strategic business analysts would also like to do a trend analysis of the kind of data I discussed earlier in the category of process improvement. The potential of what you could analyze is almost unlimited.

As an aside, organizations have started collecting an enormous amount of information on you and me. For instance, by using a supermarket card they can keep track of everything you buy at their stores. But it's not so clear they know what to do with this information. There is a well-known story that a data mining query of supermarket data revealed that many people who buy diapers also buy beer—it's the men on their way home from work, so the theory goes. Ever since I read this, every time I go into a supermarket I have a look to see if the diapers are near the beer and they never are. There is a great temptation to analyze this data in enormous detail and, while finding many interesting trends and associations, I wonder how much it has actually made much of a difference. (There is even a term for analyzing the data every way and doing nothing—"Information Paralysis.")

12.1.6   Summary of requirements for information access

There are several points that come out from this quick review.

- The requirements are varied. It ranges from access of a single object and simple reports on a collection of objects, to highly complex searches over many objects. There is no single solution; you need a blend of strategies for the different requirements.

- The requirements are changing constantly. You can try to stop the continual flow of change requests by giving people the whole data and let them get on with it, but even this may not work; the people may ask for information that isn't in the database, will ask for explanations of how the data got to be as it is, and they might need help on the query tools.

- Many of the reporting requirements are reports about business processes. The data is a record of current and past business processes, and business management is trying to reconstruct what happened from the data. If there is no understanding in the IT department of the business processes it will be hard to communicate well with the users.

- If IT support for a single business process is dispersed over several systems there will be a requirement to bring the data together to create a total view of the process.

- There is a requirement to reformat data to be more understandable, but people want to see the raw data as well.

What this amounts to is that you cannot manage information access projects the same way you build a transaction processing system.

Sometimes there seems to be an insatiable demand for information. Provide a good service for information access and you will get many more requests for change.

12.2   Information accuracy

Information access is only as good as the data. One of the largest and most frustrating problems with many IT systems is inaccuracies in the data.

Information inaccuracies have several sources:

- Information is out of date. The customer's name has changed and no one has updated the database. As a general comment, if the database is telling you a fact, it is useful to know when that fact was recorded.

- Drawing wrong conclusions from the data. For instance, you might know what you've sold and what you still maintain, but that doesn't tell you who uses the product, because without maintenance you don't know who has gotten your product.

- Information is duplicated and you don't know which is the right version.

- Information was input incorrectly.

A subtle example of something halfway between "drawing the wrong conclusions" and "inputting wrong data" is synonyms. Say there is a customer called "Really Big Things Corporation." It might be input in the database as "RBT," "R. B. T.," "RBT Corp," "Really Big Things," and so on. You can't say any are really wrong. Furthermore, if you are dealing with a large organization you are likely to have several customer numbers, many contact names, and several delivery addresses, especially if you are dealing with them internationally. Finally, with all the merger and demerger activity, names will change and what were two customers become one, and what was one becomes two.

But while there are some inherent problems with data accuracy, IT applications often make it much worse. It is very common that most of the information about a business process is gathered right at the beginning of the business process (for example, renting a car). The person entering the data just wants to get their job done with a minimum of fuss. For instance, the name of the customer may be entered on the order form—hence all the different spellings of the customer's name. Also if the order has many order lines, the salesperson might enter the price for all the items as zero, except for one, just because they can't be bothered to split the price out among the items. The fundamental problem is that the person entering the data has no incentive to get it right. The solution is to force the data entry to be good but try to do it in such a way that the user is being helped rather than being hindered. For instance, for the customer name problem, the system could provide a list of customers rather than have the user type the name. To be really effective, the application could analyze the name as typed and suggest customers it might be. This is similar to how most e-mail systems work with names these days. Adding a new customer should only be possible from one system (with possibly the information being disseminated to others). The problem of prices in the order lines could be solved by the application picking up the price automatically from the price file. The only price manipulation from the sales staff would then be to fill in the discount field. Unfortunately, these changes add considerably to the complexity of the data entry application and the investment can be hard to justify (the sales department is happy with the system as it is!).

Many organizations have data duplication, especially of product data and customer data. Customer data is particularly prone to problems. In a financial institution, it is likely that every financial product (investments, loans, mortgages, etc.) has their own customer data. What organizations want now is a consolidated view of all the customer's accounts. This is essential for "customer relationship management" systems, which is about having a better understanding of the customer by knowing more about the extent of their dealings with the organization. Suppose we have two customer tables in two different databases, how do you merge the data to form one table of good data? With great difficulty, is the answer. There are at least three major problems to overcome:

- How do you know you are talking about the same object—for instance, how do we know the customer "Fred" in table A is the same as customer "Fred" in table B?
- How do you know whether an attribute is the same? Matching attributes can become quite complex. For instance, an address attribute might be {LINE1, LINE2, LINE3} in one database and {HOUSE NUMBER, ROAD NAME, CITY, STATE, ZIP} in another. (Even if both were in the latter format, you would still have problems with international addresses as they don't have the same structure.)
- If the data from the same attribute of the same object is different, what then?

The last problem is unsolvable. The notion of taking the name from one database, the address from another, and the telephone number from a third is laughable. It could be solved in theory if every attribute (yes every attribute, not every object) has a timestamp that indicates when it was last updated. The latest attribute from all candidate records would be taken. I have never heard of anyone doing this for the obvious reason that it would require a good deal of coding, a massive increase in disk space, and would incur considerable processor overhead.

As an aside, this example looked at two databases, but I have heard of a financial organization that had 13 sets of customer records and a telephone company that had 65.

In the next section I will examine the issue from the perspective of someone developing a new application. In the section after that I look at the issues of information accuracy in existing systems.

12.3   Shared data or controlled duplication

There are two basic approaches to keeping common data: shared data and controlled duplication. These are illustrated in the Figure 12-3.

12.3.1   Shared data

The shared data solution implies a common database, typically separate from other databases. There are three ways of implementing shared data, which are illustrated in Figure 12-4.

Shared data solution

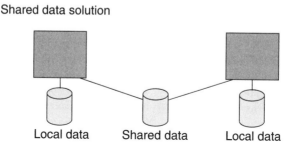

Controlled duplication solution

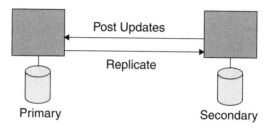

Figure 12-3   Shared data vs. controlled duplication

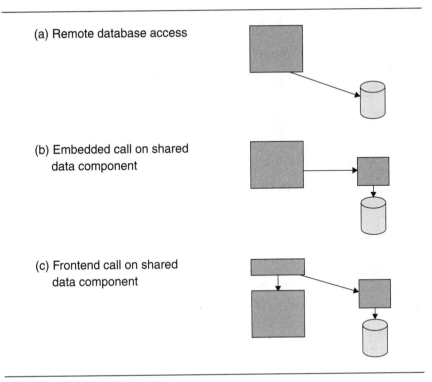

(a) Remote database access

(b) Embedded call on shared
    data component

(c) Frontend call on shared
    data component

Figure 12-4   Shared data configurations

Remote database access has the main application calling the shared data using technology like ODBC or OLE DB. While superficially attractive, there are some good reasons for not taking this approach:

- It has poor performance since network traffic is greater than other solutions especially if SQL commands must be parsed by the database server.
- Some remote database access technology does not support two-phase commits so updates cannot be synchronized.
- The structure of the shared database is hard coded into many dispersed applications making schema changes difficult to manage and implement. Put another way, the SQL commands, that access the shared data, are scattered everywhere.

The first two reasons are why, wherever possible, the database should be on the same machine as the transaction server. The last reason is why we should hide the SQL behind a component interface.

The other two solutions, (b) and (c) in Figure 12-4, are similar to each other in that they call a component that manages access to the remote database. The database is hidden behind the component interface and hence can be changed with minimum disruption to the other applications.

The difference between the embedded call and the frontend call are seen in the programs. The embedded call has the shared data component called from within the main application program. The frontend solution has a frontend program, possibly written in a script language like Visual Basic or Java, calling both the shared data component to access the data and the main program to do the main task.

In the layering presented at the end of Chapter 10 (see Figure 10-5), the front end is the presentation logic component or a mediator component, and the components calling the database are the business object components. If the business object components require a lot of data from the shared data component then passing all that data through the front end is an unnecessary complexity. In many cases, though, all the business object needs is a reference to the shared data. For instance in an order-entry processing, all the order entry object itself might need is the primary key (say, the customer number) of the customer data. If so, passing a primary key value through the front end gives flexibility. In one case the key might come from a customer search screen, in another case the key might come from a charge card. The main body of the order-entry processing is the same for both. Note it is desirable to be able to search the order data by customer key value because we want to be able to take some sensible action if the customer disappears. This is an instance of a general rule: With shared data we should always ensure that the links go both ways so you can handle deletions of the shared data.

Where possible, though, you should try and standardize one or a few interfaces to the shared data access routines. You want to be able to move the application around so if the shared data is accessible through the same interface on many machines, there is no hindrance.

12.3.2   Controlled duplication

Controlled duplication, as its name implies, has the same data in two or more databases. The advantages of controlled duplication are better resiliency and, in many cases, better performance. The disadvantages are that the data is slightly out of date and the application is more complex.

Remember that in this section I am only talking about green-field development, not existing production data (that comes in a later section). In particular, I am assuming that all the problems of reconciling data discussed earlier are solved. Thus I am assuming that you can match the objects from one database with objects in another, because they both have the same primary key. I am also assuming that it is possible to match the attributes, albeit maybe with a bit of reformatting. In short, I am assuming the database schemas have been designed to make controlled duplication possible because, if these two conditions aren't met, it isn't.

You will observe from Figure 12-3 that I have one copy of the data designated as the "primary" and the other as the "secondary." Many people will be tempted to have both copies with equal status by allowing updates on both copies, which are then propagated to the other copy. The problem with this idea is that the two copies can diverge. Consider the following scenario:

Update "ABC" on object X on copy A.

Update "ABC" sent to the copy B.

Update "LMN" on object X on copy B.

Update "LMN" sent to copy A.

Copy B processes updates from A—object X on B now has "ABC"

Copy A processes updates from B—object X on A now has "LMN"

Sometimes you don't care; if the data is known to have errors in it, one or two more might not hurt. You can of course write a program to arbitrarily fix up the data to be consistent.

(A technical aside: the notion of equal status requires that the transformation of attributes from A to B is reversible from B to A.)

It would be possible for both systems to be of equal status by using two-phase commits to update all copies of the data. However, the disadvantage of that approach is that if one system is down then the other system is badly impacted. It would be impossibly clunky to maintain synchronicity across, say, ten duplicate copies of the data. I discussed these issues in more detail when I described the dual active configuration in Chapter 7. In theory, there are some circumstances where completely synchronous duplication of data is required and two-phase commit would be the solution.

So if you don't mind the data being slightly asynchronous but you do need it to be consistent, the solution is to do all your updates on one machine first and propagate the updates using message queuing. The first updated database is the primary. Updates are sent to the secondary where they are processed in exactly the same order as on the primary. The next question is—are there constraints about how quickly the data must be updated? In most cases, while it is desirable for the data to be updated at nearly the same time, it is better for the system to be up and running with slightly old data than be down waiting for the updates to come through. This is an ideal application for message queuing.

For the most part, you can get away with a small timing window for common data because the common data contains resource objects not tracking objects (see Figure 11-2). Let me give two examples.

Suppose the common data is a product data and the price changes. There is a possibility that the order is made after the price change but before the local copy of the price changed on the system. The reason why this does not matter is that there is a much wider window of time between telling the customer the price and sending an invoice. Thus, there will always be prices on the order that do not reflect the current price in the current product database and it is something you have to live with.

The second example is: Suppose we have customer data in a Web order processing system and in a delivery system. The biggest danger would be for a customer to change their address on the Web system but still get their order delivered to the wrong address. This could happen if the delivery note was sent before the address update got through, but with a message queuing system working well, this is a timing window of less than a second. In any case, given the likelihood of sending the delivery to the wrong address, business processes should already be in place to handle this unfortunate happenstance.

As with shared data, if the primary and the secondary hold exactly the same data then the interface should be the same. This allows us to move an application from the machine that holds the primary to the machine that holds the secondary without recompilation.

It is possible, though, to have controlled duplication even though the format of the data on the primary and secondary is different. For instance, codes can be converted to text to make them more understandable. For performance, different attributes can be indexed. The simplest solution is to make the primary a complete master copy of all attributes, that is, hold all the data from all the secondaries. In other words, the secondaries can leave out data from the master but not the other way around.

The alternative solution is for the secondary to hold additional data but the programmer has to know which updates should be sent to the primary first and which are processed in place. It is easy to go wrong—for instance, if an attribute is added to the primary that already exists on the secondary. It helps to stay out of trouble if you put the additional fields into a separate table in the database with a reference to the duplicated data from the primary.

12.3.3   Hybrid strategy

It is possible to both share data and have controlled duplication. For instance, you could share data if the two applications are in the same machine but use controlled duplication between machines. Thus, there might be ten applications on three machines but only three copies of the data—one on each machine. If the interface to the data was the same on all machines, the applications could be moved from machine to machine at will.

12.4   Creating consistency in existing databases

Creating consistency in the data is one of the most important issues facing IT organizations today. It is also one of the most difficult.

The basic assumption of this section is that you want to convert existing applications that have data in silos to use either data sharing or controlled duplication of common data.

There are three problems:

1. A technical problem—converting old code to use a new component interface or equivalent.

2. A data migration problem—moving data from old databases into new databases that may be formatted in a very different way.

3. A business process problem—changing the business processes to use the new data.

I will discuss each in turn and then pull the threads of the argument together.

First, however, the easy way! Many so-called legacy systems have ODBC and OLE DB interfaces, and facilities for copying updates to data mart or data warehouse systems. You could choose one production system as the primary and have the others access the data through say OLE DB. This is the shared data strategy and has all the advantages and disadvantages of that approach. A further disadvantage is that other existing applications will have to be fixed up to use the shared data. This is the "technical problem" and is explored below. Where this strategy breaks down is situations like a large financial institution where data like customer data is dispersed over ten or more applications. In these situations the effort of changing so much existing code, and the poor performance of the final system, mitigates against this solution.

Second, an easy way that sometimes doesn't work: A strategy that is gaining some credence at the moment is called the information broker. It works as follows. When one system updates its customer data it broadcasts an "update a customer" message to all other systems. This is done by having a grand central station of a system that transforms the data into a standard format ("canonical form" is the technical expression) and then reformats the data for all the destination hosts. This sounds great; assume there are n copies of the data, then instead of "n times $(n-1)$" transformations to maintain, there are "$2n$" (for each host, one in and one out) transformations to maintain.

If you look back at the section above on "Controlled duplication" you will see the problem with this notion. Recall that we had three reasons for data inconsistency—data value inconsistency, inability to match attributes, and inability to match objects. The grand central station idea partially fixes the data value inconsistencies. I say partially because there is no primary copy of the data and, as the example at the beginning of the section on controlled duplication illustrates, there is a problem when the same data is updated at the same time on different databases. On the question of matching attributes the assumption behind the information broker concept is that this is possible. And it is—sometimes. But look at the example given earlier for matching addresses (for example, does street name equal line one?). Clearly it is often not simple. Sometimes it is impossible; for instance, if one of the attributes in one system does not exist in another.

The killer problem with information brokers is that it does not solve the problem of matching objects. That this is a serious problem is illustrated by a brewery, which wanted to know how many pubs it had (this is England). Three different systems gave three different answers (depending on whether they counted clubs, hotels, pubs that weren't owned by the brewery, etc.). This is a simple example. A much more problematic example is a bank that has many accounts and the customer data is stored with the account. In this example there is no customer number, only names to go on which to do the mapping. If the address for a "Chris Britton" changes for one account, it would be risky to change the address for a "Mr. C. G. Britton" in another account. In summary, if you have a reliable object identifier key with which to do the mapping from one object to another, you only have a small(ish) problem. If you don't have a reliable object identifier with which to do the mapping your problem is unsolvable (even by artificial intelligence programs because you don't dare take the risk of heuristic rules getting it wrong).

There are two messages from this discussion. First, we cannot avoid changing the applications and the business processes. Second, if you change the grand central station into a grand central database you have the kernel of something that works. The grand central database would implement the primary copy as in the controlled duplication strategy outlined in the previous section. The next three subsections are built around this idea.

12.4.1   The technical problem

In the green-field scenario, access to common data was hidden behind a component interface. Picture trying to implement the same strategy in an existing COBOL application. The first step would be to try and identify all the code that updates the data in question and put it into a clean interface. This might be extremely easy or impossibly hard, depending on how the code was written. Let us suppose it is done; the extracted code has been put into a COBOL copy library and the rest of the code fixed to call the copy library instead of using the data directly. The process must be repeated on all applications that want to use the same data. It is highly desirable that all applications use the same copy library for the shared data, but that might mean much greater changes to the applications. The next step is to decide which application has the primary copy of the data. The copy libraries in the secondary copies then need to send messages to the primary copy to make updates, and the primary copy needs to send updates to all the secondaries.

If we can create a component interface should we go for a shared data strategy or a controlled duplication strategy? It might be possible to implement a shared data strategy but there is a wrinkle. It could be that the updates to the shared data are embedded in transactions that do something else as well. This means splitting off the shared data would require converting a simple transaction into a distributed transaction. Some COBOL environments cannot easily support a program initiating the second leg of a distributed transaction. (The COBOL program here would be both a distributed transaction server and a distributed transaction client.)

So what if creating a component interface is too difficult? An alternative was suggested by the information broker idea; use the transaction interface. Say we have an existing system that has customer data. There are likely to be existing transactions for creating, updating, and deleting customers. The message from grand central database to the local system can become calls on these existing transactions. It is advantageous for performance and resiliency to send the messages through a message queuing, so you need a small program to read the queue and call the transactions. What you have to ensure is that the existing user interface for updating the customer data does not call these transactions. Instead they send a message to the grand central database. Ideally, you want to ensure the users never call the old transactions but instead call the update routines on the grand central database directly.

12.4.2   The data migration problem

If you have a grand central database for common data (and you only want it for common data, not everything), then you will be able to migrate applications to the new database one at a time rather than all at once.

There is obviously a logistical problem of converting the data, loading it into the new database, and putting in the new application at the same time. The logistics can be alleviated to some extent if there is a time period when the old application updates its old data and, at the same time, sends updates to the grand central database. This way you can do the data migration before the application migration and, for a while, be able to do parallel running on the old and new databases.

The problems of converting the data and loading it to the new database are not too bad for the first application but for subsequent applications there is the issue of trying to match data to see if it refers to the same object. What you probably will need to do is load the old data into the new database and then do a manual reconciliation job in the new location. You might want to develop a program that identifies possible matches. You may find that the grand central database needs to record aliases (hopefully temporary) rather than always eliminating one object in favor of another.

12.4.3   The business process problem

The point about a grand central database is to turn it into the primary and only authority of that piece of information. Inevitably this changes the business process. Instead of updating the common data as before, the primary data will have its own update routines. We are back to the point made right at the beginning of the section on information accuracy—information accuracy is a business-process issue. No amount of technology will change that. However, one reason I am so keen on having a primary copy of the database is that it provides a focus for business-process change. For instance, if it is customer data being consolidated, the grand central database of customer information will ultimately become the one and only way of maintaining customer details, which is just how we want it to be.

Observe that this strategy implements the notion of business processes controlling resource data, illustrated in Figure 11-3.

12.5   The information controller

Data administration is frequently seen as the systems manager for the database system; the person who runs recovery and reorganization routines and actually types in the schema changes. This worked fine with traditional silo application development. Each silo had its own database and the design of the database was entirely the responsibility of the silo application development manager. But with integrated applications that is no longer possible. Someone must take responsibility for the data layer as a whole to ensure consistency and quality, otherwise it won't happen.

This wider role I shall call the **information controller**. The information controller's responsibility can be easily stated; he or she is responsible for information access and information accuracy. Exactly what that means in practice includes

- Data mart and data warehouse development
- A say in online inquiry development (to resolve issues about when to use a data mart)
- Control of the database schema
- Control of the development of data access interfaces and components
- A say in the application development to ensure system-wide data quality

In other words, when a designer wants to provide data update to shared data or someone in the organization has a complaint about the quality of the data, they go to the information controller.

Note that the information controller is looking after common data, not all data. Otherwise the job is just too big and gets in the way of everybody else. What I suggest is that the information controller gradually takes control of data as the common data is synchronized. In other words, if there are ten customer databases, the information controller takes command of the customer databases one by one as they are brought under the control of the common data strategy.

But before taking control of the data, the information controller needs to have an understanding of the severity of the problem. Repositories and modeling tools are important aids. The repository should hold the schema information from the various databases and the new object models of the common data. It could also hold all the interface definitions. Modeling tools could be used to give a pictorial representation of the objects and the business processes.

As I noted earlier, many of the issues of data quality can best be fixed when the data is input, which means that the information controller is not some back room administrator but a very visible member of the IT management team.

A key skill of the information controller must be a deep understanding of the difference between an information access project and a transaction development project. In an information access project there may be little or no programming because off-the-shelf tools meet most of your requirements. But in spite of that, these projects are not easy. For instance, you can forget about a clear statement of requirements. Also, what tools will be successful will depend on training the end user, but are the end users willing to be trained? Even at the business level, your average manager will very clearly tell you what data he or she needs but, when it is provided, will immediately change his or her mind. The information controller needs to communicate well and have excellent personal relationship skills.

The final point is that information access and accuracy is not a one-time fix. It will be a slow incremental process of improvement. The information controller is in many ways like the program management function described earlier but for information access projects. These projects will tend to be short but there will be many of them. Information controller is a challenging job.

12.6   Conclusions

Understand that there is no one fix for data access; different users have different requirements. The best place to start is to position the user on the Timeliness/Data to Information chart. You also need to access their need for doing ad-hoc queries and getting the data themselves or have someone get it for them.

Wherever possible, data should belong to the transaction server.

There are two strategies for common data, like customer data or product data. Either share the data or have controlled duplication. In both cases hide the data behind a component interface. For shared data have a primary database and always update the primary first before propagating the updates to the secondaries.

For common data in an existing database, migrate the common data to a central primary store one at a time and implement either a shared data or a controlled duplication strategy.

Someone, whom I have called the information controller, should be in control of shared data. They should also be in charge of the overall data access strategy for the enterprise.

13

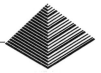

Change—Integration

There is plenty of literature about implementation design for new applications. There is very little on the very real problem of implementation design where applications already exist. This chapter and the next address this problem. They are about changing existing applications, in particular mainframe systems. Many of the points are generally applicable to any situation where you are handling significant change.

In the previous chapter the subject of changing existing applications was addressed in the context of the data layer. In this chapter the concern is the presentation layer and transaction integration; it is about programs, not data. In the next chapter I will look at the issue of program flexibility.

I will start by discussing again the order processing example used in Chapter 1. First let us recall the "before" state (see Figure 13-1).

From a business-process perspective what we are trying to achieve is illustrated in Figure 13-2.

What Figure 13-2 shows is that order processing, delivery, and billing are part of one large business process, let us call it the order handling process. In the terminology used in Chapter 11, the order tracking object is the tracking object for the order handling business process. Figure 13-2 also illustrates the need to maintain product and customer resource objects. Finally, Figure 13-2 shows the real time and deferrable links between the applications.

Figure 13-2 is only a process view. It does not show the data inquiry requirements. To show this I will redraw the diagram to show how the customer interacts with the system. This is shown in Figure 13-3.

Figure 13-3 shows that the customer has a fixed inquiry link to the customer, product, and order tracking data. Calling these links "fixed inquiry" links indicates that the inquiry is tailored to the customer demands (other situations might call for specifying "ad-hoc query" links and "push" links).

If this is what I need, how can I get there?

Clearly a major issue is multiple applications sharing the same data. Since I discussed this at length in the previous chapter, I won't discuss further the synchronization of customer and product data.

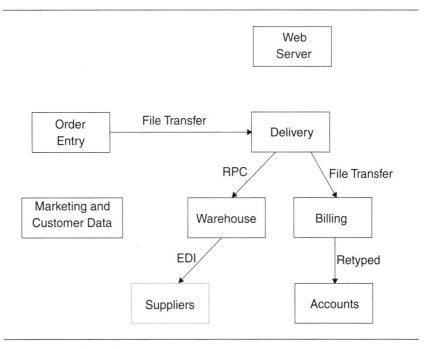

Figure 13-1 Example—before Web commerce server

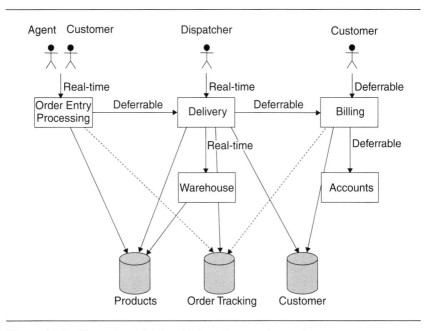

Figure 13-2 Example—high-level integration requirements

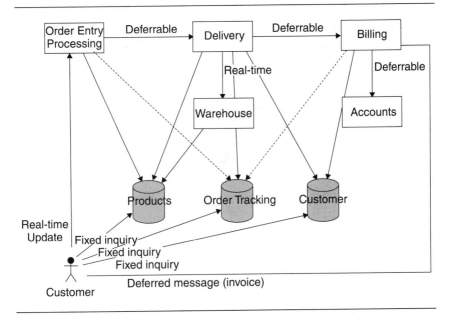

Figure 13-3   Example—the customer view

In Figure 13-3 the order tracking data is represented as a disk file and hence as a passive data source, but this is not necessarily the case. As previously described, it is usually best if the logic for updating the data goes with the data, and with the order tracking objects would go the logic for such complex issues such as multiple deliveries or replacement deliveries. Put another way, this logic is the order handling business process logic.

In this example there are four sizeable projects:

1. The implementation of order tracking data and an order handling process.

2. The consolidation of product data.

3. The consolidation of customer data.

4. The creation of a Web interface.

The first priority is probably number 4 since, as soon as the others are ready, the Web interface can quickly be adapted to make use of them. We might also want to split the customer and product consolidation projects into small deliverable chunks because the alternative of doing the whole thing as one large project would mean a long wait for delivery.

Note that part of the skill of the evolutionary process is splitting the work into small projects that deliver the most benefit early on. This juggling of project content and order is the job of the program managers (described in Chapter 10). This sometimes means implementing interim solutions that have a short life. That's all right because first, there is benefit to the organization from having functionality early, and second, if we try and design the total new system in one go we probably over engineer, so whichever way you look at it, you always do too much work.

13.1 Creating a presentation layer

This section is about carving out a clean transaction server interface from existing applications so that a new interface for the presentation layer can be created that allows for maximum flexibility.

The first question is: To what degree should we make changes? Consider Figure 13-4.

In Figure 13-4:

- Diagram (a) is the old terminal interface.
- Diagram (b) is a new interface built to talk to the old interface without changing the original interface. This is often called "screen-scraping."
- Diagram (c) shows a transaction server interface.

There are two classes of problems with screen-scraping. It puts a large workload on the frontend presentation layer and there are problems associated with the mismatch of the size of the interface device. I look at these issues in the next two subsections and then discuss option (c).

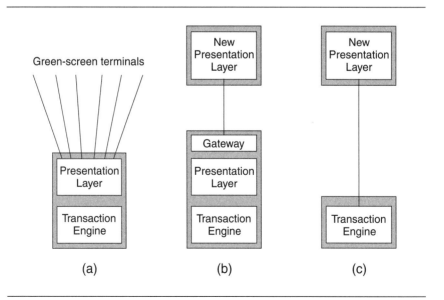

Figure 13-4 Adding a presentation layer to an existing application

13.1.1   Screen-scraping task

Consider a frontend Web server calling an existing application by screen-scraping. As well as sending and receiving the data for inquiries and transactions, it must also do the following:

- Log on to the backend system.
- Do any menu traversal required.
- Reformat the data into a string of text that precisely conforms to the format expected by the existing application.
- Take out the fields from exactly the right place in the received message.
- Keep track of the position in the dialogue (that is, which screen the dialogue is at) of many end users simultaneously.

Error handling makes these problems more difficult, since the screen output may indicate the field in error by positioning the cursor in front of it and sending a highlighting character. On the other hand, if the error is a network error, the frontend program may have to log on again and go through all the menu traversal again.

The impact of screen-scraping is to set the existing application in concrete since any change to the screen layout now has ramifications for the frontend program. This is an instance of what Gerald Weinberg calls the "Fast-Food Fallacy," which states that "No difference plus no difference plus no difference plus no difference . . . eventually equals a clear difference." (The name comes from the notion that reducing the number of sesame seeds on a bun from 100 to 99 is unnoticeable, likewise 99 to 98, 98 to 97 . . . 51 to 50.) In this case, screen-scraping on one screen won't be noticeable but screen-scraping on even ten screens will be a major headache.

13.1.2   Interface size mismatch

Some error handling situations will be even harder to implement. Look at Figure 13-5.

This illustrates the problem of large messages. A large message from the Web may correspond to many terminal-sized messages to the production system. Say a large message corresponds to five messages at the back end and, while processing the third message, the transaction aborts. Now the frontend program must undo the work of the first two messages that completed without a hitch. The simplest solution is to process the entire large message in one two-phase commit transaction (probably on one database), but if you are emulating a terminal you are unlikely to have a two-phase commit capability. Instead you have to review what the human operator would do in a similar situation. In some cases, like updating a record on the system, it could be that there is no clear answer—the human operator makes a value judgment that some of the updates are okay and some aren't. They may even resubmit the input, just leaving out the single field that caused the

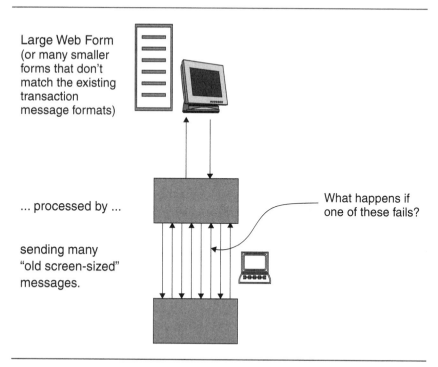

Large Web Form (or many smaller forms that don't match the existing transaction message formats)

... processed by ...

sending many "old screen-sized" messages.

What happens if one of these fails?

Figure 13-5   The device size problem

error. The Web server is unlikely to know enough to make these judgments so must instead reverse all the transactions already completed. In the worst case, there may not be any explicit reversal transaction types.

13.1.3   Turning existing applications into transaction servers

Thus, there is a strong case for moving to option (c) in Figure 13-4—a transaction server. I will look at this issue from three angles:

1. What needs to be done to the existing production code

2. Wrapping the old technology with new, and

3. The impact on the business processes

In this subsection I look at the first of these. The next subsection looks at wrapping, and the impact on business processes gets a whole section to itself.

Changing the existing code is largely a process of elimination. Obviously the presentation code—building the screen messages—can go, as we only need to send raw data. Most security checking code can go as well, since the user will be authenticated at the presentation layer. Security information is only required by a transaction server if the application itself is doing additional security checks, perhaps giving different users access to different customers. As discussed in Chapter 9, the ideal solution is to add extra input fields for the user and role identifiers to the messages for the transaction server.

Menu traversal code can go. In many terminal applications, the applications guided the user, but now the presentation layer does all the guiding; the transaction server should only process inquiries and update transactions without any regard for the ordering.

Unfortunately many existing online transaction processing applications do have ordering dependencies. The programmer knew the terminal screens would be submitted in a certain order and have exploited this fact. For example, one screen might add a new customer or find an existing customer, and a later screen adds a new order. The customer identifier might be stored in local storage and used in the new order transaction without doing any further checks.

Storing the customer identifier in local storage is an example of the session holding state. Note that state is being held on a per terminal dialogue basis. Typically, the transaction monitor will have facilities for storing small amounts of data in the output message. This data is never sent to the user but can be retrieved by any application that receives the next input from the same terminal.

Before leaving this example, observe what happens when there is a failure—the session state is lost. The user must therefore start the session from the beginning, hopefully finding the customer on the database rather than adding it again. When we re-implement the application using a different presentation, we might not want to carry this recovery strategy forward. In this example, the simplest solution is to store the customer identifier in the client and pass it as a parameter to the transaction server. That way, on any server failure, the client can go straight in and carry on processing where they left off.

Ordering dependencies are one example of storing state. Two other common reasons for storing state are security, which was discussed above, and temporary data gathering. An example of the latter could be an order entry application that stores all the order information locally until the final "It's done" command is sent when all the data is stored in the database in one transaction.

Sometimes these problems turn out to be non-problems. Look again at Figure 13-5 and the issue of the mismatch of sizes of the channel. With a transaction server there is an easy solution without a two-phase commit. Create a new transaction that takes all the data and calls the existing code within one transaction. There is no need to collect data in the session state because all the data comes in one transaction.

Where there is still a problem, the session states should be stored in the database, as discussed in Chapter 7 on resiliency.

Let me summarize the argument so far. Think of it as a three-step process.

1. The terminal forms handling code and the menu traversal is taken out of the application.

2. Security code is taken out of the application.

3. Any remaining session state must reviewed and if necessary stored in the database.

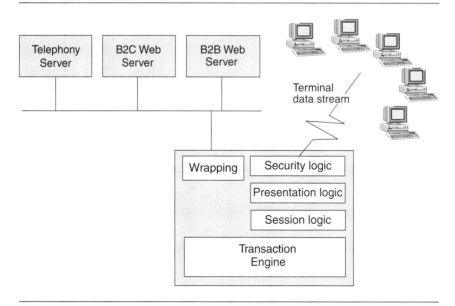

Figure 13-6 The old and the new presentation layers

With these steps done, the application is ready for wrapping.

How difficult is this whole process? It depends (you knew I was going to say that). Sometimes it is easy—sometimes there is no code to change. Sometimes it is hard. The only way to find out is to find a programmer and let them try.

Even if it turns out to be hard to make comprehensive changes, all is not lost. Often the old must co-exist with the new, as in Figure 13-6.

The number of transaction types that need to be wrapped is often very small, maybe five or ten transaction types out of a total population of several hundred. It is not so hard to clone the few transactions that need to be changed, change them, and leave the rest as before.

Of course if it really does turn out to be hard, then it is time to review replacing the complete application. Even so, the old must co-exist with the new. Adding a new order-entry process to our example at the top of this chapter and we get Figure 13-7. This shows how an alternative order entry application can be introduced without changing anything else.

I have seen very few cases where this has needed to be done. Many organizations take the far more difficult step of implementing a package solution.

13.1.4 Wrapping

Wrapping is the name for creating a new interface for an application by installing some software that converts the old interface to the new interface.

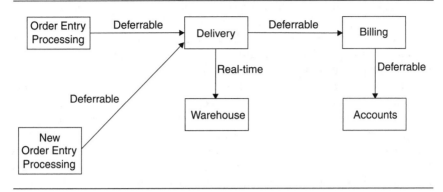

Figure 13-7   Example—two order entry processes

The technology aspect of taking a mainframe transaction processing application and giving it an interface to the world of components is relatively straightforward. For instance, in Unisys you can use BEA Tuxedo as a gateway and a product called BEA eLink OSI to communicate to the transaction monitors running on the ClearPath mainframes. Unisys have created a product called OpenTI for wrapping Tuxedo applications by Microsoft COM+ components. This gives two-phase commit capability across Tuxedo, COM+, and mainframe applications. For IBM MVS, the Microsoft product COMTI wraps CICS transactions with COM+.

There are similar products for Enterprise Java Beans. BEA themselves have all the links from Tuxedo and their eLink products to Enterprise Java Beans. The bottom line is that, technically, wrapping is not hard.

The catch with all this technology is that the applications on the mainframe transaction monitor must be stateless. In most cases this is inevitable. Because there is no terminal and because a Web session is so different from a terminal session, all the baggage that comes with a terminal interface must be eliminated.

13.1.5   Building a middle tier

A key question is how complex to make the wrapping. Should it be a minimal wrapping, simply converting one technology to another with minimal overhead, or should it create a new object view of the interface, in essence creating the business object components as described in Chapter 10 (see Figure 10-5)?

The second approach is advocated by the Microsoft DNA and Sun J2EE architectures, described in Chapter 4. Both these three-tier architectures perpetuate a strange conceit that transaction logic implemented on mainframe systems is part of the data layer, in contrast to transaction logic implemented in COM+ or EJB, which is part of the middle tier.

Strange conceit or not, this approach has some merit. The idea of implementing business object components was to increase the likelihood of reuse, especially across different presentation channels, and there are good examples of the idea working well in practice. As the architecture develops, more and more code is likely to use the business object components.

It is usually not difficult either. If you look at an existing online transaction, you will almost always see that one of the fields is something like account number or product number and identifies an object. The transaction call easily converts to an operation on an object by taking the rest of the transaction input and turning them into parameters. For instance, all transactions that change account details become operations on the account object. The actual code in the business object components is typically little more than calls on the old mainframe applications.

Sometimes the logic in the business object components becomes more complex. For instance, the data you want to expose in the object may be physically located in several backend transaction systems. Another complex scenario would be trying to make a batch system look like an online system by storing a local copy of the data more up-to-date than the backend system (a notion referred to as pseudo updating or memo updating). When you are faced with difficulties such as these you have to ask yourself the question of whether you want to add complex code to the new business object component, or whether it would be better to fix up the backend systems to be more supportive of the new functionality.

The disadvantage of creating an object-oriented middle tier is that the business objects have to be designed with care. Some organizations have developed good solutions using non-object middleware, such as Tuxedo or MQSeries. Having any common middleware-based infrastructure seems to be a more important factor for success than having an object foundation.

But it might be too early to judge. Most of the experience with multiple presentation channels is very recent (a few years old) and it is hard to tell how truly flexible and effective a solution is until the original implementers have moved on to other things and others have to grapple with their creation.

13.2   Business processing change with new interfaces

Let us return to the order handling process and look at the details of the order entry application. It is very common that old terminal based applications are rigid. The order form screens are presented in a fixed order; customer information, such as shipping address and billing details, are retyped with every order; and, if the user finds that some information is missing, the complete order is aborted. It does not have to be like that. A flexible solution is illustrated in Figure 13-8.

When I discussed business processes in Chapter 11, I contrasted, on the one hand, a military process—doing it by the numbers—and, on the other hand, a flexible rule-based definition of a process. Suppose we have several channels. For

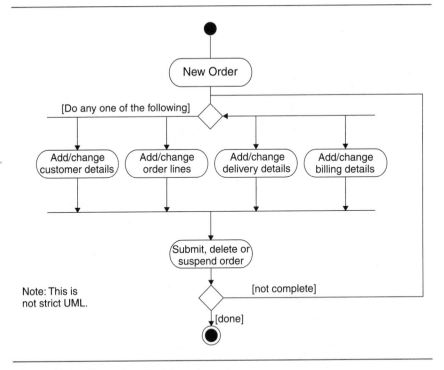

Figure 13-8   Example—flexible order entry

instance, order entry might have a Web interface, a call center, and a traditional terminal interface. While all of these channels share the fundamental logic of order entry, illustrated in Figure 13-8, they may have additional ordering constraints and additional processes. For instance, the call center might have a script that guides the telephone user through the steps of the ordering process, and the script imposes an order that isn't there in the most general case. The core process should implement the flexible rule-based definition of the business process, while the specific presentation channels might impose some military order to the process. Furthermore, the call center may be only available for specially registered customers for which the customer, delivery, and billing details may have already been entered, so some steps may be missing. The notion of a general, flexible process and specific, presentation-based processes is illustrated in Figure 13-9.

There are various ways to implement Figure 13-9.

One extreme is to implement the core process activities as a transaction server. All the different activities would map to one or more operations on an order object. Within the order object there would need to be status flags that indicate whether the customer details, the delivery details, and the billing details have been set. Only when all the status flags indicate success can the order be submitted. Presentation A and B are handled by separate logic in the Web server or call center

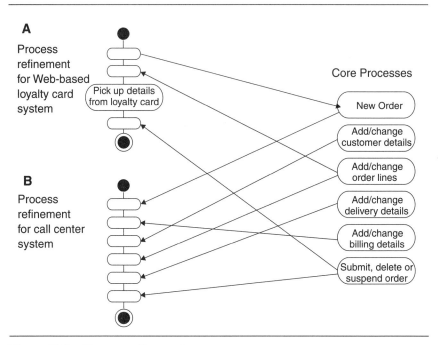

A

Process
refinement
for Web-based
loyalty card
system

Pick up details
from loyalty card

Core Processes

New Order

Add/change
customer details

Add/change
order lines

B

Process
refinement
for call center
system

Add/change
delivery details

Add/change
billing details

Submit, delete or
suspend order

Figure 13-9   Process refinement

server or whatever. The logic in A and B is little more than handling the dialogue
flow and calling the core-process activities.

I will call this style of implementation the **core server model**.

There are some advantages to the core server model.

- The core server itself is a stateless server, which, you have probably realized
  by now, I like.
- Core process rules are implemented in one place and, once implemented,
  immediately apply to all kinds of data entry.
- It is not difficult to mix presentation modes. For instance, the order can
  be initially entered over the Web, suspended, and then changed by a telephone call.
- Different core activities can be physically located on different servers. Any customer details updates may be actually implemented on the customer data server.

The alternative to the core server model is the **reuse model**. Each presentation
layer refinement is implemented as a separate application and, instead of calling the
core processes, the core processes are incorporated into the application. To avoid
developing the core processes multiple times, reuse is used. Two forms of reuse are
relevant in this model, component reuse and module reuse. (Component reuse is
reuse of runtime components and module reuse is reuse of program language source

files.) The key characteristic of the reuse model is that each application has its own private data.

The advantages of the reuse model are

- It is fast—data is stored locally for the duration of the dialogue.
- Processes are easier to change since you don't have to ensure your changes are compatible with the core process implementation.

But there are disadvantages:

- Processes are easier to change only because there is no control to ensure consistency between the different forms of the process.
- It is impossible to mix presentation modes in the business process under consideration.
- It may be hard to reuse components and modules because different presentation servers may be using different technology, for instance, one may need COM+ components, the other Java Beans.

Which model is best? In general the core server model has better control and flexibility but it is more complex. For order entry processing the core server model allows mixing up presentation channels, which is an attractive feature. But take another example, like the new car rental process discussed in Chapter 11, and there is no possibility of mixing up the presentation channels, so the reuse model may be a better solution.

So what should be done about existing applications? Typically, existing applications will combine a single implementation of the core process activities and one process refinement for one presentation channel. The ideal solution would be to pick out from the code a clean core server model.

13.3 Changing the middleware between transaction servers

You probably noticed that in Figure 13-1 the "middleware" used is file transfer and remote procedure calls (RPC). Figure 13-2 in contrast had the messages between the applications described as deferrable and real-time. The implication is that file transfer is used to implement deferrable messages and RPCs are used to implement real-time messages. In the early chapters of this book I described message queuing as the best solution to deferrable messages, and transaction component middleware as the best solution for real-time. Is it important to introduce the new middleware? Why? And how should it be done?

The tasks required to move from a file-transfer implementation to message queuing include training, installation, configuration, development of operating procedures, and program changes to the existing applications. It is a task of sufficient size not to be undertaken without significant benefits. The benefits of moving to message queuing are in the areas of responsiveness and integrity. Responsiveness because although a message queuing solution is unlikely to have less overhead than file transfer the messages are sent immediately rather than when the next file is transferred. Integrity because in message queuing there is a built-in mechanism for ensuring the messages are sent and sent only once. With file transfer there are normally manual procedures to ensure both these conditions are met. Many organizations have implemented file-transfer solutions that work well if nothing goes wrong, but, if there is a failure during file creation, file transfer, or file processing, messages can be lost or processed twice. Obviously in our order processing example, either lost orders or duplicate orders have a serious business impact.

Similarly, there is a case for moving from RPCs to transactional component middleware. The chief benefits of transactional component middleware are that:

- The use of components helps reuse in the server.
- The use of object interfaces may help simplify the client code.
- The use of distributed transactional processing makes it possible to call many operations in one transaction.

But in the conversion from RPC to transactional component middleware, all of these advantages are in the box marked "possible future benefits" rather than the box marked "immediate return on investment." I don't know many organizations that will make such a move. The reality is that something—possibly the need for integration to a Web server—needs to be added to the project before it will be justifiable.

A further difficulty with moving to transactional component middleware is that, in contrast to message queuing and RPC, the client must be written in an object-oriented language, or at least use a gateway that is written in an object-oriented language. In our example in which RPC is being used between the delivery application and the warehouse application, this could be a serious concern if the existing applications aren't object-oriented.

Even in a newly developed system we would expect that there are several forms of middleware in use, for instance, message queuing, transactional component middleware, and remote database access for ad-hoc queries. In a real organization, there will be a number of other middleware products and various ad-hoc solutions such as file transfer. We are looking at an environment of considerable complexity that is not likely to become much easier anytime soon.

When changes are made, it is advisable to put in mediator components as discussed in Chapter 6 and Chapter 10. Change will be that much easier in the future.

13.4   Runtime integration products

Integration has been recognized by the computer industry as a major problem, and where there are problems there are opportunities. Being the computer industry, there are also buzzwords. Thus we have Wrapping, Gateways, IntegrationWare, Enterprise Application Integration (EAI), Straight-Through processing, EDI, Messaging, XML, B2B, Process integration, Bridges, Workflow, hub-and-spoke, pipes, message backplanes, and much else besides. Surely somewhere in here must be a solution to the problems of integration?

None of these concepts are invalid. The problem is that they overlap and the quantity of acronyms people are inventing with such abandon has led to a situation where we don't know what people are talking about any longer. Well I don't at any rate.

One of the popular marketing themes is put a big box in the middle. The basic idea is that feeding everything through a big box reduces the number of connections (because every box has only one connection), which must be simpler, right?

The only popular middleware, that I am aware of, in which there is a significant effort in setting up inter-machine connections is IBM's MQSeries, which requires connections (and queues) to be set up statically. Thus for MQSeries it is simpler to send all the messages through a big (highly resilient and secure) box in the middle. But as the Internet proves, managing a large number of connections per se is not necessarily particularly difficult. All you need is one or more centralized directories which, in the case of the Internet, are the Domain Name Servers. What IBM developers have got against directories is one of the abiding mysteries of the present day IT scene.

A second reason for a centralized box is for broadcasts. One variation on this theme is the information broker concept discussed in Chapter 12. I noted there that the concept is not problem free. But the vast majority of middleware messages use point-to-point messages not broadcasts.

The real effort for administrators is controlling the message formats. For inter-server traffic there are far more message formats than there are machine connections. The ideal solution is centralized compile-time control; specifically, it is the control of the IDL and Cobol 01 record formats. A centralized runtime box does not achieve centralized compile-time control. What it does is convert message data from one format to another. The advantage of this approach above centralized compile-time control is that it gives you the ability to change the conversion routines without recompiling the programs at either end. The downside is an extra box to manage. You must ensure the extra box is neither a bottleneck nor a point of failure.

Is the extra runtime flexibility worth it? The first point is that when you change application integration from, say, using file transfer to using message queuing, you must do some programming at either end of the message flow. I have suggested before that you take the opportunity to put in mediator components to hide the middleware and to ensure that subsequent changes have a minimum disruptive effect. The mediator component can and should do any reformatting. If there are technical difficulties with converting different data formats the problems can almost certainly be overcome by putting all the data into character format (and see below on XML). Therefore runtime conversion does not help you convert a program to a new middleware technology—you have to convert the program in any case. The advantages of runtime conversion come into play when you want to make subsequent changes to the message format. My reservation on the technology is that making format changes is not something to do lightly; it could easily break a business process. I am wary about giving the deployment team the ability to mess with the business processes—that is the application developer's job.

But there are three good reasons for sometimes putting in an additional box, perhaps a hardware box or perhaps just a software element, between two applications.

One I have discussed already—the wrapper or gateway. The purpose is to convert from one middleware technology to another. I tend to use the term "gateway" if it is in a separate box, and the term "wrapper" if the software is in the same box as the application. Wrappers are preferable to gateways, but you might be forced to use a gateway because the box you would have used to run the wrapper does not support one of the middleware technologies.

Second, some vendors have now combined the idea of a data conversion box with the workflow manager. This implements the high-level business process object like the order handling process described in the order-processing example used earlier in this chapter. This is a good strategy. In our example it would require that the communication from the order entry to the delivery application is done through the order tracking object. You have to assess these workflow products like you would assess any application package or application generator, because that is what they are.

The third reason for a separate box is for what I call an integration server. They are used when the client needs to access many servers and you are hiding the complexity of routing the message to the right server. It is probably more common for an integration server to sit between the presentation layer and the transaction servers rather than between transaction servers. Integration servers will undoubtedly become more important as companies enter into more alliances. An integration server between a manufacturing system and a number of suppliers is a distinct possibility, for instance.

In summary, sometimes there are reasons for an integration box in the middle but it is not something to do as a matter of course. The cases where an integration box become important are when the box does something more than just reformatting, like routing or managing the workflow.

13.5   Extensible markup language (XML)

The other fashionable solution to the problem of integration is XML. XML is a way of encoding data into text—it is about message content, not how it is sent. Let us contrast XML with old-fashioned EDI (Electronic Data Interchange), in which there were fixed message formats. XML has a number of advantages:

- A number of different middleware standards can be used to send the message.
- XML is flexible; it can easily represent lists, and values can be of any length.
- Humans can read the message with a simple text editor.

But for application B to understand and act on a message it received form application A, several things must happen:

- It must know which part of the message corresponds to which data item. XML does this by tags, EDI does it by field location.
- The designers and programmers of both applications must have the same understanding of what a field really means.
- The message must contain all the fields application B requires.

XML, per se, does not solve these problem. The only solution is for applications A and B to agree on a common message format standard. The good news is that XML standards are being developed for many different industries.

The fact that tools are being developed around XML could potentially make the integration much easier. For instance, it will probably be the death knell of the notion of a separate data conversion box, because why would you need one when both sides of the conversation are talking XML? But it is too early to say how important XML will be in practice.

The main conclusion from both this section and the previous one is simple. Real integration is an application development problem and there is no magic run-time solution.

13.6   Conclusions

This chapter is about creating a presentation layer from existing applications and about application-to-application integration.

The first step for both of these tasks is to document the high-level business process model of the complete system and the mapping from that to the current IT applications (as in Figure 13-2 and 13-3). From this information you will be able to identify necessary shared data and the integration dependencies (real time and deferrable) between the applications.

The second step is to decide on the business priorities for change. Most changes will be in the areas of data consolidation and adding a new presentation-layer channel.

Having focused on a particular application you need to do a more detailed business process model and pick out the difference between the core process activities and one or more presentation-layer refinements. From this information you can explore various strategies for changing the code. The only way to really understand how easy it is to change existing code is to try. In most cases, you will find that only a few transactions need to be adapted to support a new presentation-layer channel.

Wrapping and gateways are effective technologies for interfacing new technology with old mainframe applications. The presentation logic, security logic, and session-control logic in these programs will have to be removed, typically by creating new transaction types from the old code rather than changing existing transaction type code.

There are a large number of integration software vendors whose products sometimes have a tactical use. XML will make many of these products irrelevant. But workflow management products might provide a good way of implementing tracking objects where the business process spans many applications. Integration servers are useful when the presentation layer must access many backend transaction servers, particularly if the transaction servers belong to different companies. In general, standard middleware with the intelligent use of directories is sufficient for most use. The outstanding problem is the control of the message formats themselves. This is an application development problem and no runtime solution stops it from being an application development problem.

14

Change—Flexibility

This chapter is the second of two devoted to the problem of implementation design when we have to contend with existing production applications. The last chapter focused on integration. It was about taking the silos, cutting out the presentation code from them, and building links across them. This chapter is about flexibility; it is about understanding and possibly breaking up large applications.

Very simplistically, there are three problem configurations:

1. Fragmented applications—too many small applications. This leads to data duplication and consequently poor data accuracy. There are also problems with introducing user interfaces or business processes that span multiple applications.

2. Large monoliths—applications that are too large. The issue here is flexibility; our ability to change the application fast enough to support new business change.

3. Batch—while sometimes batch is required, other times batch is a hindrance to change.

Some large organizations have all three problems. This chapter is particularly focused on the large monoliths and the batch applications where the problems of flexibility are particularly severe.

There are obvious disadvantages to large monolithic applications. If the application is down, nothing is working. The applications cannot be physically located near the users. The application itself is complex. But some of these monoliths are magnificent structures. The business is already reaping the benefits from application integration. The applications tend to be fast and well managed—they have to be, otherwise the organization would have been in serious trouble years ago. The actual volume of code is often considerably less than their fragmented counterparts. Finally, a few large systems are frequently cheaper to operate than many small ones.

The real issue with large monolithic applications is that they are hard to change. Often they are implemented using old technology and the original designers have moved on to other jobs. Testing takes a long time. Sometimes the code has many interdependencies, which must be understood and managed.

First however, let us look at one of the scariest problems for IT management today—the lack of skills. IT systems today are using a large number of different technologies. They will probably have mainframe, Unix, and NT server platforms. They are likely to have many COBOL applications, but possibly some Assembler, Fortran, Pascal, C, C++, PL/1, RPG, and various 4GLs. They will probably have a variety of database systems both relational and non-relational. And so it goes on. Clearly, joining every new IT industry fashion is only going to make it worse, because IT fashions change much more quickly than it takes to re-implement your applications. This is a real problem and a serious one, and, as the older generation of programmers retire over the next ten or twenty years, it is about to get much worse. It is not only a mainframe problem. DOS programs, Unix C programs, applications written with poorly supported application generators, the program written for Notes by the contractor who left, and the Web CGI script written in Perl two years ago are all part of the problem.

Many organizations have a strategy to solve this problem but no plan. The strategy is to "standardize" on a few platforms and technology. Thus you go in to see a CIO and they will tell you that their strategy is to move to MVS/COBOL/CICS/DB2 or SUN/C/Oracle or Microsoft or whatever. The problem is that the costs and risks of actually implementing this strategy makes the year 2000 effort look like a children's tea party, whereas the benefits are hard to quantify and long term. It is also interesting that whenever I listen to these platform strategies, the target technology is rarely at the cutting edge. The strategists have made a genuine effort to choose the best technology for today, but arguably they should be choosing the technology that is most future proof, which may be the technology now on the sharpest part of the cutting edge.

Organizations should start by building a matrix of applications against technology and, for each technology, a skills retention plan for its support. In general, factor the reduction of technologies into your plans but don't fool yourself that it is driving the plans. In other words, when you need to change an application the fact that it is using old technology adds to your desire to rewrite it, but if you don't need to change the application then leave it alone. It is not quite as black and white as that. Occasionally, you might be able to have a small project to get rid of some old code, for instance to replace all remaining Assembler code. But for major transaction-processing systems, I regret to inform you that you are doomed to support them for many years to come.

Many IT graduates understandably want to play with the latest and greatest tools, but a technique I have seen used effectively in a few organizations is to train non-IT employees from end-user departments in COBOL or other key tools. They are more interested in the application than the technology and they see that understanding what it takes to build any IT application is a valuable skill.

14.1   Understanding large applications

Let us imagine ourselves in the position of a programmer in a few years time coming into a big bank or an airline and being faced with an application with say somewhere between 100,000 to 1,000,000 lines of code. What documentation does the newcomer need to help him or her understand the system?

The first important point is that the computer language does not make much of a difference. I have seen beautifully constructed COBOL programs and COBOL programs that are a mess. It is the same with C++ and Java. (Actually picking up some code and trying to understand it, is worse in C++ than in any other language I know because with C++ you can use Defines and Overriding to develop a private dialect of your own.) The wider point is that to understand a large program we need to look at the whole picture, and the programming language code is just the brush strokes.

To see the whole picture, we need to understand the relationship between the business processes, the business objects, the runtime application, the compile-time source files, and the data. This is illustrated in Figure 14-1.

The rest of this section explores this diagram in more detail, starting at the top.

There is no way that you are going to be able to understand all the elements in Figure 14-1 for a large program. In a complex system, it is very important to be able to eliminate all the parts that are not affected by the change you are focused

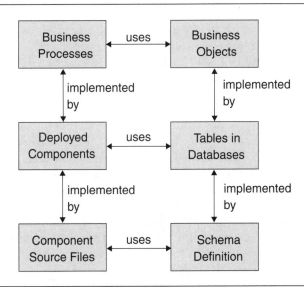

Figure 14-1   The relationship between design and implementation

on, so you can concentrate on the parts that are. I know this is a really obvious point, but there is an important implication that is often missed—the description of the system must be hierarchical. It is only with a hierarchical description that you can look at the big picture and immediately discard great chunks of it, and then by looking at the remaining parts in more detail discard much of that as well, and so on in more and more detail until you find the part to change.

Unfortunately many of our modeling brethren are not too keen on hierarchies. I remember being on an (ill-fated) team bidding for a large government contract and the account manager coming in with a big roll of paper that turned out to be a drawing of their data model (which was developed at great cost—not by us). It was about three feet by two and half feet of entity-relationship diagram and it basically told us that everything was connected to everything.

You will have realized by now that I am very keen on business-process models. This is by no means a strongly held view among modelers. There is a view that the properties of a business emerge from an examination of the business objects. I hold the contrary view that processes and objects are strongly linked and, if anything, the objects emerge from an examination of the business processes. I hope I have stressed the importance of a business process view in understanding implementation issues such as data distribution, performance requirements, integrity, and error recovery. But I have another reason for liking business processes—they are hierarchical. They are not purely hierarchical but they are hierarchical enough for our purpose, which is to provide a tool for helping us understand large complex systems.

If we look at many organizations from a business-process perspective we see two extremes. On the one hand there are large integrated business processes. The order-process example in the previous chapter (Figures 13-1 and 13-2) is an example but, by way of variation, the example I will take in this chapter is an airline system. The other extreme is many small, unconnected business processes, and the classic example of this is a bank.

14.1.1   Airline example

Airline business processes are complex, mainly because there are so many things that can go wrong, like passengers disappearing after check-in but before departure, planes being cancelled, and planes being replaced by ones with a different seating plan. Furthermore, they have high up-time requirements and high volumes of transactions. For historical reasons, airline applications have often been built in unique technology like IBM's TPF operating system and often as a single monolithic application. At least one airline has developed its own operating system (and it is still running, as of summer 2000 AD).

A partial view of an airline system is illustrated in Figure 14-2. I say partial because it ignores cargo, maintenance, financial, loyalty card, human resource systems, and much else besides.

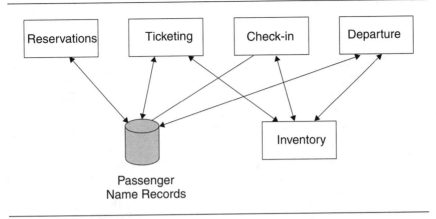

Figure 14-2   A partial airline picture

I think the names of the applications explain their purpose except for inventory, which is about an inventory of seats, in other words, it is about seat allocation (not about spare parts or aircraft). This confused me somewhat when I first heard it. Like our ordering system in the previous chapter, there is business-process integration across the different applications, but instead of explicit messages sent from one application to another, integration is achieved through shared data—the Passenger Name Record or PNR. The PNR holds all the information you see on an airline ticket. As an aside, note that it is quite common to integrate business processes through data rather than explicit message passing from one activity to another. All it means is that the flow is in the hands of an external agent, in this case the customer.

The second step is to document the business processes we plan to change. Let us suppose we want to change the check-in. The business process for check-in has a relatively simple main path—standard checks (did you pack this bag yourself? do you plan to hijack the plane? etc.), seat assignment, luggage handling—but numerous branches from the main path for errors. Many of the activities in the business process will not be computerized. Each individual task will correspond to one update transaction, maybe preceded by several inquiries.

Alongside the business-process description we need to build the IT description. For check-in we obviously have the check-in workstations and we also have a central system that holds the PNR data. Everything else could be implemented in a number of different ways. For instance, there may be intermediate servers or there could be one check-in server for everything. Alternatively, the check-in application could be part of a bigger application and share the database with the reservation, ticketing, and departure applications. A possible implementation is illustrated in Figure 14-3.

There are all kinds of interesting decisions to be made on how much data to load onto the airport system rather than the central airline system. Ideally, of

Implementation   Business Processes

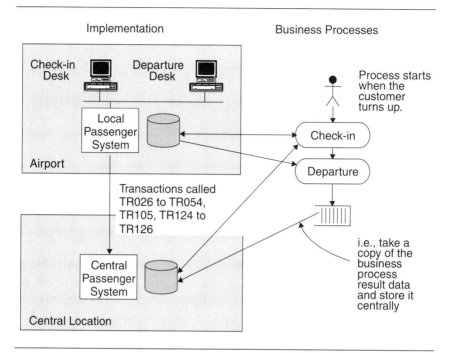

Figure 14-3   Partial airline systems configuration

course, the data should be stored in the airport server in case the long distance connection to the central IT system is down. There are difficulties though; since people can sometimes check in on the outward journey for the return trip, or check in on the second leg of a two-leg journey at the first check-in point, there does need to be facilities for passing check-in information around. It is probably easier to implement the whole system centrally.

We can draw a diagram like this for a complete application or for part of an application. We can go into greater and greater detail on less and less by breaking the business process into activities and drawing a similar diagram on the activities we want. We need to be able to visualize both the business processes and the implementation. Furthermore, we need to be able to do this down to the level of detail of a single transaction. In the old days it was straightforward; tasks mapped to one or more screen formats and one or more transaction types. The only difficulty was that format names and transaction type names tended to be meaningless codes like TR0043. But in today's distributed environment it is harder, simply because there are more layers.

The mapping from business process to implementation makes us understand the scope of change. For instance, if the change is to implement an automatic check-in machine there will be a new business process. The high-level views of the business processes and implementation tell you how the new business process fits into the existing system. The detailed picture tells you what parts of the existing application can be reused in the new process.

As well as tracing the business tasks to transaction types, we would like to trace business objects to database tables. In most cases there is a straightforward mapping but not always. Business objects might map to more than one table. Business objects may be dispersed over several databases. They could be embedded in another database record. They could be transient objects that are never stored on the database. Business objects might not be there. There will also be database tables that don't implement any business objects but instead store data internal to the IT infrastructure, like recovery data or security data. Note, if we had just looked directly at the database schema, the chances are that what we would have seen would be a massive spider's web with the PNR at the center.

By looking at the business processes we can mentally segment the database into logic application groupings, such as the data to support ticketing, the data for reservations, and so on. Of course the PNR data will be in the most logical application grouping because it is shared data. Also the data that supports the IT infrastructure will not fit in any of the logical application groupings. The importance of this analysis is apparent if we decide to split the application. The split will take a logical grouping and move it to a new database. The shared data needs a strategy for either sharing or controlling duplication. The infrastructure data can probably be duplicated as it is unlikely to have any meaning outside the new application. If it cannot be duplicated, then there is some shared infrastructure service that owns the shared infrastructure data.

The next stage is to understand the relationship between the runtime structure and the program source files. Again there is a need to trace the linkage but this time between runtime transaction types to source code file or files. This is a many-to-many relationship, one transaction type might be implemented by many source files, and one source file might be compiled into many transaction types. If you use components there could be a many-to-many-to-many linkage from transaction type to component to source file! Having a transaction type implemented by many source files is no problem (as long as you can find them easily enough), but we do have to understand why one source file is used by many transaction types. Some reasons why this might be so are

- The shared source file implements a common routine like an interest calculation or a data conversion.
- The shared source file implements access routines to shared data.
- The shared source file implements common infrastructure code like security handling code or middleware interfaces.

There are two aspects to understanding the source code—understanding how it implements the business logic and how it implements the infrastructure. We are building two models in our heads (and hopefully on paper)—the business-process model and the implementation infrastructure model.

Ideally all the business-process models, the runtime application structure, the source code file, and all the traceability information (Figure 14-1 in fact) should be stored in a repository. Even more ideally (bad English I know, but I'm sure you get my point), there should be facilities for drawing all these diagrams automatically.

14.1.2   Bank example

Bank systems are similarly complex but in many ways very different. The key difference is at the business-process level. Modern financial organizations offer a large number of different services such as checking accounts, savings accounts, unsecured loans, mortgages, investments, insurance, treasury, and so on. Each service has its own business processes, like opening an account, closing an account, moving an account, crediting an account, debiting an account, changing credit limits, and so on. But there is little integration between the different business processes; there is no overarching business process tying different applications together. Viewing a bank as a big business process is impossible, you must view it as a collection of independent services. But they are not entirely separate. The bank's general ledger—the bank's bank account is a simple way of thinking of it—takes input from everywhere. The bank needs to know, not only your balance, but also the balance at the branch (the amount of cash left in the branch) and the sum of all balances in all accounts. The bank wants this information every night so they can put spare money in the overnight money market. A very general picture of a bank business is shown in Figure 14-4. It shows the separate products, the central customer, the general ledger, and the many channels—the many ways money can come in and out.

I haven't drawn the linkages because it would look like a bowl of spaghetti.

In many banks there is no central customer data, and in the ones that do have central customer data the data quality is very poor because when opening a new account the clerk added a new customer record rather than connecting to an existing customer record. I discussed this issue in Chapter 12 so I won't belabor the point here, but it is probably today's bank's number one problem because having good customer data is critical to turning banks from account-service organizations to customer-oriented organizations.

In Figure 14-4 there is one box for checking accounts and one for savings accounts and so on, but that is a simplification. There is a range of different checking account and savings account products, mostly very similar. They differ in factors like interest rates, overdraft limit, and so on. Generalizing grossly, a bank's number two IT priority is being able to create new banking products more quickly, so they can respond more swiftly to changing marketing conditions.

A more recent phenomena is banking products that combine a number of different services, like a savings account with a mortgage.

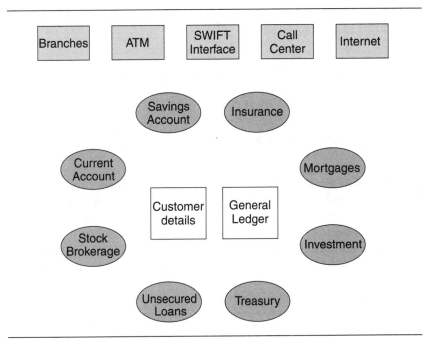

Figure 14-4   Banking systems

In summary, we have bank services, each with many variants. Financial products are formed from one of these variants or from several, each taken from a different service bucket (my term, not a bank's). Each product has its own set of business processes. From the business processes we can trace the IT runtime and source code assets as we did for the airline applications.

The key questions I want to address are: how should a bank structure its IT applications for maximum flexibility, and how should existing IT applications be restructured?

One solution is component reuse. For each product, create a new application with a scripting language (Visual Basic or JavaScript) and have components for all the basic banking functions like credits and debits. But this is a poor solution, because there are a large number of banking products and managing a large number of separate applications is not to be recommended. (Remember the bank's IT system must store information about all the old products that are no longer being marketed.) Also, it is hard to stop the applications diverging, perhaps introducing different technologies, different database design, and different system infrastructure routines. Changing any shared resource does not bear thinking about.

An alternative model is to use object-oriented polymorphism (calling different methods for the same operation, according to which subclass the object belongs). This can be illustrated by thinking of the steps taken when a customer comes along to do something.

1. Identify action
2. Identify account
3. Identify customer
4. Security check
5. Do polymorphic action on account

For instance, if the action is an account credit then the application could do a different action for different types of account, but the higher-level code would not have to worry about that because the object-oriented polymorphism would ensure the right method is called.

The problem with this solution is that for every new product you must create a new account subclass, which means recompiling the application. But the difference between some products is trivial—different interest rates, for example.

A third solution is to use parameters. For instance, interest rates and the amount at which they kick in can easily be parameterized. The product table would hold the set of parameters and the account operations would read the data and act accordingly. The downside is that the original designer must anticipate all points where the account products might differ in the future, without being too extravagant by having so many parameters that the code is unreadable. What is especially hard to anticipate are changes that require new operations or radically different business processes.

Let us try to generalize and come up with a generic solution. Consider how products differ from each other. Within each service there are a number of standard business processes, for instance, opening an account, credits, debits, going overdrawn, paying standing orders, paying interest, and closing an account. A business process like opening an account is complex and might consist of a number of tasks, but a business process like account credit is simple, a single task in fact. Products can be tailored in three ways:

1. They may do an action in a slightly different way.
2. They may use different parameters, for instance, different interest rates.
3. They may leave out some steps.

But all are driven from the account's product.

This is illustrated in Figure 14-5.

Put another way, a service defined a series of actions, each of which might be performed in several different ways, which I call variants. Variants can sometimes be implemented by polymorphism, but we should expect that sometimes the parameters for calling different variants is so different, it is impossible. A product may span one or more services, and from each may leave out one or more actions, and

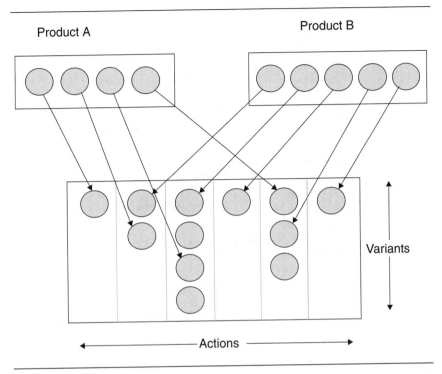

Figure 14-5   Products assembled from variants

may choose one of the variants for performing a particular action. The steps in processing a single task become:

1. Identify action
2. Identify account
3. Identify customer
4. Security check
5. Identify product and identify which action variant to call
6. Do variant action on account, passing product parameters

Many financial organizations talk about business rules or business process layer. I believe what they need is a "product" layer. A product layer specifies rules, but it is far from specifying all the rules. The structure they are looking to implement looks like Figure 14-6.

You could implement this structure by a series of servers or identifiable software layers, each possibly with different technologies. Ideally, many banks would like to have some specialized visual tool that would allow them to add or modify the product information quickly and accurately. Unfortunately, both the product

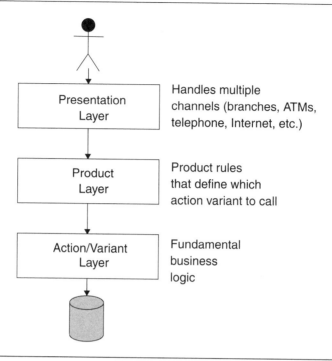

Figure 14-6   The product layer

layer and the action/variant layer must both access the account information; one to find out which product the account supports and the other to process the action. It is more efficient if the two layers are in one implementation.

When we come to look at existing applications, the structure illustrated in Figure 14-6 suggests an approach for making the application more flexible. In an existing application the three layers are probably mixed up. It may easily be possible to reduce the existing application to turn it into the action/variant layer and add new code for the product layer. Alternatively, it is possible to leave the existing code but to create a separate action/variant layer for use by new products. Over a period of time, old accounts can be moved to new products (or old products re-implemented) and the old code can be removed.

This discussion of banking systems has illustrated the requirement for business-process variation. This is not unique to banks. In Unisys for instance, we have processes for ordering and delivery, but the processes are very different depending on whether the product is a hardware product, a software product, or a services product.

Where is this taking us? Before being carried away with our wonderful model for handling product flexibility, consider that this might only be a phase in the evolution of banks, not a permanent innovation. Perhaps in the future the products will be tailored to your requirements; conceptually a product for one. Instead of a product layer we could have a "customer layer." However we look at it though, the notion of highly flexible business processes, is with us to stay.

14.2   Batch

While we are on the subject of banks, many existing banks have batch processing at the heart of their system—from a business perspective they are not real-time banks. All account updates are collected during the day and processed against the accounts during an overnight batch run.

Of course, it is not so simple; the bank must prevent someone from going around from ATM machine to ATM machine taking money out. One solution is simply to prevent more than, say, $200 being taken out during any one day. This does not help with Internet banking and telephone banking or using debit cards. There are so many ways these days of extracting money that a bank is more exposed than ever. Unless the bank is going to offer a seriously limited service (or allow very large overdrafts) the only solution is to have real-time bank balances. Some banks still retain their batch processes but calculate a "pseudo real-time balance" by updating an account balance when the data is input without doing a full debit/credit on the account.

Another difficulty with processing accounts in batch is more subtle. Suppose a bank product is set up to move money from a checking account to a savings account above a certain limit, and also to move money from a savings account to pay the mortgage when it goes above another limit. There are four batch updates—a debit on the checking account, a credit on the savings, a debit on the savings, and a credit on the mortgage. But the batch run may not process all these kinds of transactions in that order; for instance all saving account updates may be done before checking account updates. Therefore a whole day passes between posting the money from the checking account and updating the savings account. There may be another day's delay before the mortgage account is updated. Not only is the service therefore slow, but also, from the customer's perspective, money is debited from one account one night and not credited to another account for 24 hours. (And the day's interest is foregone—but banks might view this as an advantage.)

From a technical point of view there are advantages and disadvantages. The main performance advantage is that totals can be calculated during the batch run (being careful to capture any running totals in the restart area). In an online transaction, calculating totals would require an update to statistics stored in a database record or posting the data to another application. Also, bank IT operations have become very comfortable with recovery procedures that rely on a consistent copy of the account data after the batch run is complete.

A major concern for large batch runs is the time it takes. As business becomes more and more a 24-hour affair, the batch window—the time set aside for running batch programs—becomes shorter and shorter. The problem is illustrated in Figure 14-7.

There are four approaches to shortening the batch window: shorten or eliminate the batch administraton tasks, shorten the batch application's elapse time, run batch applications alongside the online process and eliminate batch applications altogether, replacing them with online applications. All four can be done; you need to attack the problem of the batch window from multiple angles.

The first approach—shortening the administration—has already been discussed in Chapter 7.

The key step in the second approach—shortening the batch process—is usually running many programs in parallel. Conceptually this is usually simple—split your input data into multiple inputs. The difficulties are merging any running totals and, more problematically, long transactions. The most common reason long transactions exist in batch is not because the business processes require them, but to simplify restart code. Programs can only recover to a point where they are out of transaction state (after a commit). It is much easier to update a whole file in

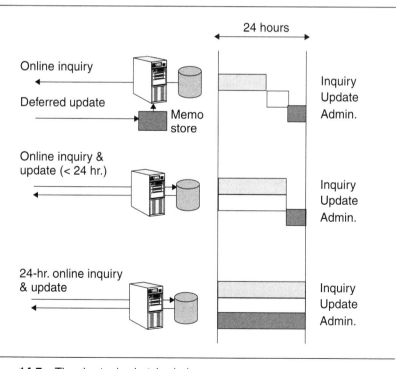

Figure 14-7   The shortening batch window

one transaction because then you don't have to write restart code to reposition the program in the middle of the file. Most of these long transactions can be eliminated, albeit with a bit of work.

The third approach is simply to run batch alongside the online processing and this too can be done—so long as the transactions are short. Ideally, what you want is a throttle mechanism where batch can do more or less work according to how busy the online processing is. This is easier to do using message queues rather than files since you can put all your input into one queue and have multiple programs processing the queue. The number of programs can be increased or decreased according to the load. A program reading a queue is also easy to recover so long as the dequeue operation is done in transaction state.

Sometimes though, the batch program requires that the database is frozen. Many of these cases are a convenience rather than an absolute requirement. For example, suppose a financial system needs a new set of interest rates every day. At some point, you need to give the system the new data and the easiest way is to replace the old file and restart the program. Obviously it is possible to implement an online change of the data, but with additional effort. Typically moving to 24 by 7 operation requires making a lot of these kinds of changes.

But some cases of having a frozen database are real. Reports are one example—for example, closing the accounts at the end of a quarter. The time can be minimized. For example, you can use technology like the EMC Business Volumes in which disk volumes are mirrored and then broken off as a snapshot copy of the data. This can be done online, but you must close the database to ensure that the database buffer pool is all written to disk to ensure a clean copy of the database. The copy can then be used for reports.

The fourth approach—replacing batch applications by online programs—can also sometimes be done. But, as I have already noted, batch cannot be eliminated entirely because some business processes are triggered by time events like payroll or interest payment accrual.

Changing a process from batch to online is not just a change in technology, it is a change to the business process (almost always for the better, unless the performance hit is too high). It may not be easy. A batch application and its online equivalent usually consist of the same basic operations but they may be processed in a totally different order. This is illustrated in Figure 14-8.

A batch run is in many ways like a giant transaction and this allows subtle optimizations. A group of operations that in business terms are one transaction, and must be implemented as one transaction in an online implementation, can be rearranged in a batch run. Thus the online transaction to move money from a savings account to a checking account may update both accounts in one transaction, the equivalent batch application has two input files, one for checking account updates and another for savings account updates. Furthermore, all the updates to one account—which in business terms were separate transactions—are implemented as one transaction in the batch process to improve performance.

Online

Transaction1	Transaction2	Transaction3
Update A1	Update A2	Update A3
Update B1	Update B2	Update B3
Update C1	Update C2	Update C3

Batch

...followed by... ...followed by...

Update A1		Update B1		Update C1	
Update A2		Update B2		Update C2	
Update A3		Update B3		Update C3	

Figure 14-8 Batch processing vs. online transactions

Clearly in some circumstances there may be no simple way to change a batch program to an online program. The best you will achieve is to salvage some of the code.

In general, therefore, while it is not possible to eliminate batch it is possible to have it run alongside the online system. In doing so, what you end up with is a set of transaction routines that are written with short transactions and are essentially the same as online transaction routines. The eventual goal should be to have one set of routines callable from either batch or online. This is illustrated in Figure 14-9.

Essentially the model is a transaction server with a bunch of feeder programs. You can think of batch as a weird type of presentation layer if you like.

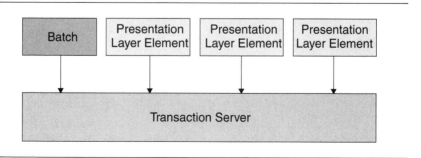

Figure 14-9 Batch as a presentation layer

14.3   Conclusions

To understand a large system you must first identify the large business-spanning business processes, or, if there aren't any (like in a bank) the functional areas. For each business process you must identify the applications and databases. Use the business-process decomposition activities to focus on the area of the part of the implementation you want to change.

Within an activity we need to document

- Sub-activities
- Business objects
- Deployed components
- Database tables
- User roles
- Computer systems

All of the relationships between these different elements must be recorded.

Finally, at the detail level we must note the relationship between the runtime structure and the compile-time source files and repository information.

We want to use the natural hierarchy imposed by business-process decomposition to figure out what to ignore and what areas to focus on.

Some batch programs are necessary, but batch programs in business processes that could be online are still common. There are various way of shortening the batch window—run batch alongside online, run batch in parallel, and shorten the batch housekeeping activities. Converting batch to online is often hard due to the fact that batch runs often treat the whole of the night's processing as logically a single business transaction.

15

Building an
IT Architecture

In this book I have covered middleware technology, the principles of distributed systems technology, and many of the issues with implementation design. Broadly speaking, for each topic I have discussed what you have to do and why. What I have not covered is how.

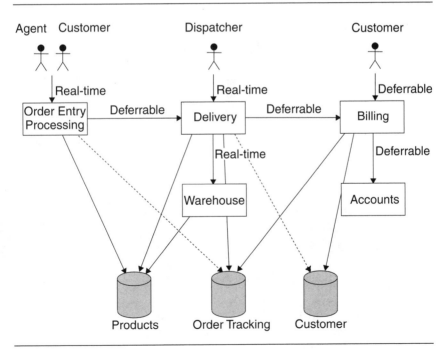

Figure 15-1 Order processing example

In this chapter I look at the questions: How does an IT organization start to implement an integrated architecture approach and what does the organization need to do differently thereafter? I will start by discussing the latter question first and return at the end of the chapter to the question of how to get off the ground. This chapter also serves as an overview of the arguments in the rest of the book.

Throughout this chapter we will use the example given at the start of Chapter 1 and discussed further in Chapter 13. By way of a reminder, Figure 15-1 is a diagram of the system.

The idea is to implement this system, incorporating existing systems where possible, using the architectural principles discussed in this book.

15.1 Integrated applications architecture

The integrated applications architecture is illustrated again in Figure 15-2.

The driving principle of this architecture is a clean presentation layer that allows you to implement additional presentation channels. The most immediate pressure is probably an e-business Web interface, but a mobile phone interface,

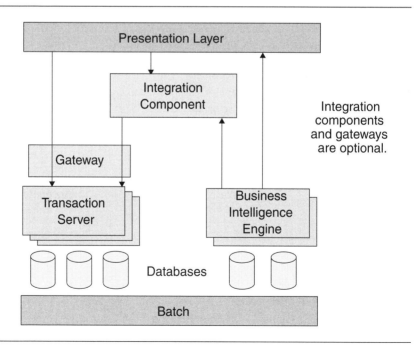

Figure 15-2 Integrated applications architecture

self-service terminals, call centers, IVR (interactive voice recognition) interface, and many specialized interfaces are likely to follow. In our example, this is an especially strong requirement for the order entry process and the order tracking objects.

The transaction servers in our example include the order entry, delivery, warehouse, billing, and accounts systems. The good news is that you don't necessarily have to rewrite all your existing applications. There is a good chance that existing transaction systems can be easily converted or wrapped to provide an object-oriented interface; for instance, all transactions that use an order number as a key are likely to map easily to operations on an order object. Also, there is a good chance that only a few of the existing transaction types need to be exposed to the new interface, especially in internal systems like the accounts and warehouse applications. The existing application can carry on servicing the existing terminal or workstation interfaces for as long as required.

There is a big reservation on the above; creating an online object view is much more difficult if the existing application is heavily batch oriented. Batch is required in the new world, because business processes need batch for regular activities (for example, payroll or interest accrual). But it is not easy to turn an application that uses batch for all updates into an online system ready for e-business. That does not mean you cannot achieve a great deal—it makes it more difficult, not impossible. This was discussed in Chapter 14.

The details of the presentation depend of course on the presentation device. The middleware between the presentation layer and the transaction servers needs to support either real-time or deferrable messages (sometimes characterized as "send and forget"). Of course, everyone wants every message to get through as fast as possible. The key difference between real-time and deferrable messages is what happens if there is a failure. For real-time messages the sender wants to be informed of any failure because they will go ahead and do something else. A deferrable message on the other hand must get through—eventually. Likewise, transaction servers also communicate with one another and again they communicate by sending either real-time or deferrable messages.

The most recent technology for real-time messages is transactional component middleware. There are two dominant technologies, Microsoft COM+ and Enterprise Java Beans. Both technologies are new, but both are likely to support large, scalable, resilient systems, if not now, at least in the near future. But you have to be careful. You cannot write an application the same way as you would in a single machine and expect it to perform well over a network.

The best technology for deferrable messages is message queuing. It is possible to use message queuing for real-time (unless you want the sender and the receiver to belong to one distributed transaction) and transactional component middleware for deferrable messages (that is, the messages are always processed immediately). My view is that you should use both technologies. It is easier to develop and administer real-time applications using transaction component middleware. It is important to use the resiliency features of message queuing for deferrable messages.

There is more, much more, to building a scalable, fast, resilient, manageable, and secure infrastructure than choosing one or a few middleware products. Some of the issues were discussed in Chapters 7, 8, and 9.

Some of the effort to implement a middleware infrastructure requires writing some code. Examples include building debugging routines, reporting errors, monitoring performance, and perhaps some additional security enforcement. It is best to hide the middleware within routines so that additional code can be added without incurring a rewrite of the application logic. I call these routines mediator components. In theory, this principle allows you to change the middleware without changing the applications.

In our example, you cannot implement all these features, for instance changing all these systems to use an object interface, all at once. The role of the architecture, per se, is just to point the organization in the right direction, to give the IT departments a sense of where it is going. The architecture can be little more than a presentation. The real manifestation of the architecture is embodied in the role of the IT architect, who should guide the implementation design on each project. In particular, the IT architect should enforce architectural component reuse. In our example architectural reuse should be important for:

- Reusing infrastructure code to build common security and systems management, and
- Reusing interfaces for common data, like customer and product data

The architecture is not a one-off exercise. Not everything can happen at once. Probably the Web interface will need to be developed first and data consistency later. The skill lies in dividing the work into projects that are relatively short (aim for 6-month length or shorter) and deliver business benefit. The infrastructure code should be implemented as required, rather than all up-front. This may mean implementing some interim code that you later intend to remove, but that is preferable to a long delay before business benefits accrue. Short projects like this also help to avoid the temptation to over-engineer.

15.2 Business process design

This book has taken a strong view on the importance of understanding business processes in design. I believe the IT architect will only be effective if he or she has a good understanding of business process design.

The fundamental reason is that IT systems have to be integrated only because business processes are integrated. Business processes are related to each other in several ways, for instance:

- Embedded business processes—an activity in a business process may itself be a business process. For instance, in an airline, the check-in process is part of the wider passenger-handling process.

- Send-and-forget—a business process may initiate another business process. For instance, finishing a customer service may initiate the task of sending an invoice.
- Real-time call—an activity in one business process may be another business process. For instance, there may be a common process for taking things out of the warehouse used by many different processes. The difference between this and send-and-forget is that the calling business process can't proceed until it has had an answer.
- Shared resource—business processes may share a common resource data. In our example, many of the business processes share the common product data. The product data is itself maintained by business processes.

It is these relationships that lead to the requirement for integration between the different applications. In particular, by analyzing the business processes you come to understand the data distribution requirements.

Embedded business processes have a particularly key part in the application structure. There is a fundamental decision on whether to implement the embedded process by shipping the required data to a local machine, acting on it locally, and shipping the result back. The alternative is to do all the processing in the central site. The "handling it remotely" scenario is particularly applicable to the first activity in a process, like creating an order or renting a car. Only when the order is complete or the car is rented, does the information need to be given to a central location.

The need for business-process analysis is important in many areas. For instance,

- It provides a tool for improving the quality of data by letting you understand where the data comes from, how it is used, and its impact on the business.
- It provides the fault lines where the system will change, which has a direct bearing on deciding how to split an application into components.
- It defines which message flows between processes are deferrable and which must be in real time. This is essential information for building a good middleware implementation.
- It provides the rationale for resiliency requirements.
- It provides the rationale for performance criteria.
- It provides the underlying basis for the discussion on security requirements, especially if we are seeking to protect against internal threats.
- It provides the underlying basis for the discussion on data distribution.

In other words, business-process analysis helps in application partitioning, helps in building data quality into the applications, and helps in understanding the non-functional requirements (performance, reliability, etc.).

It is important for the IT architect to understand the relationship between business processes and data. From the business-process perspective objects play a distinctive role, in particular there are

- Tracking objects—that keep the state of the progress of an instance of a business process.
- Resource objects—objects that provide data for input to the business process.
- Plan objects—objects that tell the process how it will be done.
- Result objects—objects that are the output from the process.

In a manufacturing process, the tracking object would keep track of a thing being manufactured. Resource objects would record things like product information and stock levels.

It was suggested that the tracking object should contain the logic for the business process. This way the business-process logic is stored with the data. The transaction servers, broadly speaking, implement the tracking objects. But most database technology is relational rather than object oriented. The implementation objects are proxies for the business objects and come into existence only when the object is used. The proxies hide the mapping from object to relational structure. The actual implementation may be by calling an existing online application. None of this prevents the database being accessed by normal relational database query tools.

Business-process analysis is particularly important for managing change. There are three reasons. First and most important, business processes are the unit of change in the business. By aligning your application structure with business processes, the system should be more flexible because change should be more localized.

Second, business processes provide a tool for understanding complex systems by using hierarchical decomposition. Some hierarchical tools are essential—otherwise you don't know what to ignore. You can split business processes down into activities and tasks, and figure out how the tasks relate to the runtime entities and the source code. This allows you quickly to focus on what needs to change.

Finally, change is better understood and catered for if you understand variant business processes.

One form of variant business process is associated with different presentation channels. Banks, for instance, are more willing to assume a bank clerk is putting data in correctly than someone at the end of an Internet connection and will therefore build in additional checks and balances to the Internet user. The clean structure illustrated in Figure 15-1 is therefore something of a simplification.

Another form of variant processes is particularly prevalent in financial organizations where there are numerous account types. This has to be handled by both object-oriented subclasses and by parameterization, subclassing for major functional differences, and parameterization especially for numerical figures like interest rates. Banks also want to assemble different account types into products, for instance moving money automatically between different accounts according to predefined rules. The solution found was to have a "product layer," which called variant operations on the "account layer" (see Figure 14-5). I expect that solutions along these lines will be increasingly popular in other organizations.

The IT architect must understand the business processes and use the information to build an effective implementation design. The IT organization should build and maintain business process models starting with a top-level view of the major business processes in the organization. As different systems take on an architectural approach the business-process models for that system should be expanded into fine detail.

15.3   Managing information

There is a wide range of information access requirements ranging from online inquiry, nightly reports, and simple queries on production data to data mining, statistical analysis, trend analysis, and so on. There is no one single solution. When you analyze these requirements you find that four basic questions (and lots of follow-up questions) are asked time and time again:

1. What are the data sources? For instance, is there a need to create a new data source such as one to collect historic records?

2. What is the requirement for the data to be completely up-to-date? If a delay is acceptable, how long can it be?

3. What is the requirement to change the data format? Is the existing data intelligible to the outsider?

4. What is the nature of the inquiry? Do you want the data sent to you (push) or do you want to get it yourself (pull)? Is a fixed inquiry required or do you need ad-hoc searching?

I have suggested that a person in your organization take on a role that I called the information controller. This person helps end users understand their requirements and create an information strategy for satisfying the requirements.

But there is a limit on how effective any information-access project can be, which is set by the completeness and the accuracy of the data. Information accuracy and completeness can be improved by:

- Sharing common data or ensuring duplicate data is controlled in such a way as to ensure consistency.

- Changing the applications to ensure (a) shared data is used rather than needlessly rekeyed and (b) all data is input correctly.

Having a separate data layer by separating all databases from the transaction logic should be avoided as it is so inefficient. Where possible, data should be in the same machine as the transaction server. Shared data access should be carefully hidden behind a component interface. This is illustrated in Figure 15-3.

This architecture forces the updates to the shared data to be done in one place, by one set of update routines. Old applications that have their own copy of the data

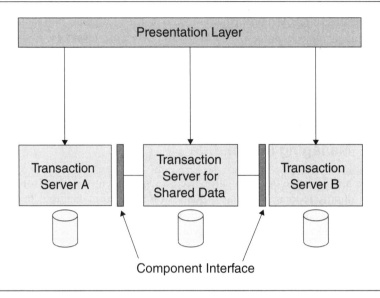

Figure 15-3 Shared data access

should be changed to use the shared data and its update routines. Also note that since old applications are likely to use old technology the notion of a component interface is a broad one and includes things like COBOL copy libraries.

The alternative to shared data is controlled duplication. It is better to have a primary database and have it process all the updates first, and then feed data from the primary to one or more secondary databases. The difficulty with doing updates on any copy of the data and sending the updates to all the other copies is that inconsistencies can arise from the same data being updated on two machines at the same time. This was described in Chapter 12.

Choosing between shared data or controlled duplication of data is a matter of weighing the merits of efficiency and resiliency (controlled duplication) against having the data completely up-to-date (shared data). Controlled duplication also makes it possible to restructure the data differently in different local copies.

There can be considerable resistance to making the above happen. The information controller needs to be a diplomat as well as a good data analyst.

15.4   The organizational and project management context

An Integrated Applications Architecture can only happen if there is strong cross-project control of the whole of IT. This is illustrated in Figure 15-4.

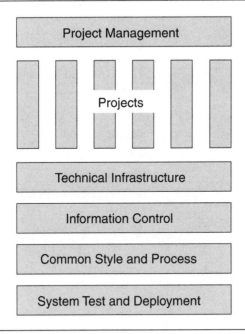

Figure 15-4   Cross-project IT functions

The technical infrastructure is the responsibility of the IT architect.

Information control is the responsibility of the information controller.

Systems test and deployment are the responsibility of the systems administrator.

Project management has the task of synchronizing the IT projects with the business and setting the IT project business requirements.

The box marked "Common Style and Process" is meant to capture the notion of common development processes, programming reuse, programming standards, and visual presentation standards. To some extent this is enforced by the IT architect during implementation design, but it should ideally have the full support of the programming staff.

This method of management will work best if:

- There are numerous small projects rather than a few big ones as discussed earlier.
- The first projects aim at simple functionality but excellent technical characteristics (fast and reliable), because it is much easier to add functionality to a good technical foundation than it is to change the technical foundation.

Following these guidelines allows program management to blend the IT projects with non-IT change and to change priorities according to business needs.

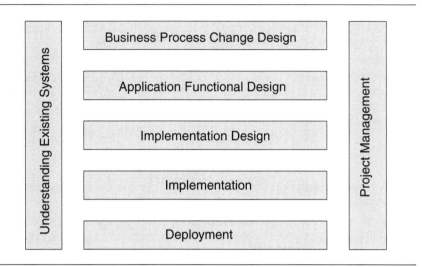

Figure 15-5   Project tasks

How do these cross-project functions relate to project tasks? I have illustrated the project tasks in Figure 15-5.

As we noted in Chapter 10, these are simple divisions into tasks, and other authorities have different splits. We also noted that when we delve into the details, different projects have different detailed tasks and some tasks that are substantial in one project are negligible or nonexistent in others.

For the rest of this section I will discuss all the large tasks illustrated in Figure 15-5.

15.4.1   Understanding existing systems

One of the consequences of the Integrated Applications Architecture is that almost all projects require changing existing systems, in contrast to developing a new silo application. Understanding the existing system can be a lengthy task, especially if the system is complex and the designers haven't worked on it before.

The key to understanding complex systems is to use the business-process description as a tool for hierarchical decomposition and to understand the traceability between business processes, business objects, runtime components, databases, and source code. This was described in Chapter 14.

It is highly desirable that, as systems are discovered and understood, they are documented in a repository. You may want to have another cross-project function for the maintenance of the common respository.

15.4.2   Business process change design

This is the responsibility of the program manager. It is from here that the functional and nonfunctional requirements of the system are developed.

The output from the business process change design is a model of the business processes. It is important that the business-process model documents the difference between real-time and deferrable messages.

15.4.3   Application functional design

This would normally be the responsibility of an application design specialist.

The outputs from the application functional design include

- The object model view
- The user interface design
- A functional description of all tasks

The design should be reviewed by the program manager, the IT architect, and the information controller.

As noted in Chapter 10, the application functional design may not be firm until a prototype has been done and the design has been fully analyzed for technical implications by the IT architect. Although I am presenting the tasks top to bottom, so to speak, development is usually iterative.

15.4.4   Implementation design

This would normally be the responsibility of the IT architect working in conjunction with the application functional designer and the programmer(s). The design needs to be reviewed by the information controller and the systems administrator.

The output from the implementation design should include

- Choice of technology
- Identification and design of new infrastructure code requirements
- Identification of reusable components
- Mapping between business objects and components
- The database design
- The data distribution design
- The component interface design

The overall architecture of the system in most cases does not need to change, but, when it does, the change is often radical; a new requirement initiates a rethink of the whole architecture. Examples are changing to a different middleware technology or the implementation of a clean presentation layer.

The natural temptation is to resist such radical thoughts and find a kludge. However, if the system is going to live for a long time, some architectural change is inevitable. You have to find a balance between making too many architectural changes and making none at all. I cannot give a simple formula for when to change and when not too, but points to ponder are

- Are similar requirements likely in the future?
- How ugly is the kludge?
- How extensive and costly is the proposed change?

What typically happens in practice is that reasons for change slowly build up, and all the management start getting nervous, worried (justifiably so) about committing their organization to radically new technology and new ways of development.

The way to tackle these questions is to do an "architectural prototype." That is, take all or part of the application and try to make the change. This will tell you if it is easy or difficult and reveal some of the pitfalls. Because the ease or difficulty is so dependent on the quality of the code, you do not know until you try. In many cases, the effort is less than you think. For example, the change might require modifying all database statements, but this could be a relatively mechanical change. The change may require introducing wrapping technology that could also be relatively straightforward. Many of the problems you come against—like changes to the security procedures—can be solved once and then mechanically implemented in many other applications. So get a few bright programmers, lock them up in a room with a few powerful PCs, slide pizzas under the door when they are hungry, and see what they can do in a few weeks.

You may need to do several architectural prototypes to try out different options. When you know enough about the practicalities of the technology, it is time to do detailed planning.

15.4.5   Implementation—coding

Coding will require writing new components and changing or deleting old ones. On the actual subject of coding itself there is nothing I want to add to the mountain of literature that already exists on the subject.

But there is a subject that is commonly forgotten—managing change and reuse. Say we have two applications that both use component A. The time might come when one of the applications wants to use a new version of component A while the other application does not. Clearly a decision must be made to either "fork the component" (my expression) and create two components each with their own source files, or change the component once, perhaps having it supply both an old and a new interface. The bias should be toward the second alternative because that reduces the amount of code in the long run. However it may (almost certainly, will) require two runtime versions of the component, because the testing and deployment cycle of one application will not be synchronized with the testing and deployment cycle of the other application. What is likely to happen is this:

1. Start with applications X and Y using component A1.

2. Application X needs a change and new version A2 is created. Application Y continues with A1.

3. Application Y is being changed so they try and incorporate component A2. But there's a bug, so component A3 is created. Application X continues with component A2.

4. And so on.

If you are serious about reusing components, you must have very good configuration management support to manage complex component dependencies.

15.4.6   Implementation—testing

The better the testing environment, the easier it is to make changes.

Many organizations test at the component level and at the complete system level. When the complete environment is assembled from perhaps a hundred or more components this becomes unwieldy. A symptom of this malaise is that systems testing takes too long. The irony is that the organization is then forced to put more untested changes into production since some bug fixes cannot wait for systems tests to be completed.

Many systems tests are linear. They start with compiling the programs, then do a deployment, and finally run the tests. If any stage fails you go back to the beginning—it's like the game of snakes and ladders without any ladders.

This is not a book on testing but here are a few ideas, the chief purpose of which is to try and show that something can be done.

- Optimize the process—treat it as a business process, see where the delays are and find out ways of fixing them. In particular, seek to ensure that early problems are quickly overcome and one test run finds the maximum of errors.

- Test assemblies of components smaller than the full system as well as the full system. Ideally you should have the programmer run the tests on the component assemblies since the tests can then be done immediately.

- Review the test scripts. System test is frequently a big bucket in which every test that has ever run is put in irrespective of its real value. "If it found a bug once, it must be valuable" is the motto. Tests should be reviewed to see if they are duplicates, to see if they can be improved to test more, and to see if they can be optimized to test faster.

- Optimize the systems test just like you would optimize a large batch process by using parallelism.

- Keep a record to find out which tests find bugs regularly and run them first.
- Find out which areas of the systems have the most bugs in them and review the testing procedures of that area.

Perhaps also keep a league table of bugs found in systems tests with prizes for the most accurate code submitted.

15.4.7   Deployment

Technically, deployment for change is not much different from deployment in a new development environment. The practical difference is complexity. In particular, you need to find all the elements you need to change, change them all, and change them accurately.

Ideally you also need to be able to revert to the previous system. This is much more difficult in a distributed environment than it ever was on a mainframe.

I have no panacea for this difficult problem. It depends a great deal on the capabilities of the operating systems and the system software and the availability of tools to help you. Here are a few pointers:

- You must have an accurate inventory of all the software running on all the boxes. This information should be stored in an online database.
- You need a laboratory environment where you can test out deployment ideas and see what happens if you get it wrong.
- You need ways to check the actual deployment fast. Write "sniffer" programs to check that the configuration is correct.
- Where possible use directories for configuration information so it is much easier to control.
- Ensure all your interfaces have version information in them so if a program sends a message in the wrong format it is caught immediately. This should be checked during the systems test.

This is not a complete list, only a few pointers. A bit of paranoia here is probably in order.

15.4.8   Project management

Project management is not much different than before. Since we are trying to aim for small projects that makes it easier, but since there are so many cross-project people to appease, that makes it harder.

Two other points need emphasis.

First, version control is extremely important, much more so with a large integrated application built with components than in the past with a silo application. The whole point of using components is to be able to change a component without having to change everything else around it, but this is only possible with good configuration management. The discussion in the subsection on "Coding" has already stressed this point.

Second, there is the thorny subject of documentation. Ideally, at each stage of the process, you should document the starting point (what you found), the end point (how you left it), and the changes you made. In practice this hardly ever happens. I believe there are three reasons why people don't document:

1. Lack of effective repository support. It is often hard to find the documentation, especially documentation of recent changes.

2. Drawing diagrams is tedious. Specialist tools help ease the workload but only up to a point. The purpose of diagrams is to be a clear and concise expression of the model. This puts an onus on tidiness and visual impact.

3. It's in the mind.

The last point is very important. You use a diagram to express a design but once you understand the system you don't need the diagram again until you come to explain the design to someone else. If the same person is going to work on an application for a long period of time then documentation becomes effort for very little gain. It is in the long run that documentation pays off. There are many organizations with large complex systems that only a few of their employees understand. As these people move on, understanding decreases, and the system becomes more and more unchangeable. This is how IT applications die. The major criticism of modern design models is that programmers feel they don't add enough value to justify keeping them current. Programmers would rather just change the code.

So what's to be done? Enforcing documentation is not the answer—it is easy to produce trivial, unhelpful documentation sufficient to please management, who don't understand the system in any case. Somehow we have to make documentation useful to the designers and coders. Since I have yet to see a large, complex application adequately documented, it would be dishonest of me to claim that I have a tried and tested solution to this problem. However I think the key points are

- Keep the modeling and the maintenance of the model with the designer. Programmers work with code not with models.
- Use the models as the means for communicating between the designer and the programmer, thereby forcing the designer to maintain the models.
- Don't be too detailed; document what components do, not how they do it. Leave that to the programmer. Designers should define the component interface and what each method does and stop.
- We must have comprehensive repository support. Trying to keep a paper trail of changes across multiple tools and multiple versions of a complex system would be a nightmare.
- Send the few who understand the application on a short "train the trainer" course and have them teach the system to others. For some teaching may be more fun than writing, and the course material could be the starting point for a professional documenter.

(As an aside for those with skills in UML—and because I like a bit of contro-versy—the above two points imply that diagrams like sequence diagrams should only be used by programmers to help them think through a problem. The reason is that sequence diagrams are prescriptive on how to code the solution rather than a description of the nature of the problem. Don't expect such programming-level diagrams to be kept up-to-date. In an ideal world, programming-level diagrams should be generated from the source code.)

(As a further aside, we should start designing tools to generate all UML dia-grams from language text because text is far easier to change and maintain than diagrams.)

15.5   Breaking down the barriers

But silo thinking is deeply embedded in the business psyche. How do we get the business and the IT department moving?

Let us review some of the barriers.

One barrier is the bean counters. Work toward improvement of internal processes always has difficulties with finance because it is so hard to estimate the payback. I would recommend going to the chief financial officer and asking how they fund infrastructure projects outside of IT. How is upgrading the telephone paid for and how is moving offices paid for? If you have a series of small projects, some of which are infrastructure projects, you can track the dependencies between the projects, you may be able to divide the costs of the infrastructure improvement over the dependent projects. A few infrastructure projects require a major invest-ment (for example, upgrading the network) but many are small. While you must have a consistent architectural goal, you rarely have to implement the whole grand plan to implement one project. Restrict your techies to implementing the task in hand; you must prevent them over-engineering too.

Another barrier is user departments who want to control their own costs and have their projects developed fast without waiting for IT delays. The key benefits for them are that better flexibility means faster development, and better integra-tion means that they benefit from improvements elsewhere they didn't pay for, like more accurate customer information.

Program management plays a key role in the above. They must be close to the business department and listening to their real concerns.

Perhaps the biggest barriers are within the IT department. They like it how it is. So cycle people around projects; give everyone the chance to work with new technology. For instance, get your mainframe systems test team to help design your distributed systems test.

But let us not get too gloomy. Two factors are playing to your advantage. The e-business revolution is forcing the pace on integration. It is more difficult for people inside and outside of the IT department to get in the way, because the

Quantum Management

In all these high-level discussions with senior management you should not forget the theory of quantum management. This is founded on the observation that the way management operates in practice is remarkably similar to the quantum mechanical description of particles. For instance, there is always uncertainty about direction and speed. If you absolutely know the direction, you have no idea of the speed. If you absolutely know the speed, you don't know the direction. More often than not you don't know either. If you try and measure either direction or speed then the act of measurement itself disrupts the thing being measured, usually to your detriment, I might add.

Then there is the curious phenomenon of quantum decision making. Management stays in one state, a quantum state if you will, its mind presumably unalterable, fixed on one purpose. Then it switches instantaneously to another state with, curiously, no measurable level of uncertainty in between. Sometimes light is given off at the same time as the transition but more often than not light is absorbed.

The most dangerous state to recognize is quantum superposition. This is when the management holds two contrary opinions simultaneously. Eventually reality dawns and, in the phrase of the physicists, there is a collapse of the wave function, one of the states is true, and the alternative never existed.

Is management rational? Well, what do you expect from a particle that can be up, down, charmed, strange, and has spin?

organization's viability is on the line. Second, your key weapon is information integrity. The lack of data accuracy is almost certainly a great annoyance to senior management. Fixing data accuracy requires greater integration. Finally, if you can push your organization to take a business-process perspective (for instance, by always playing back their requirements as business-process diagrams) then ultimately you will force them to take a wider view.

That said, management is not always predictable (see Quantum Management box).

15.6   The future

IT technology has changed enormously in the past five years; it seems unlikely that the rate of change is going to slow down appreciably over the next five years. This means—don't worry about the competitive wars going on among the IT vendors; don't build a strategy based on selecting technologies; and build your applications to expect change.

But at some time in the future a more stable world (with regard to IT) will set in. This is not because the IT vendors are suddenly going to become friends; it is because the world in general will come to grips with the electronic business. People will know what it takes to deliver successful electronic retail, banking, manufacturing, government, and so on. People will know what works and what doesn't. They will know the pitfalls. The chances are that the tools used to develop the electronic future will be more capable versions of the tools we see today but it could be that some revolutionary development comes along that none of us have thought about.

My guess, for what it is worth, is that the major area for change will be in application development tools. There will be an increased emphasis on modeling. The tools will improve. There will be better system verification. There will be dynamic visualizing of the system. You will be able to select a business process and the tool will show you, dynamically, how it works. You will be able to select an area and drill down to the code. There will be better ways of integrating technology frameworks in the system so that you will have much improved control over systems generation. This makes it possible to build systems that are flexible, robust, and scalable. Reuse will be handled by the tools rather than relying on manual searches. Above all, there will be better integration of a wide variety of tools in one repository and with the runtime system management system.

But whatever the future holds, there should be three principles to guide you:

1. Make evolution work for you.

2. Build an integrated application not silos.

3. Have the techies and the modelers understand each other and work together.

No one said it was easy, but it can be fun.

Index

Access (Microsoft), 27
Account layer, 272–273
Accuracy, of information, 211, 218–220
ACID properties, 30–32, 37
Active Data Objects (Microsoft), 27, 85
Active Directory (Microsoft), 78
Active Server Pages (Microsoft), 71, 179
ActiveX controls (Microsoft), 85
Activity Diagrams, 175
ADO (Active Data Objects), 27, 85
Agents, 152
Algorithms, 158, 202
Amazon.com, 1–4
American Standard Code for Informa-
    tion Interchange (ASCII), 77
Application(s)
    development, rapid (RAD), 174, 178
    failures, 121–123
    fragmented, 249
    GUI, as session-based, 65
    Internet, 62–66
    monolithic, 249–250
    programming interfaces (APIs), 23, 33, 77, 83, 86
    security, building, 161–166
    silo, 8–9, 199, 228–229, 284

transforming, into servers, 236–328
understanding large, 250–251
Architecture(s). *See also* CORBA
    (Common Object Request Broker
    Architecture); Design; Integrated
    Applications Architecture
basic description of, 75–91
BNA (Burroughs' Network
    Architecture), 20
building, 266–284
DCA (Distributed Communication
    Architecture), 20
design phase for, 173
DNA (Distributed Network
    Architecture), 14, 20
effect of improving, 128–130
gap, HW architecture, 128–129
generic functional, 103–105
implicit, 89–90
OMA (Object Management
    Architecture), 85
reuse of, 185–186
SAA (Systems Application
    Architecture), 85
Smother Architecture, 12–13
SNA (Systems Network Architec-
    ture), 20, 22, 32, 76, 80, 85
vendor, 84–89

ARPANET, 20, 22–23

ASCII (American Standard Code for Information Interchange), 77

ASP (Active Server Pages), 71, 179

Assembler, 250

AT&T (American Telephone & Telegraph), 22, 25, 32

Attributes
  basic description of, 24
  improving performance and, 135
  information accuracy and, 219

B2B (business-to-business), 3–4, 245

Baan, 89

Backup systems
  activating, 110–112
  clean-up work and, 110
  detecting failures and, 108–110
  dual active strategies and, 114–118, 119
  improving performance and, 144–146
  planning downtime and, 120–121
  reprocessing "lost" messages, 113–114

Batch processing, 207, 279
  flexibility and, 249, 261–264
  performance and, 139–140

BEA, 32, 89, 239

Benchmarks, 127–130, 138, 147. *See also* Performance

BNA (Burroughs' Network Architecture), 20

Browsers, 118–119, 138

Burroughs, 20

Business
  intelligence systems, 143–144
  logic, 191
  rules, 191, 202–203

Business Volumes (EMC), 263

C (high-level language), 250

C++ (high-level language)
  flexibility and, 25
  implementation design and, 187
  Java and, relation of, 61
  object middleware and, 41, 42, 51

Caching, 128–129, 134. *See also* Memory

Call-back objects, 57–58

CA Unicenter, 154

CDocument class, 42

Certificates, 157

CGI (Common Gateway Interface), 250

CICS (IBM), 32, 239, 250

CIM, 153

Class(es)
  basic description of, 42
  diagrams, 175
  identifiers, 55–56
  inheritance and, 43
  Microsoft Foundation (MFC), 42–43
  polymorphism and, 44–45
  sub-, 208

ClearPath mainframes, 239

Client(s)
  rich, 137
  /server configurations, 24, 81–82, 137–138
  thick, 137

CLSIDs (class identifiers), 55–56

Clustering, 114–115

COBOL, 41, 61, 226, 245
  flexibility and, 250
  Java and, 16

Collaboration, 97–98

Columns, 24

COM (Component Object Model), 67, 85. *See also* COM+ (Component Object Model +)
  Distributed (DCOM), 16, 52–56, 67
  implementation design and, 178

object middleware and, 52–58
operation calls and, 83–84
COM+ (Component Object Model +),
    62, 67–70, 239, 243, 269. *See
    also* COM (Component Object
    Model)
Common Gateway Interface (CGI),
    250
Common Object Request Broker
    Architecture (CORBA).
    See CORBA (Common
    Object Request Broker
    Architecture)
Communication, use of the term,
    78–84
Component(s). *See also* COM
    (Component Object Model)
    basic description of, 61–74, 181
    containers, 135–136
    dependencies, 184
    diagrams, 176
    formatting, 187
    grouping objects into, 181–182
    implementation design and,
        174–178
    layers, 186–187
    middleware, transactional (TCM),
        66–71
    presentation logic, 187
    reusable, 182–187, 279
    testing, 279
Component Object Model (COM).
    See COM (Component Object
    Model)
COMTI, 239
COMWare, 66
Consistency, creating, 224–227
Construction phase, 173
Controlled duplication, 220–224
Cookies, 65–66, 71–73, 157
Copied tracking objects, 201

CORBA (Common Object Request
    Broker Architecture), 13, 16
    APIs and, 77
    component containers and, 135–136
    EJB and, 70
    implementation design and, 180
    object middleware and, 50, 52–56, 58
    Object Transaction Service, 68
    operation calls and, 83–84
Core server models, 243
CRM (customer relationship
    management), 198
CView class, 42

Data
    consolidation of, 223
    duplication, 273
    historical, format changes and, 214
    mart, 213, 215–216, 228
    migration, 227
    mining, 213, 273
    replication technology, 213
    shared, 220–224
    warehouses, 213, 228
Data layer, 101–103
Data link layer, 79
DB2 (IBM), 250
DCA (Distributed Communication
    Architecture), 20
DCE (Distributed Computing
    Environment), 13, 27, 85
DCOM (Distributed COM), 16, 52–56,
    67. *See also* COM (Component
    Object Model)
Deactivation, 69–70
DEC, 20, 25
Deferrable messages, 93, 95–96
Defines, 250
Department of Defense (United States),
    20
Deployment phase, 172–173, 275, 280

Design. *See also* Architecture
  business processes and, 191–205,
    270–273
  completing, 187–188
  functional, 172, 277
  general comments on, 171–178
  implementation, 171–189, 191–205,
    251–252, 277–278
  interfaces and, 181, 185–186, 187
  for performance and scalability,
    146–147
DHCP (Dynamic Host Configuration
    Protocol), 63
DHTML (Dynamic HTML), 85. *See also*
    HTML (HyperText Markup
    Language)
Directory services, 78
Disks, speed of, 134
Display Manager, 153
Distributed COM (DCOM), 16, 52–56,
    67
Distributed Computing Environment
    (DCE), 27, 85
Distributed Communication Architecture
    (DCA), 20
Distributed Management Task Force
    (DMTF), 153
Distributed Network Architecture
    (DNA), 14, 20
Distributed transaction processing,
    30–34, 36–39
DLLs (Dynamic Link Libraries), 66, 181
DMTF (Distributed Management Task
    Force), 153
DNS (Domain Name Service), 78
DNS (Domain Name Servers), 62, 76,
    111
Documentation, 172, 281
Downtime, planning, 120–121
DRDA (IBM), 27
Dual active strategies, 114–118, 119

Duplication, controlled, 220–224
Dynamic Host Configuration Protocol
    (DHCP), 63
Dynamic Link Libraries (DLLs), 66, 181

EAI (Enterprise Application Integration),
    89, 245
Ease of use, 23
EBCDIC, 77
EDI (Electronic Data Interchange), 98,
    245, 246–247
Efficiency, 195–196
EJB (Enterprise Java Beans), 13, 16, 62,
    66, 68–70, 86
  basic description of, 70–71
  components and, 68
  load balancing and, 142
Electronic Data Interchange (EDI), 98,
    245, 246–247
eLink OSI, 239. *See also* OSI (Open
    Systems Interconnection)
EMC Business Volumes, 263
Encapsulation, 42
Encina, 34
Encryption, 157–158
Enterprise Application Integration (EAI),
    89, 245
Enterprise Java Beans (EJB). *See* EJB
    (Enterprise Java Beans)
Errors, 215–216, 235, 253
Excel (Microsoft), 42
eXtensible Markup Language (XML).
    See XML (eXtensible Markup
    Language)

Failures
  application software, 121–123
  detecting, 108–110
  system software, 119–120
Fast-Food Fallacy, 235
FDDI, 165

Firewalls, 64. *See also* Security
Flexibility, 206–207, 234, 249–265, 284
Formatting components, 187
Fortran, 250
Fragmented applications, 249
FTP (File Transfer Protocol), 23, 76
Functional
    analysis, 197–199
    design, 172, 277

GUI (Graphical User Interface)
    applications, as session-based, 65
    object middleware and, 41, 57
    implementation design and, 175
    presentation layer and, 99

HTML (HyperText Markup Language),
    65, 85
    Dynamic (DHTML), 85
    editors, 179
    implementation design and, 179
HW architecture gap, 128–129
Hybrid strategies, 224

IATA (International Air Transport
    Association), 20
IBM (International Business Machines),
    25, 36, 62
    CICS, 32, 239, 250
    DB2, 250
    DRDA, 27
    MQSeries, 35, 40, 240, 245
    MVS, 30
    SNA (Systems Network Architec-
        ture), 20, 22, 32, 76, 80, 85
    TPF operating system, 255
IDL (Interface Definition Language), 28,
    77, 83
    basic description of, 26
    integration and, 245
    message queuing and, 35

object middleware and, 50
    RPC and, 26, 27
IETF (Internet Engineering Task Force),
    158
IIS (Microsoft Internet Information
    Server), 85
Information
    access, 211–212, 217–218
    accuracy, 211, 218–220
    bases, 152
    basic process, 214–215
    controllers, 228–229
    managing, 273–274
    retrieval, 96–97
Inheritance
    basic description of, 43
    multiple, 43
Integrated Applications Architecture.
    See also Architectures
    alternatives to, 11–13
    basic description of, 9–18
    building, 268–270
    business process change design and,
        277
    development of, 17–18
    project management and, 274–282
    understanding existing systems and,
        276
Intelligence systems, 143–144
Interactive Voice Recognition (IVR),
    179, 269
Interface(s)
    basic description of, 42, 181
    business processing change with new,
        240–243
    classification of, 83–84
    converting old into new, 238–249
    implementation design and, 181,
        185–186, 187
    improving performance and,
        133–135

Interface(s) (*cont.*)
  size mismatches, 235–236
  using, 56–58
International Organization for
    Standardization (ISO), 21–22, 79
Internet
  applications, 62–66
  origins of, 20, 61–74
  Service Providers (ISPs), 155
Internet Engineering Task Force (IETF),
    158
Internet Protocol (IP). *See* IP (Internet
    Protocol)
Interoperability, 76–77
Intranets, 62
IP (Internet Protocol), 23, 62, 79
  backup systems and, 111
  security and, 155
  servers and, 65–66
  network layer and, 81
ISO (International Organization for
    Standardization), 21–22, 79
ISPs (Internet Service Providers), 155
IVR (Interactive Voice Recognition),
    179, 269

Java, 24, 28, 52, 65, 250. *See also* Java
    Beans, Enterprise (EJB)
  2 Enterprise Environment (J2EE), 75,
    83, 85–88, 239
  C++ and, relation of, 61
  Database Connectivity (JDBC), 86
  implementation design and, 178–179
  Messaging Services (JMS), 86, 88
  RMI (Remote Method Invocation),
    52, 67, 70
  security and, 155
  Server Pages (JSP), 71, 86, 179
  Servlets, 178–179
  shared data and, 222
  Virtual Machine (JVM), 61, 155

Java Beans, Enterprise (EJB), 13, 16, 62,
    66–70, 86
  basic description of, 70–71
  components and, 68
  load balancing and, 142
JavaScript, 257
JDBC (Java Database Connectivity), 86
JINI, 155
JMS (Java Messaging Services), 86, 88
JSP (Java Server Pages), 71, 86, 179
JVM (Java Virtual Machine), 61, 155

KDC (Key Distribution Center), 158, 159
Kerberos, 159, 161

LANs (local area networks), 63, 81, 98
  improving performance and,
    131–139, 144
  replication and, 144
  security and, 157
Layers. *See also* Presentation layer
  Account layer, 272–273
  Data layer, 101–103
  Data link layer, 79
  Network layer, 79
  Physical layer, 79
  Product layer, 260, 272–273
  Secure Sockets Layer (SSL),
    157–159
  Transaction Server layer, 100–101
  Transport layer, 79
Leadership, 177
Legacy systems, 225
Lisp, 41
Load balancing, 141–143
Locking, 149
Logic, business, 191
LU6.2 protocol, 32

Mainframes, 239
Managed Object, 152

Mapping objects, 179–181, 277
Marketing, 88–89, 216–217
Markup languages. *See* XML
    (eXtensible Markup Language);
    HTML (HyperText Markup
    Language)
Marshalling, 26, 77
Mediator(s), 105–106
    components, 187–188
    routines, 16
Memory
    caching, 128–129, 134
    improving performance and,
        128–129, 132–134, 136, 143
    mapping objects and, 179–180
Message(s)
    deferrable, 93, 95–96
    formats, 152
    queuing, 34–39
    real-time, 93–94
Methods, basic description of, 42
MFC (Microsoft Foundation Classes),
    42–43
MIB formats, 153
Microsoft Access, 27
Microsoft Active Data Objects (ADO),
    27, 85
Microsoft Active Directory, 78
Microsoft Active Server Pages (ASP),
    71, 179
Microsoft ActiveX controls, 85
Microsoft DNA (Distributed
    Network Architecture), 75,
    84–88, 239
Microsoft Excel, 42
Microsoft IIS (Internet Information
    Server), 85
Microsoft MFC (Microsoft Foundation
    Classes), 42–43
Microsoft MTS (Microsoft Transaction
    Server), 69

Microsoft Visual Basic
    attributes and, 135
    flexibility and, 257
    object middleware and, 41, 51
    shared data and, 222
Microsoft Windows 2000, 23
Microsoft Windows NT, 107, 250
Microsoft Word, 42
Middleware
    architectures, 75–91
    basic concepts of, 23–24
    changing, between transaction
        servers, 243–244
    classification of, 75–91
    early days of, 19–23
    elements of, 75–78
    evolution of, 19–40
    history of, 41–59, 51–74
    object-oriented concepts and, 42–49
    purpose of, 91–106
    support for business processes, 92–96
Mining data, 213, 273
Monolithic applications, 249–250
MQSeries (IBM), 35, 40, 240, 245
MTS (Microsoft Transaction Server), 69
Multi-threading
    basic description of, 24
    RPC and, 26
MVS (IBM), 30

Naming services, 78
NDS (Netware Directory Services), 78
Network layer, 79

Object(s). *See also* OLE (Object Linking
    and Embedding)
    active data objects (ADO), 27, 85
    basic description of, 41–59
    call-back objects, 57–58
    mapping, 179–181, 277
    grouping, 181–182

Object(s) (*cont.*)
   Plan objects, 199–201, 272
   Resource objects, 199–201, 272
   Result objects, 199–201, 272
   Tracking objects, 199–201, 203–204,
     231–232, 272
Object Pascal, 41
Object Transaction Managers (OTM), 66
ODBC (Open Database Connectivity),
   17, 27
   consistency and, 225
   shared data and, 221
OLE (Object Linking and Embedding).
   See also Objects
   COM developers and, 56
   consistency and, 225
   DB, 27, 57, 85, 221, 225
OLTP (Online Transaction Processing),
   132–133
OMA (Object Management
   Architecture), 85
OMG (Object Management Group), 85
Online Transaction Processing (OLTP),
   132–133
OODB (object-oriented databases),
   46–49
Open Database Connectivity (ODBC).
   See ODBC (Open Database
   Connectivity)
Open Group, 32
OpenTI, 239
Operations, basic description of, 42
Oracle, 27, 62, 250
Organizational management, 274–282
OSF (Open Software Foundation), 25, 85
OSI (Open Systems Interconnection),
   21–22, 28, 34, 80, 239
Overriding, 251

Packages, 13
Parallelism, 279

Parallel Sysplex, 107
Parameterized routines, 208
Passwords, 156–157
PCI bus, 129
PeopleSoft, 89
Performance
   basic description of, 127–149
   batch processing and, 139–140
   benchmarks, 127–130, 138, 147
   business intelligence systems and,
     143–144
   caching and, 128–129, 134
   design for, 146–147
   load balancing and, 141–145
   object interfaces and, 133–135
   replication and, 144
Perl, 250
Physical layer, 79
PKI (Public Key Infrastructure), 157
PL/1, 250
Plan objects, 199–201, 272
Polymorphism, 44–45
Positioning, 87–88
Presentation layer, 98–100, 161–162,
   208
   batch processing and, 264
   creating, 234–240
   implementation design and, 178–179,
     188
   information management and,
     273–274
Presentation logic components, 187
Primary keys, 24
Process(es)
   basic description of, 24, 193–106
   change definition, 171–172
   computer applications and, 202–207
   control of, 77–78
   data distribution and, 203–204
   flexibility and, 206–207
   functional approach to, 197–199

function versus, 176–177
generic, 206
implementation design and, 171–172
implementing, 191–205
improvement, 216
information and, 199–201, 214–215
long transactions and, 204–206
management, 215–216
refinement of, 242
sub-, 184, 201, 203
Product layer, 260, 272–273
Program elements, 181
Project management, 172, 177, 274–282
Prototypes, 278
Public Key Infrastructure (PKI), 157
Push protocol, 82

QuadCycle, 173
Quantum management, 283
Queries
ad-hoc, 143–144
business intelligence systems and,
143–144
Queuing
basic description of, 34–39, 136–137
improving performance and, 131,
136–137

RAD (Rapid Application Development),
174, 178
Real-time, 203, 271
transactions, 137–139
messages, 93–94
Recovery, of data, 144–146. *See also*
Backup systems
Relational databases, 24
Remote database access, 27–30
Remote Method Invocation (RMI), 52,
67, 70
Remote procedure calls (RPC). *See* RPC
(remote procedure calls)

Replication, 144
Requirements phase, 173–174
Resiliency
basic description of, 107–126
backup servers and, 108–114
planning downtime and, 120–121
system software failures and,
119–120
strategy, developing, 123–125
techniques, applying, 118–119
Resource objects, 199–201, 272
Result objects, 199–201, 272
Reuse of code, 182–187, 242–243, 279
Rewrite option, 13–15
RFP (Request For Proposals), 209
Rich clients, 137
RMI (Remote Method Invocation), 52,
67, 70
Rows, 24
RPC (remote procedure calls), 28, 34
basic description of, 25–27
integration and, 243–244
message queuing and, 34
object middleware and, 49–51
replacement of, by component
middleware, 39
RPG, 250
RSA algorithm, 158
Rules, business, 191, 202–203
Rules engine, 153
Runtime integration products,
244–246

SAA (Systems Application
Architecture), 85
SAP, 89
Scalability, 127, 146–147, 284
Schema, 24
Screen-scraping, 235
SCSI (Small Computer Systems
Interface), 131–133

Security
    algorithms, 158
    applications, building, 161–166
    application support for, 166–168
    basic description of, 151–169
    circumventing, 163–165
    encryption, 157–158
    existing applications and, 165–166
    firewalls, 64
    passwords, 156–157
    technology, 156–161
    violations, handling, 165
Sequence Diagrams, 176
Serendipitous reuse, 183, 185
Server(s). *See also* Client/server
        configurations; Transaction
        servers
    backup, 108–114
    changing middleware between,
        243–244
    clustered, 114–115
    control of, 77–78
    improving performance and, 139,
        141–145
    load balancing and, 141–145
    Microsoft IIS (Internet Information
        Server), 85
    resiliency and, 108–114, 114–115
    skeletons, 26
    Secure Sockets Layer and, 157–159
    turning existing applications into,
        236–328
Shared data, 220–224
Shared tracking objects, 201
Silo applications, 8–9, 199, 228–229,
        284
Skeletons, server, 26
Smalltalk, 41
Smother Architecture, 12–13
SMTP (Simple Mail Transfer Protocol),
        76

SNA (System Network Architecture),
        20, 22, 32, 76, 80, 85
SNMP (Simple Network Management
        Protocol), 23, 153, 154
SOAP (Simple Object Access Protocol),
        69
Sperry, 20
SPO (Single Point Operations), 154
SQL (Structured Query Language),
        28, 83
    basic description of, 24
    Check statement, 160
    distributed databases and, 31
    information access and, 215
    information retrieval and, 96–97
    parsing, 29–30
    security and, 160
    shared data and, 221
SQL View, 160
SSL (Secure Sockets Layer),
        157–159
State(s)
    basic description of, 42
    issues of, 71–73
Statistics, 215–216, 273
Status reports, 215–216
Stone, Christopher, 19
Straight-Through processing, 245
Strategies
    business analysis, 216–217
    developing, 123–125
    Dual active strategies, 114–118,
        119
    hybrid, 224
    resiliency, 123–125
Stubs, 26
Sun J2EE (Java 2 Enterprise Environ-
        ment), 75, 83, 85–88, 239
Sun Microsystems, 62, 72. *See also*
        Sun J2EE (Java 2 Enterprise
        Environment)

SunSoft, 155

System. *See also* Systems management
    software, failures and, 119–120
    tests, 279–280
    verification, 283

Systems management
    application support for, 166–168
    security and, 151–169
    technology, 151–156
    vertical, 166–167

Systems Network Architecture (SNA),
    22, 76, 80

System Tuning Union, 131

Tables, 24

TCM (transactional component
    middleware), 66–71

TCP (Transmission Control Protocol),
    23, 81–83. *See also* TCP/IP
    (Transmission Control
    Protocol/Internet Protocol)

TCP/IP (Transmission Control
    Protocol/Internet Protocol),
    22, 23, 24. *See also* TCP
    (Transmission Control
    Protocol)
    backup systems and, 111
    interoperability and, 76–77
    layering and, 79, 80
    message queuing and, 34–35
    the rise of Internet applications
    and, 62
    security and, 153, 155, 158

Testing, 172, 279–280

Test scripts, 279

TGT (Ticket Granting Ticket),
    158

Thick clients, 137

Threads
    basic description of, 24
    blocked, 24

Throughput requirements, 131–132

Timeliness, information versus,
    96–97

Tivoli, 154

TLS (Transport Layer Security), 158

TpcC benchmark, 127, 147

TPF operating system (IBM), 255

Tracking objects, 199–201, 203–204,
    231–232, 272

Transaction monitors, 34

Transaction processing. *See also*
    Transaction servers
    component containers and,
    135–136
    distributed, 30–34, 36–39
    long transactions and, 205–207
    online (OLTP), 132–133
    optimizing, 131–139

Transaction server(s). *See also* Servers;
    Transaction processing
    changing middleware between,
    243–244
    layer, 100–101
    information management and,
    273–274
    transaction monitors and, 34
    turning existing applications into,
    236–328

Transmission Control Protocol (TCP).
    See TCP (Transmission Control
    Protocol)

Transmission Control Protocol/Internet
    Protocol (TCP/IP). *See* TCP/IP
    (Transmission Control
    Protocol/Internet Protocol)

Transparency, location, 23–24

Transport layer, 79

Trend analysis, 215–216, 273

Tuxedo, 32–36, 89, 239, 240

Two-phase commit protocol, 31,
    116–117, 135–136, 235

UDP (User Datagram Protocol), 81, 159

UML (Unified Modeling Language), 176, 191, 208, 282

UNICODE, 77

Unisys, 154

Unix, 22, 23, 159
   flexibility and, 250
   resiliency and, 107

UREP, 175

URLs (Uniform Resource Locators), 62–63

Use Case Diagrams, 176

Vendor architectures, 84–89

Verification, 283

Version control, 280–281

Visual Basic (Microsoft)
   attributes and, 135
   flexibility and, 257
   object middleware and, 41, 51
   shared data and, 222

Voice recognition, 179, 269

WANs (wide area networks), 98

WBEM (Web-Based Enterprise Management), 153

Web browsers, 118–119, 138

Weinberg, Gerald, 235

Windows 2000 (Microsoft), 23

Windows NT (Microsoft), 107, 250

Winsock on Windows, 23

Word (Microsoft), 42

Wrapping, 238–239, 245–246

X.25 protocol, 21

X.509 certificate standard, 157

XATMI protocol, 32

XML (eXtensible Markup Language), 69, 77, 98
   basic description of, 246–247
   integration and, 245–247
   security and, 153

X/Open, 32, 33

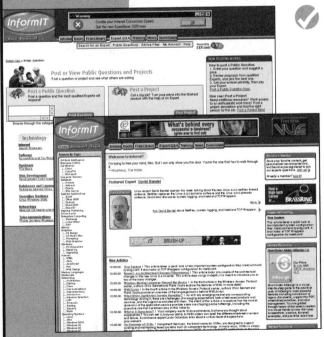

Register
Your Book
at www.aw.com/cseng/register

You may be eligible to receive:

- Advance notice of forthcoming editions of the book
- Related book recommendations
- Chapter excerpts and supplements of forthcoming titles
- Information about special contests and promotions throughout the year
- Notices and reminders about author appearances, tradeshows, and online chats with special guests

Contact us

If you are interested in writing a book or reviewing manuscripts prior to publication, please write to us at:

Editorial Department
Addison-Wesley Professional
75 Arlington Street, Suite 300
Boston, MA 02116 USA
Email: AWPro@aw.com

Visit us on the Web: http://www.aw.com/cseng